Photograph by Vandyk

Major-General The VISCOUNT BRIDGEMAN, C.B., D.S.O., M.C.,
Director-General of the Home Guard.

BUREAUCRATS IN BATTLEDRESS

A History of the Ministry of Food
Home Guard

By
HENRY SMITH

With a Foreword by
MAJOR-GENERAL THE RIGHT HONOURABLE
VISCOUNT BRIDGEMAN
C.B., D.S.O., M.C.

"*They also serve who only stand and wait*"

The Naval & Military Press Ltd

Published by

The Naval & Military Press Ltd
Unit 10 Ridgewood Industrial Park,
Uckfield, East Sussex,
TN22 5QE England

Tel: +44 (0) 1825 749494
Fax: +44 (0) 1825 765701

www.naval-military-press.com
www.nmarchive.com

In reprinting in facsimile from the original, any imperfections are inevitably reproduced and the quality may fall short of modern type and cartographic standards.

CONTENTS

FOREWORD by Major-General The Right Hon. The Viscount Bridgeman, C.B., D.S.O., M.C., Director-General, Home Guard, 1941–44.

AUTHOR'S PREFACE

		Page
Chapter 1.	INTRODUCTION	11
Chapter 2.	THE MINISTRY OF FOOD HOME GUARD IN DEFENCE	18
Chapter 3.	TRAINING AND ORGANISATION I.— May, 1940, to April, 1941 The L.D.V. Unit London and Colwyn Bay "F" Coy., 1st Bn. Denbighshire Home Guard	27
Chapter 4.	TRAINING AND ORGANISATION II.— March 28th, 1941, to June 1st, 1942 "E" and "F" Companies 1st Bn. Denbighshire Home Guard Training outside the parade ground	44
Chapter 5.	TRAINING AND ORGANISATION III.— June 1st, 1942, to December 31st, 1942 The Ministry of Food Wing Directed Men	72
Chapter 6.	TRAINING AND ORGANISATION IV.— 11th Battalion Denbighshire Home Guard The Wing takes flight	81
Chapter 7.	THE SPECIALIST SERVICES	97
Chapter 8.	THE BATTALION IN THE FIELD	128
Chapter 9.	STANDING DOWN	147

APPENDICES

1.	Roll of Honour	153
2.	Honours and Awards	153
3.	Nominal roll of the Unit	154

ILLUSTRATIONS

All the photographs accompanying this history are (with the exception of two specifically acknowledged) by Corporal A. Wrigley, Battalion Photographer

❧

Major-General The Viscount Bridgeman, C.B., D.S.O., M.C., Director-General of the Home Guard	*Frontispiece*
L.D.V. Days—Bureaucrats without Battledress	*Following p.* 24
In the Dark Days	,, 24
The first Uniforms—Lord Woolton inspects	,, 24
"Standing Easy"	,, 24
Cooking under difficulties	,, 40
St. John's Ambulance Unit at work	,, 40
Instruction in "Fire Control" Orders	,, 48
After the Battle	,, 48
Colonel Barton, C.B.E., M.C., takes the Salute	,, 56
The Home Guard "Salutes the Soldier"	,, 56
Ministry of Food Platoon, 2nd City of London (Civil Service) Battalion	,, 86
Inspection of Guard of Honour by Major-General Wilson, C.B., D.S.O., O.B.E., Colonel of the Royal Welch Fusiliers ...	,, 86
Colonel Llewellin presenting the Inter-Platoon Challenge Cup to Sergt. Clark and Sergt. Harris, representing No. 10 Platoon and No. 12 platoon, joint winners	,, 96
Demonstration on the Spigot Mortar	,, 96
"Cookhouse"	,, 96
Col. Shennan, Mr. A. Grieg, Major H. M. Pemberton, Lieut. Polfry, Colonel Barton and the Commanding Officer inspecting Field Kitchens	,, 96
"All our own Work"—The Runabout	,, 108
Colonel Llewellin meets the Auxiliaries	,, 108
International Gallery	,, 120
The Adjutant explains the "War"	,, 120
11th Denbighshire on Parade	,, 136

Auxiliaries inspected by Controller Chitty ... ... *Following p.*		136
The Auxiliaries March Past—Stand Down Parade 9th December, 1944	,,	148
The Last Parade—9th December, 1944	,,	148
Battalion Headquarters Officers	,,	152
The Sergeants' Mess	,,	152
H.Q. Company Officers	,,	152
No. 1 Platoon H.Q. Company	,,	152
No. 2 Platoon (Medium Machine Guns) H.Q. Company ...	,,	152
No. 3 Platoon (Signals) H.Q. Company	,,	152
No. 4 Platoon (Transport) H.Q. Company	,,	152
No. 6 Platoon H.Q. Company	,,	152
"B" Company Officers	,,	152
No. 7 Platoon "B" Company	,,	152
No. 8 Platoon "B" Company	,,	152
No. 9 Platoon "B" Company	,,	152
No. 10 Platoon "B" Company	,,	152
"C" Company Officers	,,	152
No. 11 Platoon "C" Company	,,	152
No. 12 Platoon "C" Company	,,	152
No. 14 Platoon "C" Company	,,	152
"D" Company Officers	,,	152
No. 15 Platoon "D" Company	,,	152
No. 16 Platoon "D" Company	,,	152
No. 17 Platoon "D" Company	,,	152
C.O. and Auxiliary Unit	,,	152

FOREWORD

THERE were over a thousand battalions in the Home Guard. Most of them I visited, and many of them I knew well. All of them had the same ideals, but no two of them interpreted them in quite the same way.

In one way, the 11th Denbighshire Battalion of the Home Guard had a character all its own. Unlike the rest, it did not do its duty on its Home Ground. Nominally a Welsh battalion, it was charged in fact with the defence of a strip of coast of considerable importance in the days when a German invasion of Ireland was a real possibility. But it was not a native battalion. Brought together by the accidents of service in the Ministry of Food, and of the evacuation of the Ministry to Colwyn Bay, the battalion was the nearest counterpart in the Home Guard to a unit on foreign service. Like other battalions away from their home stations, it gained a cohesion, a flexibility and a battalion spirit just a little different from those battalions whose members came each Sunday or week-night parade from the farm and the mine, and went back to their own firesides on the dismiss.

But with it all, the battalion—as this story shows—breathed the authentic Home Guard spirit.

It is written on every page of this book. Home Guard stories, Home Guard songs, Home Guard keenness, Home Guard patience, and not least, pride in the Home Guard achievement which in fact caused this book to be written as a labour of love, and will cause it to be read.

It is not the least fortunate part of the history of the Home Guard that it stood down when it did. It had served its purpose. Britain was no longer in danger of invasion, except perhaps to a few wishful warriors. So in full vigour it came to its end, with no decrepit old age or lack of favour to mar the final chapter. Its true place in the history of the times will stand out more clearly as events recede into perspective, and we see on the chessboard of war the Home Guard as the Castle guarding the King, while the Knights of the Regular Army went overseas in search of the King's enemies. Now the contest is won. The King's enemies are defeated and the Home Guard and its work have been finally justified.

Bridgeman

Director-General,
Home Guard,
1941-1944.

AUTHOR'S PREFACE

IT is among the traditions of the British Army that its organisation depends upon N.C.O.s, and its history is written by Brigadiers. In the case of the Ministry of Food Home Guard this well established procedure is, quite properly, reversed: the officers, in fact as well as in form, organised and directed, and the compilation of its history has been entrusted to an N.C.O. While the N.C.O. might well have been better chosen, the change is not without significance as a reflection of the spirit of the Home Guard and the more democratic regular army of this war. In both, ability as a soldier alone (tempered, in the case of the Home Guard by the possession of, or capacity to improvise, 'spare time') establishes the right to command. Not only is this the only proper basis on which to found armies fighting to eradicate the vicious principle that authority should reside with one race alone, and one caste within that race, but it has the supreme advantage that it works. Shop assistants, Etonians, and mechanics combined to shoot the aces of the Luftwaffe out of the sky in the Battle of Britain: the Russian army command, including ex-cavalry troopers and ex-fitters, out-generalled and out-fought the best that the Nazi staff colleges could produce. In such armies the N.C.O.s tend to be non-commissioned as a result of their relative deficiency in the essential military qualities, and the capacity to write history is not of necessity among these. As Bernard Shaw has aptly put it, in a slightly different context, 'Those who can, do: those who can't, teach.'

So much by way of excuse for my temerity in undertaking this history. I have throughout conceived it to be my task to deal with the history of the Ministry unit as the development of a fighting organisation, improvised under conditions of great difficulty, and to attempt to trace its organic connection with the changing political and military history of these momentous days, rather than to describe, with a wealth of anecdote, individual exploits and personal experiences. I am aware how much I have fallen short of this objective: it would be ambiguous to say that I am more aware of the shortcomings of this work than any of its readers, because many of them, knowing far more of the Home Guard than I, will be the more justifiably critical. But I have done my best, and no other approach was possible to one of my peace-time trade of lecturer and writer on economic subjects.

In conclusion I have to acknowledge the assistance I have been so generously accorded by everyone, from the C.O. downwards, to whom I have appealed for help: in particular I must record my profound gratitude to the Auxiliaries for the ready response with which they have invariably granted my requests for what must have seemed an endless succession of re-typing, and to the clerical staff at Headquarters. Without this help the work could not have been done, and I hasten to absolve them, and all my collaborators, from responsibility for the faults of this book, which, like the Home Guard itself, is a hasty piece of wartime improvisation.

HENRY SMITH,
Colwyn Bay, 1945.

BUREAUCRATS IN BATTLE DRESS

CHAPTER 1.

INTRODUCTION.

"Indeed if we choose to face danger with an easy mind rather than after a rigorous training, and trust rather in native manliness than in state made courage the advantage lies with us, for we are spared all the weariness of practising for future hardships, and when we find ourselves amongst them we are as brave as our plodding rivals."

Thucidides. Pericles' Funeral Oration. (*tr. Zimmern.*)

IN the Home Guard of Great Britain two historical streams run together. On the one hand, there is the long established British tradition of free men bearing arms in defence of properly constituted authority. This tradition comes down to us from the Elizabethan train bands who stood ready to confront the Spanish Armada, from the volunteers of the Napoleonic Wars, and from the Territorial Army which has done such gallant service in both of the wars which have been forced upon us within the last three decades. This is an old tradition, deeply rooted in the British character and in our political life. In this war, however, and in the Home Guard, it runs together with a new current. This war is fundamentally a conflict of ideals, marked everywhere by this spontaneous rising of free men to defend their freedom against Fascism, and from this aspect the Home Guard of Great Britain invites comparison with the untrained and half-armed People's Army of the Spanish Civil War, who proved the mettle of Italian infantry before it was finally put to the test from which it emerged so disgracefully in North Africa, and who stood up to German bombing in Madrid with the same courage and determination which London afterwards was to display. In the same way the Jugo-Slav Army of Liberation, the French Forces of the Interior, the partisans operating behind the German lines in the Soviet Union, have gone into battle, half-armed, half-trained and ill-equipped in defence of their freedom; in the same way the Local Defence Volunteers stood ready with sticks and shotguns to meet the threat of invasion on English soil in 1940. Thus the Home Guard is at once the embodiment of one of our oldest British traditions and of the newest phase of man's struggle for freedom.

There are, of course, many differences between the Home Guard and the irregular armies which came to life on the Continent. The most obvious difference is that we, in this country, have had to suffer no German occupation and no breakdown of authority. We have been able to train in public and in safety (apart from the inevitable "incidents" which make the weapon training of part-time troops somewhat eventful) and thus we have been able throughout to maintain the closest union with the Command of the regular Army. On the other hand, the Home Guard has had to combine its training and its occasional operations with the rigorous standard of industrial and professional activity which war time demands. The arming of the Home Guard has been on the same basis as that of the regular Army, although the arms arrived considerably later, while in most cases the continental partisans have armed themselves largely at the expense of the enemy, and have perforce been in the field practically all the time.

As a record of difficulties overcome, the organisation of the Home Guard is impressive. Many of these difficulties were common to all Home Guard units and mention of them, therefore, finds its appropriate place in a Battalion History. It must be remembered that the Home Guard came into being at a time when our regular troops, after Dunkirk, had lost the bulk of their equipment. The maintenance and extension of production in every conceivable field-arm, food and capital equipment were, therefore, of absolutely paramount importance at the time when the Home Guard was founded. For the same reason that made production at white-hot intensity the major consideration on the Home Front, it was impossible to divert arms from the regular Army to the Home Guard for quite a period after it had been founded. This same problem of production also meant that the claims of industry and administration on whatever leisure key men might possess were even more important than those of the Home Guard. At the same time, moreover, aerial bombardment was commencing on the "blitz" scale and the Civil Defence Services had long since claimed a very large number of the most able and patriotic citizens, particularly those who would have had sufficient leisure to have been of value in building up the Home Guard organisation. They were already doing a job which had become important as a result of the same crisis which called the Home Guard into being.

Another weakness which confronted the men who were organising the Local Defence Volunteers in the early days was the fact that, owing to the absence of compulsory military service in Great Britain, it was impossible to rely on any basic minimum of military skill in the average citizen. Our ex-professional army men were probably, owing to their longer service, considerably better trained than the Continentals who had done their year of service some time before and then retired into civilian life, but in many old soldiers the trench warfare tradition of the last war was so deeply embedded that it was not without danger to entrust them with the training of raw recruits, who had no basis of elementary knowledge, for this new and faster warfare. Moreover, some of the veterans of the last war, whose knowledge and keenness would have been of the most value, had maintained their connection with the Territorial Army through the inter-war period, and were gone with the indiscriminate drafting of the Territorial Army at the outbreak of war. These problems perhaps crystallised themselves in two shapes most apparent to those confronted with the task of organising the crowds of volunteers who were besieging the police stations in the spring of 1940. The first of these was the problem of choosing officers; the second was that of instituting discipline which should be voluntary in form and at the same time sufficiently rigorous to hold together a military force.

The men who undertook the first stages of organising the Ministry of Food Home Guard were spared none of these difficulties. On the other hand they were confronted with others which arose out of the special nature of the force they were building up and which, to a certain extent, tended to multiply in complexity as the work progressed. Before the organisation of the Local Defence Volunteers in London was anything like complete, the vast majority of the Ministry of Food moved to Colwyn Bay. This move at once destroyed, for the Ministry Unit, the one advantage which Home Guard Units operating under more normal circumstances would hold over an invader. Home Guard forces operating in areas, particularly in rural areas which they know well, have an enormous advantage; poachers and gamekeepers, fox hunters and harriers know every scrap of the countryside; errand boys and taxi drivers, milk roundsmen and insurance agents, know every scrap of the urban area where they operate. Indeed, no one who has seen the Home Guard in action on manoeuvres on their own terrain, in opposition to skilled and well-trained troops imported for the occasion to provide the opposition, can fail to realise the enormous importance of this advantage. As an operational unit, therefore, the Ministry of Food Home Guard were at one stroke condemned to lose this advantage, except in so far as they could build up for themselves, by constant exercises and by adequate intelligence work, the necessary knowledge of the countryside. This gave particular urgency to other aspects of training besides the essential weapon training, which had to form the basis for the rest, and was an important and well justified claimant upon the scarce time available for training. Moreover, not only was the Ministry of Food Home Guard operating as a 'Foreign Legion'; it was, compared with the normal town, village or works Home Guard, a heterogeneous collection of strangers who had only recently come to work together and who knew little or nothing of each other's capacity or reliability. These factors, combined with the very frequent absence necessitated by the retention of many central departments in London, of many of those whose services would have been most valuable in organising the Unit, complicated immeasurably the work involved in the building up of the Unit and increase the debt of gratitude due to those who undertook the task.

It remains to complete this introduction by out-lining the development of the Ministry of Food unit, first as a company, then as a wing, then as a battalion, against the background of the growth of the National Home Guard, and the general progress of the war.

On May the 14th, 1940, with the whole structure of Allied defence crumbling, the Prime Minister gave out his order of the day. "What is our policy? I say it is to wage war by sea, land and air; war with all our might and with all the strength that God can give us." A few hours later Mr. Eden invited recruits for the Local Defence Volunteers: before he had completed his speech the first recruits were making applications. By May 21st, with commendable speed, the Establishment Division of the Ministry of Food had caught up with the mood of the nation and published an office memorandum defining the conditions under which Civil Servants might join the Local Defence Volunteers. The apparent excess of official caution was, however, belied by the activity which had been taking place behind the scenes. Already Mr. Lachlan Maclean and Mr. G. N. Lawrence had been requested to undertake the organisation of a Ministry unit, and by May 29th a memorandum had appeared inviting volunteers. Enrolment proceeded at Great Westminster House: training parades commenced, of the same type as were taking place all over the country. Armlets, walking-sticks, shot-guns, war souvenirs, civilian gas masks and an occasional rook-rifle provided the armament available.

By June 4th the mingled defeat and betrayal of the Allied armies was well nigh complete, and the evacuation from Dunkirk was in progress. Britain stood alone. The Prime Minister, speaking for her new citizen army as well as for the regular forces, defied the enemies of man in words that will always be remembered ". . . . we shall defend our island, whatever the cost may be. We shall fight on the beaches, the landing grounds, in the fields, in the streets and on the hills. We shall never surrender." The next day General Ironside defined the duties which were expected of the Local Defence Volunteers in a blunt and matter-of-fact speech which was the practical counterpart of the Prime Minister's measured periods and generalised appeal. Organised patrolling in conjunction with the civil authorities became general. In the midst of this first phase the Ministry of Food moved, at the end of June, to Colwyn Bay, and the Local Defence Volunteer unit became part of the local organisation. Early in August the Battle of Britain commenced, merging slowly into the series of night bombardments to which the out-fought Luftwaffe had perforce to resort. About midnight on the 7th/8th September the telephones buzzed with a code word—no exercise warning preceded it—and many a Home Guard, turned out of his bed in the small hours, speculated on the chance of trying his mettle and his improvised weapons against an invader, while his officers ruminated upon the means to muster their men more rapidly in future. By September 16th the Ministry unit was guarding the Penmaen Head quarries and explosive dump, and Colwyn Bay station: the probability that German strategists were thinking in terms of Eire as a jumping-off ground for invasion, and the series of bomb outrages attributed to the I.R.A., combined to make the local duties of the Home Guard, as they had now been since July 23rd, more important than their distance from the Channel coast would appear to indicate. Through the first half of a pitiless winter the men on guard shivered, cursed, watched the bombing of Liverpool, and thought of their families in the South, while Home Guards elsewhere were helping to deal with the "blitz."

INTRODUCTION

This first period saw the distribution of the issue of uniforms and equipment, albeit gradually and piecemeal. Boots of civilian pattern, uniforms part denim and part serge, bayonets without frogs .... the Army proper, quite properly, had to come first. Weapons, too, began to arrive. Still, the O.C. writing in December, could say, "I am credibly informed that a consignment of Springfield Rifles has now arrived in Liverpool Harbour, and that some time next month we may expect to receive a full issue of .300 rifles. By 'full issue' I would point out that it is meant that we shall receive one rifle for every two enrolled men. . . . Members who may have to parade for guards in their own boots or shoes can. . . . obtain for use on guard a pair of gum boots. . . . these gum boots should be returned on the following morning." Meanwhile a small store of pikes and rubber truncheons languished unissued.

From December 13th onwards these guards were abandoned in favour of patrolling the coast, which continued until July 10th, 1942. But meanwhile much had changed. Gradually, despite the bombardment, war production began to achieve proportions so massive that equipment was available even for the Home Guard: lease/lend supplies also eased the burden. Automatic weapons started to reach the north-west: more systematic training and the appointment of specialist officers took place. First at Aber (the coldest range outside the Arctic Circle) and then at Coed Coch adequate weapon training and manoeuvres with live ammunition became possible. Exercises in combination with other Home Guard units and with the Army were conducted on an increasingly ambitious scale. Standards of proficiency were set up and achieved: even proficiency badges (popularly supposed to have some connection therewith) were issued. But still Britain stood alone: still the role of the Home Guard was understood to be that of static defence auxiliary to the regular Army when the invasion began.

In July, 1941, the Nazis sealed their fate by the invasion of Russia. It did not seem so at the time. The "over in six weeks" school was vocal (never including the Prime Minister) for some three weeks. The defence of Moscow, however, the first real check on land to the victorious Nazi armies, changed the task of the Home Guard, although that also was not apparent at the time. Henceforward the Home Guard was fated to abandon its role of static defence in alliance with supporting regular forces, in favour of training to hold the fort against nuisance counter-attacks from air and sea while the continent was reconquered from the powers of darkness. The invasion of Germany, rendered possible by the acquisition of two hundred million surprisingly tough Russians as allies, was rendered certain by the attack on Pearl Harbour, and the entry of America into the war. When, with the fall of Singapore in the February of 1942, with the Nazis at the gates of Egypt and in the foothills of the Caucasus, our fortunes seemed at their lowest ebb, it was not despair which brought about the change in the Home Guard to a compulsory force, but rather a reasoned optimism. To stand and defend one's native place against overwhelming odds is a job for volunteers: to stand by for general defence and guard duty, defending the "backdoor" of an invading Army, is a task which all may be called upon to share. From the 16th of February, 1942—the day after the fall of Singapore—service in the Home Guard became compulsory. In the Ministry of Food unit in Colwyn Bay the change in organisation did not greatly alter the character of the force or the spirit in which it approached its duties. There were some who had been instrumental in building up the unit in the days when invasion seemed immediate, who had subsequently withdrawn under pressure of official duties, which seemed to them to come first when the crisis was lessened. There were others, no doubt, who had been unable to justify to themselves the devotion of the time which the training demanded, but who were glad to "have their minds made up for them." In a surprisingly short space of time it was often hard to distinguish between the keenness and efficiency of those who had a record of unbroken service and those who came back, or who came in for the first time.

The year 1942 saw the tide turn, first with the victory of El Alamein, then with the relief of Stalingrad. It saw also the inspiring record of Soviet partisans and the Jugo-Slav and Grecian armies of liberation, pointing the way to what determined men could do, even half-armed and in isolation. In Britain the formation of the Home Guard anti-aircraft batteries was the first definite step in the release of regular forces for the role of attack. Mobile training, and the organisation of mobile units, became of increasing importance in Home Guard training. In Colwyn Bay a mobile unit was trained to a surprising pitch of toughness and efficiency, while even the less athletic acquired the unscrupulous ferocity of race-gang toughs in unarmed combat courses, and harassed instructors tried to keep pace with the changing vocabulary of battle drill.

The end of the year saw North Africa invaded in strength. By the beginning of 1943 the growth in strength of the Ministry of Food unit was such as to justify the formation of a separate Battalion, the 11th Denbighshire, recruited wholly from Ministry employees. At the same time a series of courses of instruction was set on foot with a view to enrolling a women's unit, which came officially to life in April. Meanwhile, the Nazi forces had been cleared out of North Africa. Shortly after, Sicily was invaded, an operation in which the Battalion participated in the person of Major Lawrence, who was on shore in uniform during the last week of the operation, thereby establishing a claim to be the first Home Guard to take part in the liberation of Europe. Training in the new Battalion proceeded at an accelerated tempo, and the focus of its operations changed to Pentre Foelas. During the winter of 1943/4 a general course for the proficiency badge was instituted, and the vast majority passed the examinations held in February and March, 1944. Meanwhile the specialist units of the Battalion had been built up, and become proficient. Signals, guides, intelligence, ambulance and other special services were trained and equipped.

By the time the effective 'stand down' order was given, when the successful invasion of the continent had rendered negligible the chances of counter-attack by sea or air (with the exception of the coward's weapon of the flying bomb), the Ministry of Food Home Guard had undergone the same transformation to an effective unit in the garrison forces of Great Britain as had their comrades in the rest of the country.

CHAPTER 2.

The Ministry of Food Home Guard in Defence.

"There was a little man and he had a little gun."
Old Nursery Rhyme.

Before the evacuation of the Ministry from London, already the L.D.V. unit had posted guards on Ministry buildings and made plans for their defence. On May 25th the Treasury had issued a memorandum: "It has now been decided to provide armed defence to be carried out by Civil Servant Volunteers, in certain Government Offices. Rifles and ammunition (20 rounds per rifle) and bayonets to the number of 10% and uniforms or brassards will be provided and the volunteers will be enrolled in the L.D.V." But with characteristic caution it proceeded, "specially stringent steps must be taken to exclude unsuitable volunteers. So far as possible enrolment should be from (a) established Civil Servants and (b) unestablished Civil Servants of reasonably long service who are Army, Navy or Air Force Pensioners . . . Volunteers who do not satisfy these requirements may complete the form, but unless the officer has been recently vetted (sic) from a security point of view by the appropriate authorities, the forms should be sent to the Private Secretary to the Permanent Under Secretary of State, Home Office, before enrolment."

This did not ease the task of those engaged in building up the L.D.V. unit of what Lord Woolton was subsequently to refer to as "My motley army of business men and dons," but enrolment proceeded. On May 29th, the Ministry of Food Establishment Division issued a memorandum. "It is necessary, in the present conditions, that the Ministry should be provided with armed defence and it has been decided that this service should be carried out by volunteers from the staff under the command of Mr. Lachlan Maclean, O.B.E., C.St.J. Volunteers should be men of reasonably good physique, and if possible, should have experience of firearms."

On June 1st, the issue of arms to Civil Service L.D.V. units took place: ten rifles per *Ministry*! On the 4th, the Treasury wrote: "I cannot supply four-by-two, cleaning rods or rifle oil; can Departments see to these for themselves, if necessary? We shall have to get along without belts, frogs and ammunition pouches. . . . I cannot say when more supplies will be available; you will appreciate that the needs of the moment make it quite likely that we shall have to wait some time." Not surprisingly, Captain Hope from Operations H.Q. London Area, concluded his report of a reconnaissance of the defence arrangements at Great Westminster House (in the course of which he had recommended a minimum of thirteen armed guards) by saying, "the present supply of rifles, e.g., 10, is insufficient, having regard to the great size of the building, and a further ten should, if possible, be secured."

The background was the disembarkation from Dunkirk, the hourly expectation of German landings, absence of arms, hasty improvisation of training and organisation—in short the condition of the L.D.V. all over Great Britain. Harassed majors, straight from the beaches of Dunkirk, were consulted about modern methods of street-fighting and the defence of buildings; the advice of any returned soldier of the Expeditionary Force who had come into contact with paratroops was eagerly sought. Then, for the majority of the Ministry staff, came the evacuation. The Home Guard at this time, it must be remembered, was expecting to go into action at short notice. How serious the official view of the situation was may best be illustrated by extracts from an almost contemporaneous instruction from the H.Q. Oswestry Sub-Area. "In view of the possibility of an attempt at invasion being made at an early date, all preparations for defence should be completed as soon as possible. These preparations should include a review of your operational commitments and the preparation of definite plans for manning the defences which you will have to man and preparations by each company of a list showing exactly the defensive position it intends to occupy.... It is to be impressed on any individual engaged in anti-invasion measures that once action commences, control of the tactical situation becomes largely de-centralised. Each man becomes his own 'Wavel,' personal initiative is everything, and every local opportunity to destroy or delay enemy elements must be energetically taken and continuously pursued.... Hostile parties succeeding in reaching defensive positions are to be vigorously attacked with hand grenades and the bayonet; A.F.V.s with bombs and coils of concertina wire, which should be stored in readiness at all posts in the vicinity of tracks leading off the beaches. At close quarters crowbars and picks should be used against tracks and driving sprockets. The essence of all action should be individual vigour, and initiative in meeting each local situation as it arises; this should be thoroughly inculcated into every man engaged." The little man was expecting to fire his little gun in deadly earnest, and his only anxiety was, in most cases, whether it would be his turn to have one of the very few available guns when the trouble started.

It was against this background that, shortly after the arrival of the Ministry of Food in Colwyn Bay, the Home Guard Unit of the Ministry, now attached to the 1st Denbighshire Home Guard Battalion, began to undertake what were destined to be their only operational duties in the North Wales area. These consisted, firstly, of guarding the Penmaen Head quarries and the station at Colwyn Bay, and subsequently of operating a series of patrols, based upon an inlying piquet, which covered a section of the seashore. Of these duties the one which appears to have taken the strongest hold on the imagination and memory of all who participated was the Penmaen Head guard, which was indeed carried out under conditions of difficulty and hardship sufficient to make a fairly deep impression. The first of the Penmaen Head guards was on the night of September 16th/17th, 1940, and, through the mist of legend which has already come to surround that occasion, the following facts may be discerned.

The first guard was under the command of Colonel Balfour, with McCulloch as second in command, both names subsequently to be well known in the Home Guard.[1] It should be recollected that, at this stage in the organisation of the unit, a kind of primitive communism operated in respect of most equipment. A small supply of rifles and a smaller supply of ammunition was available, adequate to arm only those Home Guards who were actually on duty. Rifles and ammunition, therefore, had to be collected and returned to a central depot whenever operational duties were undertaken. Nor was this only the case with arms and ammunition. Greatcoats, steel helmets and even boots were in similarly scarce supply, and had to be collected and returned. No transport was available for the Home Guard to call upon, other than overcrowded public vehicles; no commissariat arrangements had been completed and, while they were in course of improvisation, experiments were made of necessity upon the "vile bodies" of those who had to be fed.

On the evening of September 16th, therefore, the guard fell in and then fell out to board an omnibus in an approximately orderly manner. On the outward journey the conductor meekly accepted the assertion of Sgt. Balfour that the party consisted of Home Guardsmen on duty, and demanded no fare. On arriving at the nearest point to the quarry the party dismounted, encumbered with blankets, palliasses, rations and arms. At the quarry at Penmaen Head, the Pier and the ammunition dump which were the object of the guard are a considerable distance from the nearest road and are approached by a very steep and uneven path. The Head falls precipitately, and on the quarry face vertically towards the sea. The shore end of the jetty serving the quarry consists of a stone crushing plant and a few small cabins in which the guard had to sleep. The jetty itself consists mainly of the appurtenances of the mechanism whereby quarry boats are mechanically loaded, and was not designed as a promenade on a dark winter's night. Decanted from the bus the guard stumbled in rain and mud down the steep decline which appeared to lead directly into the faintly seen breakers below. Several journeys had to be made on this pioneer trip, but eventually the fourteen members of the guard and their impedimenta were all collected, the former were allotted sleeping space and tours of duty, and the first sentries posted. Of these, two guarded the shed in which explosives were housed, which stood on the edge of a steep cliff descending directly into the sea and which

---

(1) The following were members of the first guard mounted at Penmaen Head: —

Col. F. C. C. Balfour, C.I.E., C.B.E., M.C. (Commander),
G. McCulloch (2nd in Command),   A. V. Luscombe, M.M.,
H. C. Carter,   A. R. Parselle,
E. B. Cranfield,   J. A. Reid,
C. R. Currie,   J. Roberts,
G. R. Davis,   H. J. Sayers,
B. A. Forster,   J. W. H. Taylor.

was incidentally one of the coldest spots in North Wales. Another guarded the jetty, slippery with sea water and inadequately railed, whilst the fourth, guarding against possible landwise attack, was situated on the bend of the goat track by which alone the jetty could be approached. Inside, two rooms were at the joint disposal of the guard, a much larger number of cockroaches, and a number of rats which was never properly ascertained. Palliasses lay more or less where they fell, and competition for the extremely limited sitting accommodation, consisting of a rickety table, a broken chair and a bench, was keen, at least in the early hours of the evening .

It blew and rained all that first night. There was no moon and none of the guard, N.C.O.s or privates, had had an opportunity to learn the layout of the quarry. None, therefore, knew the whereabouts of the quarry tramlines, chunks of broken limestone and rainfilled potholes, all of which had apparently been set to catch the N.C.O. on his rounds and the sentries on their beat. Fortunately, order of some kind had been established before Huskisson, Platoon Commander, accompanied by Sir Russell Scott, then Deputy Secretary in the Ministry, came to inspect the guard and ascertain the position in respect of their (almost completely negative) comforts. He approved of the military disposition of the guards, but took a poor view, which he expressed with characteristic forcefulness, of the local contours.

Included in the orders covering the guard were instructions to make contact with the beach patrol of the Royal Corps of Signals and also to ensure that no ship was to move within a mile of the shore during the hours of darkness. Unfortunately, the Signals patrol did not appear and it was not altogether obvious what a Home Guard patrol, armed only with rifles, was to do when a coaster left the jetty further along the shore and proceeded to take advantage of a favourable tide, passing Penmaen Head in the early hours of the morning. On the way home, very weary but less burdened than when they had come out, the Guard found the conductor of the bus less co-operative. Refusing to accept the statement that the party were Home Guardsmen coming off duty, he stoutly insisted on the rights of the Crosville shareholders. This, however, made no impression on Sgt. Balfour who calmly kept his seat saying, "Yes, indeed, you can take it up with whomsoever you like," and proceeded to furnish the irate conductor with the name and address of the unit. In those days the Home Guard took themselves very seriously, and indeed the hardship which the Penmaen Head guard voluntarily underwent was sufficient to explain and justify their attitude.

This guard continued until December 12th. The only important change which took place during this time was that the weather got colder and colder. The series of logs furnished by N.C.O.s in charge indicate that a number of incidents of minor importance took place. Steamers appeared in the small hours of the morning to load at the jetty, and their Admiralty authorisation had to be checked. On one occasion a violent thunderstorm burst over the district and the Quarry

Manager, apparently somewhat more acquainted with the characteristics of the explosives under his care than were the Home Guard, rang up to suggest that the sentries might be moved from the immediate vicinity of the explosives store. (There is, incidentally, no record as to whether or not the unfortunate sentries actually were moved). Mysterious lights were observed, some of which were subsequently identified as railway signal lights. Warnings were received from the Civil Defence Authorities concerning the different types of attack which might be expected from the Luftwaffe, for it must be remembered that during this period the blitz was in full swing, and very often the sentries on the edge of the cliff could see and even feel the detonations as their comrades were bombarded in Liverpool, thirty miles away. On one occasion an enterprising N.C.O. fired his rifle in the dead of night in order to ascertain, as indeed he did, what the reaction of the guard would be. On another, the guard room was deeply flooded, and all Gair's flair for organisation was called into play.

But the central theme of the Penmaen Head guard was quite serious physical hardship and discomfort, sufficient indeed to make those who took part proudly conscious of the fact that they were indeed sharing, although in a minor key, in the direct burden of National Defence. A few extracts from reports of the N.C.O.s in charge may serve to indicate the conditions under which this guard was carried out. "There were not enough palliasses for all the men off duty to lie down." .... "Putting them on the floor not only makes them dirty, but puts the men among the beetles and cockroaches." .... "Unless reasonable sleeping accommodation is provided, I do not think the men will be able to continue during the winter to do guard and their work in the Ministry." .... "Reliable transport arrangements should be made. Unless a lorry is provided an arrangement should be made for sufficient number of cars to take the guard to Penmaen Head as it is impossible to put so many men on the buses during the rush hours."

Food also was something of a problem: it added variety to the Home Guard's night on duty, never to know if he was to be greeted on his return from a tour of duty at 2 a.m. with cold stew or cold soup (cocoa, like the poor, we had always with us: in some mysterious manner, however, the old soldiers managed to provide themselves with rum, without even a quartermaster's store in being). On one occasion indeed, half way down the steep and stony path, someone dropped the dixie containing the stew, and the still small voice of the (then) C.S.M. Selby was heard, "Go on, pick it up. You'll have to eat a lot more dirt than that before you're a soldier."

Add to the lack of accommodation and equipment the fact that the winter was the hardest for many years and that the position was so exposed that, for example, on one occasion a door blew through its frame and could not be replaced, and some measure of the hardship incurred by the troops taking part in this guard is indicated. Perhaps the best tribute which could be paid to the general spirit of the Ministry of Food Unit is that the Penmaen Head guard is still usually spoken of by the pioneers in terms of affectionate and blasphemous regret.

In addition to guards, the unit undertook one other role in defence, that of digging trenches and weapon pits. It is perhaps somewhat doubtful, in view of the siting of most of these, whether their construction should have been regarded as defence or training, but those who dug certainly thought of them in terms of defence. It is difficult to wax eloquent about digging, blisters or lumbago: suffice it to say that in an incredibly short space of time the children had destroyed all the defence works so painfully prepared. (A company recruited from the small boys and girls of Colwyn Bay might be guaranteed to burrow through the Siegfried Line within a week). And mention might be made, in passing, of the pride of a party of No. 5 Platoon who, having been instructed to dig and camouflage a weapon pit, did the latter so successfully as to be upbraided by their Platoon Commander for not having done it at all!

During the period in which the Penmaen Head guard was undertaken the Ministry of Food Unit also took over from the local railway Home Guard unit the task of guarding the main line railway station at Colwyn Bay, with its two signal boxes, and patrolling the intermediate length of line. This guard was carried out under conditions somewhat less bleak than those obtaining at Penmaen Head and its site was easier of access. It was not, however, by any means a picnic. Conditions were similar in respect of equipment; indeed at this period they were similar all over the country as far as the Home Guard went.

At this stage what uniforms were available were curiously cut objects of denim. Their general characteristics are admirably set out below.

Armlet's Soliloquy: *L.D.V., August*, 1940.

Enter Armlet, in his nightshirt, holding in one hand his newest blue serge suit, and in the other his denim uniform.

Armlet: To wear, or not to wear: that is the question :
Whether 'tis nobler in the mind to suffer
The jeers and titters of misguided females,
Or to slope arms against my natty suitings
And smear my coat with grease ; ay, there's the rub
That lends extremity to the long life
My suit was planned for. Yet should I attend
The Office in my denim uniform
I should, in truth, be fearfully arrayed—
(The clumping boots, the empty bosomed tunic,
The calf-revealing. armpit-scratching pants,
The neckband sticking out a yard in front,
The trousers sagging out a yard behind)—
The girls would snigger, and the messengers,
Looking most reverend and sagely wise
Before me, mock at me behind my back.

Yet if I wear my blue suit on parade
The desperate chance of war might ruin it.

("What dids't thou, daddy, in the Greater War?"
"My son, I got this green stain on my waistcoat
When crawling on my tummy through the grass."
Or "Wait a moment while I turn about . . .
See what a rent the envious Brechus made—
He crawled behind—his bayonet sheath fell off . . . .
This was the most unkindest cut of all.
Indubitably it was not repaired—
With a bare bodkin . . . . But of that, no more").

And yet, the thought of income-tax to come—
The urge to National Savings—and the day,
Perhaps not distant—when our puissant King
Will bid me don a permanent battle-dress—
Urge me to save the blue ; . . . . though self-respect
Will make us rather wear the clothes we choose
Than skulk in readymades that hardly fit
Thus Hitler will make scarecrows of us all,
And the proud glossiness of summer suitings
Be muddied o'er with the wormcasts of Penrhos . . .
Far better this than swelter in the garb
That would affright the fair at Pwllycrochan.
For who can bear the quips and frowns of girls.
The poets song, the dandy's contumely,

The chance of love despised—e'en Love's delay—
The insolence of street-boys, and the spurns
That patient soldiery of civilians take,
Clad à la mode ? Ay, who would rifle bear,
To itch and sweat beneath the gaberdine,
But that the dread of something worse than sweat —
That unremovable blemish at whose sight
Each passer-by will turn, and smile, and pause,
And obviously wonder why we sport,
Even in war-time such a shabby suit . . . .
And yet, it may be, he will not despise
My brave blue suit that has such smirches on it—
The egg-yolk and the thousand inky spots
That cloth is heir to, added to the scars
Of humble service with the L.D.V.—
But that's a dream ! For now I realise
That to the kerbside crowd what gleams must come
When we are shuffling past in Khaki coils
Even khaki swathings of great girth and torment :
Envy is certain. 'Tis a consummation
Devoutly to be wished. I'll brave the scoffing
Ophelia, and don the uniform.

(Does so.)

A.F.E.

Steel helmets formed a particular problem at the station, as the scanty supply available had to be shared with the railway unit, who still retained responsibility for guarding the goods yard. In consequence, occasionally the operative members of the station guard had to patrol or stand sentry in rain and snow with no more effective protection than a field service cap. The guard were housed in the station waiting room, which barely accommodated, side by side, the palliasses of those members of the guard who were off duty.

L.D.V. Days—Bureaucrats without Battledress

In the Dark Days

The first Uniforms—Lord Woolton inspects

"Standing Easy"

Frequently, moreover, during the blitz the 8.50 or the 9.40 p.m. would appear at anything from 2 to 5 a.m. and the guard would find themselves giving up their fire and palliasses to stranded wayfarers who could not reach their homes. On guard, the main difficulty was to prevent the troops breaking their shins over signal rods, rails and all the curious appliances which exist to trip the unwary foot as it proceeds across the railway. Getting on and off platforms and up and down the stairs of signal boxes in the blackout also had their dangers, while it took some time for Home Guards who were laymen as far as railways were concerned to get accustomed to walking across the tracks without the feeling that a railway engine was lurking around the corner and about to spring.

The commissariat difficulties of the Home Guard at this stage in its development also affected the station guard. Again quotations from the guard log illustrate the point. "The food provided was appreciated by the guard, but as no knives, forks, spoons or plates were issued, it was eaten under difficulties. As there are no facilities at the station for heating food I would suggest that meat pies or something similar would be a more suitable meal." . . . "When drawing our rations from the canteen we were given a brown paper bag which should have been sugar, but when we came to use it we found it was plaster of paris." . . . "I would also like to stress the point of all guards being properly clothed and would suggest in this respect that all additional equipment such as steel helmets and waterproof capes should be issued at the time of guard mounting." Even accommodation within the Ministry buildings was a problem. For a time the communal overcoats utilised by the guard were kept in the men's lavatory at the social centre, and the guard was mounted in the bar, for lack of alternative space!

The station guard also came to an end on December 12th, 1940: henceforward for some 18 months the operational duties of the Ministry of Food Unit centred upon the beach patrol, based upon the inlying piquet in the Old Sanatorium at Penrhos. By this time equipment was somewhat more plentiful and the organisation of the Home Guard was in itself more complete, while its relations with the army and civil authorities had become defined and polished by usage. It was, therefore, as compared with the other two guards, somewhat uneventful. Sentries were posted outside the guard room and patrols contacted the railway and patrolled the front from the Dingle to the end of the Cayley Promenade, making contact, in theory, with another Home Guard unit and with the regular holding forces (Signals) respectively. Occasionally reports came through on the now properly organised military telephone system, concerning escaped prisoners, fog, or other military or natural events necessitating doubling the patrol, and consequently halving the sleep of the guard. By this time also, small arms had become available in quantities sufficient for every Home Guard to have his own rifle, and in certain cases, duly recorded by holes in the guardroom ceiling, it appeared that custody had preceded familiarity. As time passed, the illuminations on the skyline happily became dimmer and less frequent, as the striking power of the Luftwaffe was worn down, and gradually the duties demanded of the patrols were lessened. It was only during the earliest period of this inlying piquet that patrols were required to examine the identity cards of late wanderers on the promenade, and by the time the piquet was finally stood down and the patrols discontinued, the operational atmosphere, which had been so strong on Penmaen Head and at the station and indeed on the beach patrol in the early days, had faded away. Henceforward, apart from the duty of appearing at the office in uniform and with arms and equipment as the tour of duty came round, the only nominally operational duty of the unit was to provide guards for the files at Battalion Headquarters. The active days for the Home Guard in Colwyn Bay were over, although its training continued and its standards and equipment continued steadily to improve.[1]

This chapter cannot, however, be concluded without reference to the men who left the unit to join His Majesty's Forces, and, more particularly, to those who gave their lives. Their names are recorded in the Roll of Honour; where all equally proved their devotion, distinction would be invidious. Their comrades remember them with pride and sorrow; their pride is heightened by memories of duties undertaken side by side with them in the past.

---

(1) The last picquet at the Old Sanatorium was furnished on 10th July, 1942, from No. 11 Platoon, and included:

Sgt. Ruff	Pte. Huntingdon
Cpl. Sermon	Pte. Mackay
L./Cpl. Reiss	Pte. Suckling
Pte. Beckett	Pte. Tyrtell
Pte. Chatfield	Pte. Wood
Pte. Harrison	

CHAPTER 3.

TRAINING AND ORGANISATION I

May, 1940, to April, 1941: The L.D.V. Unit in London and Colwyn Bay: "F" Coy. No. 1 Bn. (Denbighshire) Home Guard.

"The mind of the people is like mud,
From which arise strange and beautiful things."

W. J. Turner.

The previous chapter dealt with the operative duties of the Unit, and made reference in passing to new weapons, and improving standards of efficiency: the first described the measure in which the changing pattern of the war altered the role of the Home Guard. All this necessitated constant change in the organisation and the training programme of the Ministry of Food Unit, and the two factors are so intimately interlocked that in order to present an intelligible picture they must be taken together, phase by phase. This chapter deals with the period in which the foundations were laid.

The story of the first administrative measures taken in London has already been told. The first move made in the matter of weapon training was, as so often was the case in the early days of the Local Defence Volunteers, as a result of unofficial initiative. On the 4th of June a meeting was convened by Maclean in Great Westminster House at which a Rifle Club was formed. The new venture received enthusiastic support and at the conclusion of the meeting volunteers for the Local Defence Volunteers were enrolled, although, still operating under the somewhat timid aegis of the Treasury, only permanent members of the Civil Service were allowed to join. The next memorable date in the development of the Unit is June 11th, marked by the issue of a document headed Order (No. 1) by Maclean, Group Organiser. This order made the first appointments to the H.Q. Personnel of the Local Defence Volunteers and the names are worthy of recording.[1]

The Order terminated with the announcement that the Musketry Instructor had arranged for a detail of 20 men to parade at Great Westminster House on the following day for practice on the House of Lords miniature range. This was the first shoot actually in charge of Major Moore, who was, with the able assistance of Sherman and Twigge, to work tirelessly through the following months in installing the rudiments of weapon training into new recruits and in polishing up the memories of the old soldiers.

(1) In the following order, the appointments were:

Armourer	E. A. Lovett
Musketry Instructor	A. G. Moore, M.C.
Signalling Instructor	H. G. Vincent, C.B., C.V.O.
Group Organisers	E. P. Keeley.
	G. N. Lawrence.

C

With the move of the Ministry to Colwyn Bay, which at first involved the retention of Maclean in London, Lawrence became acting O.C. at Colwyn Bay. To his enterprise and initiative a very great deal of the success of the initial period must be attributed. As early as 3rd July we find him reporting to Maclean by letter that he had taken it upon himself to institute training parades for the Local Defence Volunteers in Penrhos College, and that he had been fortunate in enlisting the support of the O.C. of No. 1 Coy. of the Royal Corps of Signals billeted in Colwyn Bay. The latter, a foretaste of the generous co-operation which was throughout to mark relations with the Royal Corps of Signals, made available to the Local Defence Volunteers some 50 rifles and the services of seven N.C.O. instructors. With this assistance parades were arranged on every week-day evening for rifle drill and musketry instruction, and for physical training and bathing at 7 o'clock every morning. The Local Defence Volunteers of those days certainly took their training seriously! Their enthusiasm must have been infectious, for on July 8th we find Lawrence inviting the ladies of the Ministry to attend the physical training and bathing parades at 7 o'clock on Mondays, Wednesdays and Fridays; the attendance is not recorded.

In the same letter Lawrence strikes another note, which was to recur all too frequently: "In view of the general urgency of preparing our defensive arrangements, I feel that we should make every effort to obtain arms and equipment, and I shall be glad to know if there is any chance of obtaining rifles sufficient to mount a guard on this building. The minimum number of rifles for a guard for Penrhos College would be 10 rifles with supporting equipment and ammunition."

Also, in the same letter, the shadow of Aber range falls across the future. "There is a fully equipped range some 16 miles away, and the N.C.O. instructors have volunteered to take details to the range as soon as the training of these Squads is sufficiently advanced and, more particularly, as soon as the necessary ammunition can be obtained."

Training and the organisation of the Unit into sections and platoons continued. Meanwhile, the administrative work associated with the Unit began to reach formidable proportions, and to throw a heavy burden upon Lawrence, whose secretary, Miss Marston, was almost performing the duties of an adjutant. In this she was followed by Miss Smith, who carried out the paper work subsequently necessitating an orderly room staff with such effect that when she left the Ministry a presentation was made to her by the grateful "troops." Moreover, equipment was still very scarce. The equipment supplied for the whole of the Ministry of Food—that is to say for, presumably, some 500 volunteers—was 10 rifles, 10 bayonets and 250 rounds of ammunition. Even this had had to be left behind on leaving London!

Quite apart, however, from this shortage of supplies, Lawrence must inevitably have had to struggle against a sense of frustration.

He was alone at the time, in the sense that Maclean was still in London, and was fighting a solitary battle, first of all to establish and then to develop a Ministry of Food Unit, and to prevent a drift which would otherwise have taken place of the keener men in the Ministry into the local Battalion. He had no specific authority, even to organise the training of the Ministry's Unit, since his original appointment was only that of group organiser for the Neville House Unit. He was, therefore, acting beyond his powers, both in so far as he was developing a training programme for the whole of the Ministry Unit, and in so far as he was accepting and training men in advance of the Home Office authorisation (for all but permanent Civil Servants) upon which the Treasury was still insisting. Such, however, was the general sense of urgency of the time that he probably had no compunction in exercising his initiative beyond official bounds, and certainly those of us who were co-operating with him at the time had no hesitation in accepting the authority with which the logic of contemporary events invested him. As usual, real authority was in the hands of those who had the intelligence to interpret the developing pattern of history and to act accordingly.

An interesting feature of the formative period of the Unit is the enormous number of letters and other documents embodying suggestions which were being constantly passed up the ladder from the rank and file. Not only were the Volunteers training on six nights a week and Sunday morning, and doing physical training at 7 o'clock in the morning three days a week; they were proving their enthusiasm by making constant proposals for the improvement of the Unit's organisation and for bringing its training programme into line with the technique of modern warfare. Some of them wanted the Unit to be more like His Majesty's Brigade of Guards in the days of His Majesty King Edward VII.; others wanted it to be more like the Red Army in 1917. The old sailors wanted it to be more like the Navy which, like ship's tobacco, spoils a man's taste for milder things. But sifting through this mass of correspondence, which is the despair of the historian and must have been the nightmare of the officers concerned with administration, one finds a large number of ideas which have subsequently been embodied in the training and organisation of the Home Guard.

At this time, the only ammunition to which the Unit had access was .22 and, as was characteristic of the period, it could not be issued direct to the Local Defence Volunteers. This was where the Ministry Rifle Club came in handy. As a registered Rifle Club they could obtain the ammunition which was denied to the L.D.V. and they obtained also the use of the range at Rydal School. Consequently the Rifle Club undertook to provide range facilities—targets, rifles and ammunition—and the Local Defence Volunteers Unit agreed to pay a sum of 1s. per member firing on the range.

On the 26th July, for the first time, the L.D.V. Unit, in plain clothes and with forty rifles, was paraded before Lord Woolton in the grounds of Penrhos College.[1] This visit had very important and interesting repercussions, because it is very obvious, from a letter despatched only three days later, that the indefatigable Lawrence had cornered the Minister on the question of arms and equipment. We find him writing: "You will recollect that you asked me to let you have a note of my estimate of the minimum requirements of the Ministry of Food L.D.V. Unit, a detachment of which you inspected on parade in Colwyn Bay on Friday last. I am taking the opportunity to give you, in duplicate, two lists of arms and equipment which I feel we should have. List A represents what, in my opinion, is the barest minimum for the continued existence of the Unit. At the moment, as you know, we are depending entirely on the goodwill of the local Royal Corps of Signals for the rifles with which we parade, and apart from these we have not one item of arms or equipment. List B comprises such items as would bring the Unit to a more proper state of efficiency. . . . . [2] Uniforms and our own rifles will go a long way towards establishing that spirit of cohesion and esprit de corps, which I am particularly anxious to arouse. But until such time as we have had an opportunity of firing a few rounds of ball ammunition per man I am loath to take over a guard or duty which calls for a knowledge of the use of fire arms."

The Minister took the point. On the 5th August we find him writing to the Secretary of State for War in the following terms: "I think you know that the greater part of the Ministry of Food has been evacuated to Colwyn Bay. The move has inevitably been unpopular,

(1) The personnel at this first inspection was drawn from:—
    Bacon and Ham Division 62
    Sugar and Starch Division 24
    Other Offices 11
        Total 97

(2) *List A.*   450 Rifles and bayonets (with slings).
           40 Revolvers
           450 Uniforms—Denim overalls and forage caps and armlets
      15,000 Rounds of S.A.A. (10 rounds per man for practice; 20 rounds per man for internal security)
           450 Shrapnel helmets
           600 Rounds of revolver ammunition
           24 Rifle grenade attachments
           200 Mills bombs (with rifle grenade accessories for 50 grenades)
           450 Mackintosh capes.

    List B.   8 Lewis or other Light Automatic Guns
      40,000 S.A.A.
           450 Greatcoats
           450 Shrapnel helmets
           Dummy bombs for practice throwing
           Musketry Landscape targets, etc.

and quite a large number of the men feel that they may be considered to have run away from danger.

"This feeling has had its effect in causing them to form a most enthusiastic body of men for the Home Guard. I was there ten days ago and they asked me to review a section of the unit, which numbers 450. . . . they are anxious to take a part in the defence of the place, by patrolling the railway line, the sea front, etc.

"But while they are full of enthusiasm, they have no uniforms, rifles or ammunition. They begged me to ask if anything can be done to hasten the supply of these to them, so that they may be available to help their country in the case of need and may have their prestige enhanced in the district, which I am bound to admit has been very critical of the Civil Servants who have commandeered their hotels."

Two days later, however, Mr. Anthony Eden replied: "I am afraid that our resources in rifles, ammunition, uniform, etc., do not permit of immediate issues to all members of the Home Guard on the scale suggested in the enclosure to your letter. We are working on a carefully drawn up programme of priority in the issue of rifles and other items of equipment to the Home Guard and when making these issues we have to bear in mind the importance of the particular area in our general scheme of defence. I quite agree that we must do everything possible to avoid damping the enthusiasm of your people at Colwyn Bay and I am therefore having enquiries made through the Local H.G. Commander, with whom I should expect that Mr. Lawrence has already been in touch, in order to ensure that everything possible is done to further the efficient organisation and equipment of the Ministry of Food Home Guard detachment."

Lawrence had indeed been in touch with the local organisation and on the previous day he had received a note from Major I. Edwardes-Evans, M.C., the Commander of the 1st Battalion No. 3 Zone, informing him that the Ministry of Food Unit of the L.D.V. would be incorporated as a Company in his Battalion and would be designated as "F" Company. The Battalion to which the Ministry of Food Unit thus found itself assigned was attached to the Royal Welch Fusiliers, and indeed had very many old soldiers of that magnificent regiment in its ranks. Henceforward, even after the Ministry of Food Unit had become the 11th Battalion, contact was still maintained both in training and on operational duties with the 1st Battalion. Reference will frequently be made in subsequent chapters to various phases of this co-operation, but it must at this stage be recorded how cordial was their welcome on the occasion of the formal affiliation of the Ministry's Unit, and how ready was their response to our demand for assistance. Their difficulties in this respect had been no less than those of the Ministry Unit and had, in some ways, been greater, in that the Volunteers of the 1st Denbighshire Battalion had, in many cases, been training over rough mountain and moorland since the inception of the L.D.V., and undertaking patrols under very trying circumstances, with no more equipment than was at the time available for any of the Units in those areas of the country which were considered to be comparatively immune from immediate attack.

Not the least of the benefits derived from incorporation was that the unit came under the command of Colonel J. S. Barton, O.B.E., M.C., Zone Commander and later Secretary of the T.A.A. With imperturbable good humour and patience he stood up to a constant barrage of requests for equipment, by letter and telephone and, when he had them, which in the early days was seldom, delivered the goods.

One of the first operations to be undertaken jointly by Ministry Officers and N.C.O.s with those of the 1st Battalion took place some six days later, when a demonstration, arranged by the 216/S/L Training Regiment R.A., of self-igniting phosphorous bombs took place at Bryn Euryn Quarry. These weapons, which had already under the title of "Molotov Cocktails" seized the imagination of the public and the Home Guard, were on view for the first time to the Home Guard in the area, and even if they had no rifles they began to feel that equipment was on the way. Shortly after, too, an issue of Ross rifles arrived. The state of organisation and equipment at the end of August is shown in a letter from Lawrence to one of the more active members of the London Unit. This letter moreover stresses once more the extent to which the local unit of the Royal Corps of Signals was helping the Ministry Unit. "You will no doubt have heard that we are parading every evening at 6 p.m. to 6.30 p.m. . . . you should know also that there are a number of courses running which will of course have to be duplicated owing to the number of applicants exceeding the convenient number of a class that can be taken in these subjects, e.g., a course in (a) Map Reading and Scouting; (b) Signalling, buzzer, lamp and flags—given by the C.S.M. of No. 1 Coy. Royal Corps of Signals; (c) Section Leading and Fire Control. In addition I have been able to arrange an occasional Lecture by Major Hay of the Royal Corps of Signals, the next one being on Thursday, the 29th August, on the subject of 'The Defence of a Strong Point.' The last lecture was on the subject of 'The Tactics of the Home Guard.' To give you the background of our immediate activities I think that you should know that when we arrived here we had 'nothing of no sort' to work with, but I managed to borrow from the Royal Corps of Signals a number of rifles and N.C.O. Instructors. The rifles have now, unfortunately, been called in but there is a possibility that after next week I may be able to get an additional 30 or 40 of them on loan again. These were the P.14 adapted Ross rifle. The N.C.O. Instructors put in these parades in their spare time and their services are very greatly appreciated by this Unit. Our original lot of N.C.O.s have been drafted, some abroad and some on other Courses, and I have now another set of four Corporals who turn up most evenings and help in the parades. In the way of equipment I have now received 100 Ross rifles (and terrible things they are too!) and bayonets, 30 denim uniforms (which I dare not issue among 470 soldiers), 80 blankets, 60 groundsheets and 80 greatcoats. I have also got 1,000 rounds S.A.A. of which I am entitled to use 500 on the ranges." (The Ross rifles referred to above were issued on September 17th.)

Meanwhile the organisation of the unit as "F" Coy. of No. 1 Battalion had proceeded, and the first list of officers appeared in Part II. Orders on August 30th. It might at this juncture be of interest, particularly in view of those who may be tempted to think of the Home Guard as a purely amateur force, to recall the names and the achievements of these officers. All had held commissions previously in H.M. Forces and all had had fighting experience. The O.C. was, of course, Major (now Lt. Colonel) Lachlan Frederick Copeland Maclean, whose military service had commenced as a Second Lieutenant in the 6th Militia Battalion of the Manchester Regiment. He was mobilised with his Regiment on the outbreak of the Great War and served in France with the 2nd Battalion: he subsequently held staff appointments in England, France and in North Russia. He was mentioned in despatches and has an impressive collection of decorations. The Second-in-Command, Major George Napier Lawrence, was found at school in his O.T.C. Unit by the outbreak of the last war. By 1917 he was in the Army and in 1918/19 he saw service both in France and in the Army of Occupation as an ensign with the 1st Battalion, Coldstream Guards. He was subsequently Lieutenant in the Karachi Light Horse during his service in India and, later, Captain in the Madras Guards. The Officer Commanding No. 1 Platoon, Major Geoffrey Huskisson, D.S.O., M.C., joined the Army in 1914, went to Egypt, was wounded, returned to England, went to France as a Second Lieutenant with the Royal Regiment of Artillery and finally, after being wounded three times, having been mentioned in despatches and having been awarded the M.C. with Bar and the D.S.O., left the Army with the honorary rank of Major in 1919. The Commanding Officer of No. 2 Platoon, Captain Edward Capstick, M.C., was also found at school by the outbreak of the Great War, leaving his O.T.C. Unit as Senior Sergeant. He joined the Army in 1917 as a corporal in an Officers' Cadet Battalion and was posted to the Liverpool Regiment with whom he saw service in France, was wounded, invalided home and returned. He won the M.C. and Bar and rejoined the Territorial Army at the outbreak of this war. Captain Robert Hamilton Bremner, the O.C. of No. 3 Platoon, was a Second Lieutenant in the Territorial Army before the last war. He saw service with the Artillery from 1914 to 1917 when he was invalided home after service in France, being finally demobilised in the March of 1919. Major Alfred Garnett Moore, M.C. and Bar, who was Officer Commanding No. 4 Platoon, joined the 6th Manchester Regiment at the beginning of the century and saw service in South Africa. During the last war he saw service in the Western Desert and France, becoming attached to the Royal Flying Corps in 1915. He retired with the rank of Major on reaching the age limit in 1932. Captain Charles Augustine Holliday, the Officer Commanding No. 5 Platoon, was also a Territorial before the last war and saw service first in Egypt, where he was commissioned as a Second Lieutenant in the Royal Artillery in 1915, then in Mesopotamia, where he took part in the Relief of Kut, being subsequently invalided to England following typhoid, which was to prevent him from getting out to France in time for the last of the Great War. In 1919 he was demobilised but in 1920 joined the Honourable Artillery Company. He was mentioned in despatches.

By the time of the enrolment of the Ministry unit as "F" Company in the 1st Battalion, Ross rifles—as appeared from Lawrence's previously quoted letter—had become available and they were very shortly followed by Browning light machine guns and Lewis machine guns, ex-aircraft. About this time, too, shortly after the transfer to the 1st Battalion, more uniforms had started to arrive. The supply must indeed have become available very shortly before the first exercise in which the unit took part as a Company of the 1st Battalion, for we find Huskisson commenting characteristically, on 28th August, on the proposal to hold the exercise.

"With the greatest respect, I believe that with this issue of uniforms (which has not yet taken place) it would be advisable to get the uniforms issued out to the 'troops' and see that they know how to wear them. Also, if time permits, give them some indication how to deal with and roll mackintoshes or raincoats and give them an opportunity of wearing uniforms which they have never had on before. I think the time would be very well spent on Saturday afternoon tying up some loose ends of this sort, rather than putting them out on the roads like Fred Karno's Army!"

The exercise, however, took place and on 31st August Operational Order No. 001 was issued under the name of the acting O/C "F" Company. It conveyed "information" of the type with which the Home Guard were to become extremely familiar in the days to come. The traditional enemy force, estimated at 50 men, armed with the inevitable automatics and light machine guns, had been landed by the equally inevitable parachutes during the night of 30/31st August. The Ministry of Food Home Guard unit, supported by reconnaissance aircraft (represented by signals on Bryn Euryn), were to engage, attack and destroy. The exercise took place in the ground behind the quarry on Bryn Euryn and ended in a somewhat involved battle, which most of the participants appeared to enjoy, on what was subsequently the site of the buildings of the Cereals Division.

It is interesting at this stage to pause and review the level which training had already reached, remembering that the unit had only been in existence since May; it was still struggling into new uniforms and had just received its first official issue of rifles, apart from loans from the ever co-operative Signals unit. Part I. orders for the week ending 21st September give a pretty clear indication that on every night of the week, except Saturday, a detachment from one or more of the Ministry buildings was parading. The current courses of instruction included map reading and scouting, signalling—advanced and ele-

TRAINING AND ORGANISATION—I

mentary—and a course in musketry instruction, in addition to section leading and fire control; by this time, however, possibly as a result of the worsening weather, the seven a.m. physical training parades had been discontinued. A word concerning the general problem of training as it confronted the unit at this time is not perhaps irrelevant at this point. The paramount necessity of the time was to create a force, which, however heterogeneous its composition or unorthodox its methods, would be capable, if need be, of going into action at a very early date. The apparent lack of system in the training programme was neither due to lack of control nor of knowledge on the part of Commanders or Instructors (weekly lectures to all officers were a feature of the 1940/41 training programme), but to the absolute priority of getting over information which might form the basis for immediate action.

This order is also memorable in that it announces the first Penmaen Head Guards. These have already been described as part of the work of the unit in defence, but from the side of organisation, with which we are here concerned, they presented a headache. All equipment was still in short supply: night by night rifles, ammunition, blankets, greatcoats, boots and even caps and steel helmets had to be issued; every morning they had to be checked back into store. Had it not been for the constant and devoted work of Selby as C.S.M., and Battson as C.Q.M.S., it is doubtful if the guards could have been maintained.

Another angle on training is given by the record of the Ministry of Food demonstration squad which came into being about this time. Fortunately an account in the words of one of its leading spirits—Captain Hitchcock—is available:

"One week towards the end of the summer of 1940, an order was issued to the effect that on the following Sunday morning the Training Officer attached to the local companies of the Home Guard would talk to the Ministry of Food Unit at Penrhos on the subject of Street Fighting, and calling for volunteers to attend at Penrhos on the preceding Saturday afternoon to rehearse the part they would have to play on the Sunday morning. A dozen or so men volunteered, and on the Saturday afternoon were introduced to the Training Officer, Major South, newly returned from a course at Altcar. (This was, I believe, the first introduction to this unit of the man who was to become Commander of the Battalion).

"On Sunday morning these men were used to demonstrate methods of Street Fighting, and South was apparently so impressed with their performance that he asked permission to use them for demonstration purposes amongst outlying platoons. This, then, was the beginning of the Demonstration Squad.

"All through the winter of 1940/41, after attending the normal Company Parades on Sunday mornings, this band of stalwarts toured North Wales with South in the afternoons, demonstrating to units as far afield as Llanrwst, Eglwysbach, Abergele and Llangerniew. As the winter progressed, by additional coaching in the evenings, they added to their repertoire other subjects including sentry duties by day and night, camouflage and concealment, bayonet fighting, the Browning M.M.G., grenade throwing and fighting and 'recce' patrols. Towards the end of the winter it was decided to run week-end courses at Kinmel Camp for H.G. officers and N.C.O.s, and South and his party were used there each Sunday afternoon to demonstrate observation, searching ground, distance judging and open warfare.

"South was asked whether he could assist in training an outlying section of some thirty men at Llangerniew, where there were no ex-service men or other trained men to act as instructors. This task was cheerfully undertaken, and South with the squad leader and Teddy Crump (later Sub-Lt. T. Crump, R.N.V.R.) betook them-selves to Llangerniew each Wednesday evening and on occasional Saturdays throughout the early months of 1941 to the local Drill Hall at Llangerniew. There they met and trained a bunch of Welsh boys and men of all ages, from 17 to 70, most of whom tramped in through snow and rain from outlying farms for their weekly hour of foot and arms drill, and later musketry training.

"Most of these men were agricultural workers and many of them did not understand English—certainly not our English. In the more complicated drills, after a short explanation by the Major one or other of the recruits would interpret in Welsh, but for the shorter commands they would watch the next man. Thus if an order 'right turn' was given, those who understood would carry out the order and those who did not would keep an eye on their neighbour. This worked quite well up to a point, but when the order 'about turn' was given, quite a few would stop half-way.

"As the weather improved we were able to get outside, and later built an open air miniature range. We soon found that so far as aim was concerned there was nothing we could teach these lads. They could all shoot the eye out of a rabbit at 50 yards! Some years later, when No. 8 Platoon, 'B' Company, represented this Battalion in the Sector Final of a rifle shooting competition at Aber, it was this Llangerniew platoon to whom No. 8 Platoon lost and which subsequently went on to the Final round of the North Wales District.

"With the appointment of South to the Command of the 1st Denbighs., the Demonstration Squad broke up, but by this time a number of newly trained officers began to appear with the latest information on new weapons and modern methods of warfare. The Squad had by this time fulfilled its function, however, introducing methods which, in those days, were sufficiently novel to excite interest and discussion at a time when the lack of arms and ammuni-tion was wont to damp enthusiasm and induce a feeling of frustration.

"Local and Ministry Home Guardsmen owe a debt to that stout and warmhearted veteran, Tommy South (perhaps more than they realise), for his energetic and unflagging work in organising and co-ordinating the training of 1 Den. Battalion. In his 65th year, as he then was, South was as keen and fit as any of us, and the members of his Squad will always cherish happy memories of those winter days when they toured North Wales with him in an open truck under the guise of instructors, occasionally enjoying hospitality not only in private houses but at a number of hostels where South's face, even in Welsh Wales, seemed to be an open sesame—to the 'Sunday' door."[1]

Still, however, the membership of the Ministry unit was not up to what was regarded as a reasonable strength and on 15th October the Minister circulated a memorandum to all male members of the staff at Colwyn Bay in which he urged the staff of the Ministry to share in the duties which the Home Guard had undertaken.[2]

Following upon the Minister's memorandum, a recruiting campaign took place, in the course of which various officers of the company, and others, addressed meetings of the male staff. The result was a considerable influx of new volunteers and for the first time the unit had to face a problem which was to recur—that of organising a training programme for new intake superimposed upon the training of the original volunteers. Although his narrative carries the story well beyond this first stage of organisation, Sherman, then assisting Moore and subsequently to be training officer of "F" Company, provides a characteristically vivid record of the problems thus created and the solutions achieved.

(1) The members of the Demonstration Squad, who all served overseas in the last war or in this, were :—Abrams, Bartholomew, Crump, Gage, Harper. Hitchcock, Morley, Penn, Sidwell, Skilton, Warwick, Wheatley, Wilson,

(2) *Ministry of Food Unit of the Home Guard' Colwyn Bay.*
Memorandum by the Minister.

"The Secretary of State for War has recently sent me a very encouraging report upon the progress which is being made in equipping and training the Ministry of Food unit in the Home Guard.

"This Unit has recently taken over protective duties and is mounting guards at various points each night. These duties are being performed at present at frequent intervals by a relatively small number of the staff. I should be glad to see the number of Home Guard materially increased so that these duties may be more widely spread and their incidence upon individual members of the staff correspondingly reduced.

"A second company of the Unit is in process of formation. It will be for senior officers in the various Divisions of the Ministry to decide which, if any, of their staff can be borne on the strength of mobile sections of the Home Guard and be available in an emergency for military duty outside their own buildings.

"Subject to this reservation, which I am sure senior officers will exercise with discretion, I hope to see our Unit quickly increased in numbers."

W.
15*th October*, 1940.

"The method of recruitment at the outset in 1940 was nominally voluntary, but often semi-hidden coercion played its part. Certain bands of keen blokes made it quite difficult for their pals, whether with or without complete sets of limbs and organs, to remain outside the ranks. In the first two years there was little change in the faces in the H.G. and no large fluctuations in numbers occurred. This, many think, was the Home Guard at its best.

"In the Autumn of 1941, with the blessing of Establishment Division, meetings were arranged at most of the hotels, at which speakers tried to shew the light to the backward and doubting. Forms were ready at these meetings and a good many signed that they were prepared to join; many of these forms, however, were withdrawn and a number of signatories, luckily small, were told that they could not be allowed to 'waste' their time on H.G. duties. Ultimately, a considerable number of men were enrolled and allotted, according to hotel, to the two Companies.[1]

"The writer was associated with 'E' Company—later 'B' Company 11th Den.—and we had the job of training about 60 men. A long, comprehensive programme was arranged, based on the normal course at a Regular Infantry Training Centre, and in a period of about 3 months, working twice a week and Sundays, the rookies got a fair pasting. From the Instructor's point of view it was pretty hard work, as it meant, owing to lack of arms and indoor training space, taking two shifts each night. The course was run by the Company Training Officer, who had noble assistance from, to give recent Rank:—Lieuts. Coke and Harry Wilson, with Sgts. Pitcher and Connors. Attendance was very good and, once over the hurdle of lying down on the dusty floor of the Canteen and aiming at some mark they couldn't see, the new chaps almost seemed to enjoy it. There were a fair number of old sweats, including a number of ex-matelots, who livened things by explaining how much better it was the old way. The finish was a good shoot on the open range and a show, on the last Sunday morning, of all our precious new weapons, including the NARK—sorry NORTHOVER. These blokes, incidentally, were the last who were regarded in some Platoons as coming 'above the salt' and a gratifying number became N.C.O.s.

"Not long afterwards, H.G. conscription came in and the fun began. A large net was thrown around the male members of the Ministry and it was soon obvious that there were many hundreds of proper age lurking among the byeways. The net, however, was either of too large mesh or had many concealed holes, because the haul was most meagre. The sad fact remains, one is sorry to say, that the numbers in H.G. battle-rompers never swelled to the quantity needed. I would like to say here that after the first couple

---

(1) Office accommodation for the Ministry of Food staff at Colwyn Bay had been provided by the requisitioning of some forty buildings, mostly hotels and boarding houses.

TRAINING AND ORGANISATION—I

of parades with each batch, most of the men buckled to and, in their own way, lumped—if not liked it. Anyhow, commencing in July, 1942, a series of squads of 'NEW INTAKE' were trained, mostly at Penrhos, under Battalion arrangements.

"The writer again had charge, and again received grand support from Company Training Officers and N.C.O.s, and, before long, from the very able P.S.I.s. If any names are omitted, I apologise, but grand work on this job was done by Lieuts. Coke, Lovett, Chart, Wilson, H. C. Allen and Cowling; also by C.S.M. Boyle-Thomas, Sgt. Costello and others. Each squad had valuable talks from specialists such as Capt. Bowles (Security), Lieut. Essex-Lopresti (P.A.D.) and Sgt. Tyack assisted by Cpl. Alcock and his S.B. First-aiders.

"The courses usually lasted about three months, and were framed with the object of turning out men ready to take their place in the Platoons, and, we hoped, better grounded than the average. Each squad worked up to a final shoot on the open range and latterly much time was spent on grenades, stens and even a smattering of Lewis. Bayonet fighting was done pretty thoroughly, as this was being rather overlooked in the Battalion generally.

"We also put the new blokes through the mysteries (and they were mysteries even to the Instructors) of Battle Drill, with all its weird assortment of intelligent cries and studious standings-at-attention to show you aren't doing something else!!

"I—in fact I am sure on behalf of the Training Cadre it ought to be WE—are darned sorry it is over. It was rather nice to see the blokes looking less like Trade Directors and more like the Home Guard each week, and, if nothing else, it showed how appallingly neglectful the Country had been in military training. It shook us to find in the earlier and younger squads only one man here and there who had had any previous drilling, usually in a Junior O.T.C., and many who had never handled, let alone fired, a rifle.

"All this while we were receiving a small but steady influx of volunteer recruits and they, notably young men from other districts where they had been exempt for various local reasons, were trained alongside the conscripts. When numbers allowed they were formed into a separate squad.

"As soon as a new course had settled down we got the men measured, and sometimes were able to clothe and equip them before we finished with them and posted them to Companies. We sorted out those who were specialist-minded and popped them into one of the many Platoons of H.Q. Company. We were never able, however, to convince them that the Machine Gun Platoon was their obvious goal, and their O.C. waited in vain for new blood. I think we only produced four men altogether who became Gunners, and they had enlisted with that end in mind."

By this time the Unit was almost properly dressed. We find Lawrence writing to South on 17th October pointing out that 433 uniforms, 311 pairs of boots and 349 caps had been received and that the total enrolled strength of nearly 500 were more or less clothed (for the H.G.) but still found only 100 rifles a little inadequate as protection.

At the time, however, as a result of the recruiting campaign referred to above, new recruits were rolled in very rapidly, and the struggle between new intake and the Quartermaster's Store was to continue for a not inconsiderable period.

Another note, too, continues to recur through this period—that of the ungrudging co-operation of the Signals. We again find the O.C. thanking the Signals Adjutant for the loan of 50 rifles, aiming rests, Lewis guns, Mills bombs and a lecturer on gas and anti-gas measures. By this time also, training had become stepped up to a higher level; for example, in the appendix to the Platoon Orders of No. 5 Platoon, dated 1st November, covering the winter training programme, we find that instruction on some subject or another was proceeding on every evening of the week, ranging from elementary drill for new recruits, to more advanced exercises designed for the veterans of, by this time, seven months' standing. An interesting side-line also on the extent to which the Company had become organised, and indeed equipped, is given by the report of the second parade inspected by the Minister and Sir Henry French, which took place on 24th November. The O.C. reports to Platoon Commanders that—"the turn out was, I think, commendable, while the drill and march past were definitely good." More interesting, however, is the fact that for this parade a Signals Section, a Machine Gun Section, First Aid Party and a despatch rider were on parade, indicating that not only the training of individuals, but the organisation of the Company as a potential fighting unit, had gone a considerable distance. It is also impressive to realise that a Home Guard Unit, situated in one of the most remote and perhaps safest parts of the British Isles, could, within nine months of the regular army having been forced to abandon nearly all its equipment, at a time when the armed forces were growing fast, and in the midst of an unprecedented aerial bombardment, build up such a body of armament and, in the midst of their multifarious duties, acquire a sufficient degree of training. Tribute is due not only to those who organised the Ministry Home Guard, but to those mysterious and often-cursed figures at the War Office who, while apparently niggardly, were wrestling with the thankless task of rationing inadequate supplies, and also, perhaps most of all, to the men and women in the factories.

Gradually supplies of ammunition available for range practice arrived and, after a long search for a suitable shooting ground, it became possible for the Ministry Home Guard for the first time to have a properly organised shoot on a military range. As a result of a great deal of correspondence the range at Aber, normally reserved for the Caernarvon Units, was placed at the occasional disposal of the Ministry Unit. Those who took part in those early shoots at Aber remember them in much the same spirit as those who took part in

Cooking under difficulties

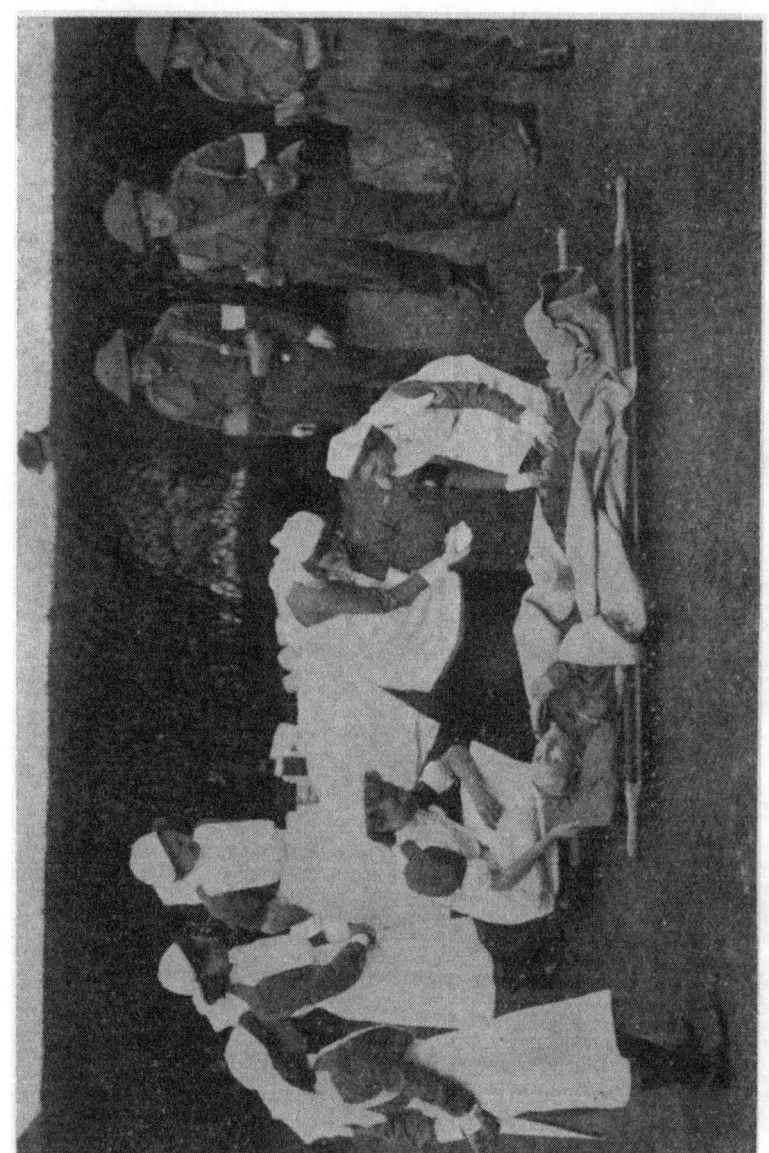

St. John's Ambulance Unit at work

the early guards at Penmaen Head. The same atmosphere prevailed and again it is impossible to improve upon the description of Captain Sherman—'The Voice that breathed o'er Aber': —

"Who does not recall, with some regret, the visits in the early days to the range at Aber; usually on a Saturday afternoon; usually in mid-winter in a howling gale or a snow storm? Usually it meant having a hurried lunch and a long bumpy ride in a lorry. Often the lorry had no cover and one keen lad, to my knowledge, got pneumonia as a result. But who did not welcome the chance? At first we had our Ross rifles, and after we had learned the sights we put on pretty decent scores. Later as there was no .300 available we were lucky to get a handful of .303 and borrowed rifles from the Signals at Rhos. That meant taking the lorry via Rhos to pick up rifles and I can remember the arguments I used to have with the C.Q.M.S. there before we could get P.14 rifles (the same action as our P.17—Springfields).

"But to get back to Aber; whichever Platoon was going, there was seldom a vacant place. On arrival someone—I used to call for the youngest man and send him, much to his disgust—had to trot about half a mile in the wrong direction to get the key to the target shed. Then we spent a profane half-hour patching out the last blokes' holes. (It indicates the average age of the unit to recall that the 'youngest man' on two occasions was 41!) Then we started to shoot. (Or did we wait and wait, until the concrete boxes that were the firing points at 200 and 300 ceased to be islands surrounded by seawater and became islands in greasy slippery mud?)

"A man when firing should have an instructor lying alongside keeping up a running commentary and helping him to apply his shots to the mark. How the blazes could more than four men at a time get on to one of those boxes? So a lot of men blazed away, happily, unconscious of what they were missing compared with the jolly arguments between coach and pupil which should have gone on. (I wonder if the shooting suffered?) A coach has to be born and it takes a lot of practice on top; I think, really, it saved a lot of time.

"One jolly variation used to be that on arrival we found some other mob from Caernarvon or Bangor there already, and quite convinced that they were in the right. When we explained that we had booked the range, and the warden was there and agreed that we had done so, he went on to say that as the booking had been done on the 'phone by a female voice (Major Lawrence's Secretary) he did not think it was genuine and let the next people have the range. Once when that happened we had to wait till about 4.30 and on another day we had to lump it and come back with the rifles still clean—more than could always be said, I am afraid, having memory of a distressing occasion when a Lewis .303 was untouched for several days and the armourer at Prestatyn wanted to charge the Battalion with over £30 for damage.

"Nevertheless we enjoyed Aber and in some ways got better results than at Coed Coch. It brought back pleasant memories to some of us when we went to the Sector Finals there."

The new year was marked by three significant innovations. The Commandant, Kinmel Park Camp, granted facilities for courses of instruction for officers and men of the Home Guard—the first residential courses of this kind under direct Army auspices to be available in the area. Only one officer and five men from each company—the first of the many—were invited, but the ice had been broken. This was in February, 1941: in January the role to be filled by "F" Company in the defence scheme had been defined. Unfortunately, the defence area originally allotted excluded Penrhos College, Meadowcroft and Mount Stewart. As the Coy. H.Q., the armoury and the canteen were all three excluded from the zone allocated to the Ministry Unit, it was considered that its efficiency might not be wholly unimpaired, and amendment was urged and accepted. From time to time other definitions of defence-zone boundaries were to be made, throughout the whole of the period in which static defence (commonly known as suicide) was considered to be the role of the Home Guard, but we were fitted amicably into the local scheme, and never again were asked to abandon our armoury or our canteen.

The third innovation was the inauguration of the rousing system. Part I. Orders, 28/1/41, cast the first shadow of the many which were to darken wet winter nights. "Arrangements are being made to establish a system of co-operative rousing in the event of an alarm at night or over a week-end. The system is based on the appointment of a number of "Rousers" in each division of the town." Then, 16/4/41, "A practice alarm will be held without preliminary notification within the next few days. Every member of the unit is requested to make certain that the Rouser of his Block is acquainted with his address and with the best manner in which he should be knocked up at night." A week later the blow fell, and so did the heaviest fall of snow known for some years in Colwyn Bay, just at the time that the unaccustomed rousers were scrambling round their unfamiliar territory, trying to find "Bryn X" and "Glynn Y" with the aid of dimmed torches!

Perhaps most characteristic of all the events of this period, when the foundations had been laid and "F" Company was finding its feet, while, at the same time, the atmosphere was experimental and improvisation reigned supreme, was the visit of the School of Guerrilla Warfare from Hurlingham, which took place on Saturday and Sunday, April 19th and 20th. Already the Unit had come into mild conflict with the military authorities by sponsoring a lecture by J. Langdon Davies, who in spite of his B.B.C. appointment and his very recent experience of guerrilla warfare in both Spain and Finland, was not then recognised by the War Office. The upshot of this was that the Unit held the lecture and then, finding themselves denied official reimbursement for the cost of the hall, reverted to civilian activities and ran a dance to pay the bill. But when it was proposed that the Hurlingham School, which was being run for the love of the job by a group of young men, most of whom had seen very recent fighting in Spain or elsewhere experienced the sort of war without effective equipment or organisation in which the Home Guard expected to find itself involved any day, should pay us a visit, the War Office showed a singular absence of enthusiasm and it took quite a lot of time and used quite a lot of paper before arrangements could be made. When, however, the School arrived to demonstrate their very effective artillery, to explain (the Ministry of Works and Buildings hastily stopped them from demonstrating) modern methods of house to house fighting by burrowing through party walls, and to bring a refreshing breath of realism into the Company's training, they were more than welcome. The personality of Captain Crisp ("the little runt," as he described himself) made a particularly deep impression, as a soldier of the contemporary type, a cultured man forced by circumstances into a mould of pitiless efficiency. For two days the School explained how the amateur soldier reacted to fear; the simple psychological weapons at his disposal; the improvisation of arms and equipment, and the essentials of training for action which was combined, disciplined, and yet individual. In the memory of a large number of the more active members of the Home Guard, the School marked the highest spot of that first period of Home Guard life. As yet, in spite of the Signals' co-operation, we were not anything like as completely under the wing of the Military Authorities as we were subsequently to be. Quite rightly so, for they were busy hatching other and more fearsome fighting cocks, in the form of the Army they were struggling to build up. But, had we had to go into action at that earlier period, had we had—as we might well have done—to have improvised our own weapons and completed our training while in battle, then our gratitude to the Hurlingham instructors would no doubt have been felt even more strongly, although perhaps for a much shorter period.

Shortly after, as the next chapter will tell, the Unit was formed into two Companies and a period commenced during which War Office direction and co-operation grew closer and more intimate. The first phase of the Home Guard in Colwyn Bay was over.

CHAPTER 4.

Training and Organisation II.

"E" and "F" Companies 1st Denbighshire Battalion: Training outside the Parade Ground: March 28th, 1941, to June 1st, 1942.

> "With a host of furious fancies
> Whereof I am commander
> With a burning spear
> And a horse of air
> To the wilderness I wander."
>
> "Tom o' Bedlam's Song (*Anon.*)

In 1940 the foundations of the Home Guard were laid. During 1941/2 two things happened which had an immense effect on the new "part-time army"; one material, the other psychological. The first was the momentum which the expansion of our war industries gained, and the resulting improvement in equipment. After the phase of the "phoney war," the truly national government formed by Churchill inaugurated a programme of expansion which was carried out at white-heat: by the end of 1940 the "tooling up" period was over, and output rose spectacularly. During the 1941/2 period the supply of guns, ammunition and army equipment in general more than doubled up on the previous year, and practically achieved the level which was to be maintained for the rest of the war.

The second, psychological, factor was the emergence of Russia as our ally, and the news of the stand made behind the invaders' lines by the partisans, or irregular force. For many, to whom the only justification for war was the championship of the democratic way of life, the Russian alliance was a final confirmation of the ideological basis of the war, while the record of popular resistance emphasised the effectiveness of the part which the Home Guard might play in the war against Fascism.

The extent to which, as compared with the rest of the country, either arms or inspiration penetrated to the Ministry unit is matter for conjecture; the period during which the new "E" Coy. came into being (its formation was announced in orders on 28th April, 1941) and operated side by side with "F" Coy., until the formation of the Ministry Wing, roughly coincides with this material and political change.

It expressed itself in the life of the Ministry Home Guard by the arrival of new weapons to master, the allotment of a definite share in the task of local defence, and by the transference of the balance of training from the parade ground to the countryside, as the progress of equipment and proficiency permitted.

The basis of organisation of the two new Companies was that Major Maclean took over the command of "E" Coy., with Captain Capstick as Second in Command, and Lieutenants Sherman and Sharp as Training Officer and Quartermaster respectively. The three Platoons of "E" Coy. were under Lieutenant Moore, Lieutenant Hitchcock and Lieutenant Holliday. Major Lawrence became Officer Commanding "F" Coy., with Captain Huskisson as Second in Command, Lieutenant Holt as Training Officer and Lieutenant Battson as Quartermaster. No. 1 Platoon was under Lieutenant Balfour, Lieutenant Bremner took over Nos. 2 and 3, and No. 4 Platoon was commanded by Lieutenant Selby. In each Company, Headquarter Officers and N.C.O.s, together with despatch riders, machine gunners and signallers and the Company Petroleum N.C.O.s, were borne on the strength of the Headquarter Section and, for general organisation and discipline, were in each case under the control of the Company Training Officer. For training and operational purposes the machine-gunners of both Companies were placed under the command of Lieutenant Sherman, and the signallers of both Companies under that of Lieutenant Holt. As far as possible the re-arrangement of the troops of the Unit into the two Companies was based on the hotels where they worked: this had been the original method employed but it had become somewhat out of date as the result of individual transfers and sectional movement within the Ministry. In certain cases, however, men who were particularly keen to remain with their old sections, and who could put up a good case, were permitted to continue to train and operate with them.

"E" Company had hardly been formed when Lt.-Col. M. H. D. Bell, O.B.E., R.A., who commanded the coastal zone of the Oswestry sub-area, asked for more recruits in order that the Ministry personnel might assume wider responsibilities in the local defence scheme. As a result "G" Company was formed, but not until the end of May, 1942.

Few changes in the leading personalities of the unit took place during the period under review, but those which did were important. Balfour and Bremner removed from the district: in both cases the loss was severe. To some extent, however, it was counterbalanced by the acquisition of Cessford, who had been prominent in the Home Guard on Merseyside and was to prove his worth in North Wales.

During this period the armament and equipment of the Ministry Unit began to approach an adequate level. In the first place, the long and unwieldy, if accurate, Ross rifles, which had made Home Guards on parade look a little like Indian trappers in the North West Territory, were withdrawn and replaced by American Springfields of the 1917 pattern, which were easier to handle as well as somewhat lighter and, moreover, were provided with a more simple and robust mechanism. In addition, ammunition supplies improved somewhat, and at the same time supplies of Mills Grenades for training were acquired. By the end of the year also, Service respirators had become available for all ranks, and with the co-operation of the Signals Unit all the more active members of the force passed through the gas chamber, had their respirators properly adjusted, and were conversant with the proper drill.

In addition to these historic weapons, the Unit had become possessed of a certain number of more experimental types designed for anti-tank defence, in the shape of several types of anti-tank grenade, the E.Y. Rifle, and the Northover Projector. The E.Y. Rifle was an ordinary Service rifle, equipped with a discharger cup fitted to the end of the barrel from which, when a ballastite cartridge was fired, an anti-tank grenade was "blown." It was moderately safe to operate and not very dangerous to tanks, because owing to its construction its aim was extremely erratic, unless it could be trained and secured in advance to cover a fixed position. It also had a kick like a mule and had to have its butt very deeply heeled-in to firm earth. It was, however, presumably the lineal ancestor of the Piat and as such no doubt served its purpose. The Northover was an altogether more temperamental and less discreet weapon. Used as a projector for Mills grenades it was comparatively accurate and had a reasonable range. The principal purpose for which it was designed, however, was to discharge S.I.P. anti-tank grenades, which were glass bottles containing a phosphorus mixture which burst into livid flames, giving off quantities of suffocating smoke, upon exposure to the air. It was when dealing with this ammunition that the least lovable characteristics of the Northover Projector became apparent. Unless the utmost care was exercised in loading and firing, and sometimes when the utmost care had been exercised, there was a natural tendency for the shock of discharge to break the glass bottle in the breech, whereupon the gun, and sometimes the gunner and troops standing to leeward, were liable to burst into flames. These had to be promptly extinguished, and the gun thoroughly washed down with soda solution before it could again be used. Those of us who had much experience of the Northover Projector prayed fervently that we might never have to employ it to betray our position when attacking a tank. It should perhaps be added that if the glass bottles were safely discharged they exploded upon arrival only if they happened to hit rock, brick or a metalled road. On one occasion it may be recollected that a certain amount of friction was caused by the very accurate revolver practice which a Captain put in, in exploding one of these, at the expense of a certain amount of equipment belonging to other officers in the Unit.

Another weapon of the same type, although belonging more exclusively to the concept of static defence, was the Fougasse. This can be described as a flame-thrower, electrically detonated and very vicious in its effects. It was designed to be dug in to re-inforce a road block; only a few members of this Unit saw demonstrations arranged in secrecy in remote places, but we all had lectures on them and most of us would have liked to see one go off.

The arrival of this new equipment, particularly the erratic artillery, necessitated a greater proportion of training time being spent on the range and less on the parade ground. Fairly soon Aber Range was abandoned, principally on account of its inaccessibility, and, after a period in which the range at the Morfa had been placed at the disposal of the Unit, most of the work on the open range was carried out at

Coed Coch. Indeed, the chance of sharing in the very excellent training facilities in pleasing surroundings offered by the Coed Coch range was one of the advantages derived from affiliation to the local Battalion. The gratitude of the Ministry Unit must here be expressed for the admirable work which had been done under the direction of the No. 1 Battalion Pioneer Officer, Lieutenant W. Williams, in constructing the four target range of 100, 200, 300 and 400 yards and also the bombing range at Coed Coch. This latter was quite indispensable in order for adequate practice with live grenades to be obtained; dummy bombs could be and were thrown on the sands, and in the grounds of Penhros College, and a certain amount of practice with live grenades took place in the quarry at Bryn Euryn, but the latter was never a satisfactory place. With the availability of an appropriate bomb pit, however, it became possible to undertake general training in the use of that invaluable weapon, the Mills Grenade, and very soon all the active members of the Unit had had some experience with it. Not all, however, are born to be bombers, and in some cases the task of the Instructor was somewhat embarrassing.

As an example of how throwing a live bomb appears to those physically or temperamentally unsuited to the task the following narrative invokes understanding and sympathy: "I watched the first pair go down to the priming pit, then the second and then . . . . after an agony of suspense came my turn. The next few moments passed quickly and I soon found myself in the bombing pit under the vigilant eyes of the Platoon Officer and Sergeant. In my anxiety to display my prowess, I had almost got the pin out when a commanding voice rang in my ears. It was the Platoon Sergeant. 'Stop,' he said, 'listen to me.' I listened patiently while he recited the drill to be performed. Then came the command, 'Get ready to throw'—out came the pin, back went the right arm. 'Throw.' I executed the perfect overarm with all my strength behind it. Something went wrong. My hand and the Mills refused to part company at the right moment. But I was blind to this at the time for, full of wishful thinking, I looked over the parapet at the target hole expecting to see the grenade landing on the bullseye. No, it wasn't there. In a split second, my eye travelled backwards. No sign anywhere. And then, three feet away half left, I spotted something, something which fascinated me. I stared hard at this object stuck there in the mud. Somehow it didn't make sense that this was a grenade, let alone my grenade. But just as I did awaken to stark reality, a whistle rang out. I knew 3 seconds had gone and deciding that discretion was the better part of valour, took the necessary action, and so officer, sergeant and private got down behind Mother Earth, all very close to the ground. The next second, our eardrums were almost split by the explosion, and we three were subjected to premature burial. The officer and sergeant, fortunately for me, took a good view of things, and even thanked me for the unusual experience, but the very red faced N.C.O. in the priming pit offered to pay my fare to Broadmoor."

In addition to this extra range work the training programme of the Ministry Unit grew wider and more varied. The previous chapter referred to the first of the courses organised as part of the regular Army training scheme to which Home Guards from this Unit were invited. In the period now under review these were rapidly multiplied, as it became apparent to the War Office authorities that the two special Home Guard training courses which had been authorised by them were hopelessly inadequate to train nearly two million Home Guards. A constant flow of officers and men of the Unit, therefore, commenced to go to and fro to specialist and general courses of all kinds, held under the aegis of the Army authorities. Moreover, Army Training Films were becoming available. Perhaps no branch of the technique of Army training has progressed more during the war than the production of instructional films. During the period in which they have been available to Home Guard audiences an enormous improvement has taken place, and although those films which were available to the Unit at the first few exhibitions were somewhat crude compared with the later productions of the War Office Film Unit, they were of very great interest and provided a welcome element of comfort and variety in the winter training programme. In addition, during the autumn of 1941 the Unit organised visits to a service aerodrome near Chester, in order to obtain information on how to release pilots from their harness and how to effect an entry into crashed aircraft. Incidentally, the first platoon to go on this demonstration saw one of the earliest specimens of an aircraft which was later to become popular in Great Britain and notorious in Germany—the Mosquito. It was then on the secret list and all members of the platoon were sworn to secrecy, both as regards its design and its name. A further innovation in the training programme was that advantage was taken of opportunities afforded by the Royal Artillery for parties to visit coastal defence batteries and watch firing. It was never expected that members of the Unit who witnessed this and other demonstrations would at any time become crack gunners or experts in aircraft salvage, but it was hoped that from among the witnesses, should the Unit ever be in action, some members of the Home Guard might in some future emergency recall the right way to lay a 25 pounder on the target, or the correct method of releasing an airman from a wrecked machine.

Reference must also here be made to the training in unarmed combat, which commenced early in 1942.

Few Home Guards will forget their first innoculation into this technique of perverted anatomy, particularly those who retained the romantic illusion that modern war (or, indeed, adds the student of history, any war) was a chivalrous business. We learned to gouge and dislocate, how to kill noiselessly and ruthlessly and very messily, and, above all, not to resist the sergeant instructor. Considered philosophically there was nothing we were learning to do which was not infinitely cleaner and more decent than that which the Nazis were

Instruction in "Fire Control" Orders

After the Battle

contemporaneously doing to captured Russian civilians, nothing so dirty as the bombing of defenceless Rotterdam. But, like getting ones ideas into perspective on most things, it was something of an ordeal for those unaccustomed to the process.

Meanwhile, policy was becoming clearer as to the way in which this painfully acquired knowledge and these slowly accumulated armaments were to be employed should the Home Guard be called upon to go into action. The quotation is here from a document on policy which appeared half way through 1941 for issue down to platoons.

"The main role of the Home Guard is observation and the rapid passing of information to local troops, especially mobile columns. When a landing party has once rallied and is ready for action Home Guards should not normally adopt the role of attackers; their doing so will probably result in their being defeated in detail, for they are not primarily either trained or equipped for the attack. There may be exceptions to this guiding principle when Home Guards can and should attack, e.g., against a small number of parachutists, but in general their main role will be observation and the passing of information. Coupled with this is the duty of containing the enemy wherever practicable until the arrival of troops, and of shadowing, sniping and generally harrassing him. This refers to the role to be carried out by the Home Guard when confronted with relatively small raiding parties. When confronted with attack on a more extensive scale in which considerable bodies of enemy troops are involved, the main role of the Home Guard becomes defence of nodal points with the object of impeding enemy movement by holding towns and large villages that the enemy cannot occupy without staging a full scale attack, which the Home Guard should have a good chance of resisting until the arrival of troops.... the nodal points will be held to the last round and the last man.... The principles set out here are in no way intended to discourage small parties of Home Guard living near areas where enemy troops have landed by air, from acting as scouts and obtaining information before they fall back to more defendable points. On the contrary, the inquisitive spirit should be encouraged, since the obtaining of information by the Home Guard will continue to be of the utmost importance at all times."

It is apparent from this document that while the job of the Home Guard was still considered to be, in the main, static defence, the possibility of more mobile action was coming to be considered. The Ministry unit may claim to have been well in the vanguard of this change. It was possibly one of the first in the country to undergo a course of Battle innoculation (almost eighteen months before such a practice was authorised by the pundits of the War Office) when at Coed Coch it was fired on by camouflaged Brownings and Lewises. This field firing and battle practice with live ammunition (with adequate safety measures) anticipated to a very marked degree of similarity, by over a year, the "Battle Drill" which was later to constitute such an important feature of training. The left flanking attack up the valley at Coed Coch with ball ammunition against falling targets, ending with a demonstration by what was then the solitary tommy gun in the unit, and a bayonet charge on the butts followed by reorganisation beyond them, was a very fair prototype of the final drill.

Another pointer in the same direction was the creation of the Mobile Column. It might be considered impertinent if any but a member of that corps d'elite were to describe it: here is the version provided by its Platoon Officer, Parselle: —

"The Mobile Column was formed in May, 1942, under the command of Lieut. R. H. Looker. In the main this Platoon was formed from young active men and their operational role demanded physical fitness as a first class essential. The average age of the Platoon was considerably lower than that of any other platoon in the Battalion. The bulk of its early training was carried out on ground which first required the ascent of King's Drive or the Old Highway, and to achieve this at regulation marching pace is no mean performance in anybody's language. Added to this, the army assault course at the back of Rydal Playing Fields was tackled at frequent intervals (the 8 foot wall provided a wealth of good-natured chaff but there were few, if any, who baulked it after a little practice) and regular P.T. and games parades were held; these became very popular and were instrumental in building up a team spirit which was second to none."

But here let a voice from the ranks make an interjection.

"Ostensibly the mobile platoon was filled up by physically fit volunteers, but the few who could not claim to be other than ejected from their old platoons entered their new ranks with as much purpose as the 'better born.' Sterner training was provided for with much guile. Quoth the platoon officer, 'We ought to have a parade ground of our own, but at the moment we must either share one or put up with a rough field—you know the place, the Army have built an assault course on part of it—we might even have a go at that course one day.' How could grown men be so simple?"

The Platoon Officer continues: —

"Map-reading contests which entailed hareing along the roads within a 10 mile radius or so of Colwyn Bay on cycles were also conducive to physical fitness—to say nothing of the fact that the first group home with the correct answers took the kitty! Unfortunately, for reasons known only to the Higher Command, the Mobile Column was never really given an opportunity to show its pace (visions of Llanrwst Cinema at 5 in the morning and St. Asaph), but with the change in the operational role of the 11th Battalion and the assumption by the Mobile Column of Garrison Mobile Reserve at Pentre Foelas, a number of strenuous tests were accomplished with considerable zest—and not a little dampness! To the end, the Mobile Column, although steadily depleted in strength, maintained its high standard and had the distinction in 1943/4 of sharing with No. 12 Platoon the Battalion Proficiency Cup and also of providing the Battalion's Lewis Gun Team (Sergeant A. C. G. Warland, Private H. J. M. Paull and Private R. E. Gemmell) in the North Wales District competition of 1944."

The Mobile Column will be heard of again as the story proceeds; at this stage what matters in the narrative is not so much its exploits as the way in which its formation is characteristic of this period in the life of the whole Unit. Now equipped, not perfectly, but adequately, and trained to a point when it was anxious to get off the parade ground, the Unit welcomed the numerous exercises in which its capacity for organised action and its fitness were tested. For this reason a fairly detailed account of one or two of them is here appropriate. The part played by the Ministry Unit in most of them was of course that of static defence. Based upon their battle Headquarters, they guarded and patrolled; the rousing organisation, the staff, despatch riders, telephonists, all had work to do most of the time and lessons to learn. The rank and file, however, of necessity found them as dull as war itself, which has been defined as long periods of intense boredom interrupted by short periods of intense fear.

The first of the two exercises at Newmarket took place on 9th November, 1941. At the northern end of the Clwydian range the little village of Newmarket reposes peacefully in the lap of Gop Hill, a sugar loaf eminence of aggressive appearance and dominating character. We were to know the features of this country well before the winter of 1941 drew to its close.

It was late in October that orders were issued by Lieut.-Colonel M. H. D. Bell, O.B.E., R.A., who was then commanding the coastal zone of the Oswestry Sub-Area, for the first of two exercises designed to test the local defences. For the purposes of this exercise it was assumed that Germany had invaded Ireland and occupied Dublin. The narrative made our concern with the operations more intimate, when it recorded the discovery early on the morning of Sunday, 9th November, of several parachutes and harness on the Denbigh Moors and of the partial wreckage of six troop-carrying gliders two miles north east of Denbigh. Such was the information at the disposal of the regular defenders. The Home Guard attackers were more fully informed. While denied exact information of the numbers and dispositions of the defence, we were aware of the probable centres of resistance and had some idea of the forces likely to be brought against us. Further, we knew the intention of our command to launch at high water (14.30 hours) an attack on the coast between Rhyl and the Dee Estuary, supported by an air offensive and a series of parachute landings. In two of the latter we were to take part, while Capstick, Cessford and Huskisson were to umpire at other incidents.

To "E" Coy. was given the task of providing a party of 3 officers and 75 other paratroops to attack Newmarket at 13.45 hours and divert attention from an assault to be delivered at 14.00 hours upon Defence Sector Headquarters at Gop Farm and the observation post at Gop Hill, by a similar party from "F" Coy. Strict adherence to the timing by the two companies was of paramount importance.

The "E" Coy. parachutists under Maclean were to be "dropped" at Terfyn at 12.45 hours. Their prescribed route to this rendezvous, in lorries provided by the 2nd Holding Battalion Royal Corps of Signals, passed by Brynglas where an enterprising gunner Subaltern was already astride the cross roads with a strong force of steel-helmeted defenders. Into this force we butted before the word "go" had been given. Argument and explanation availed not: he was there to deny the use of this centre of communications to the invader and with his vehicles broadside across the road effectually he did so. Twenty precious minutes were wasted in fruitless expostulation and vain explanation that zero hour was not yet. The deadlock was ultimately resolved by an umpire passing that way to his appointed duty. But the party was twenty minutes late at the rendezvous and twenty valuable minutes late in moving off from there.

Maclean's orders issued at Terfyn were brief and simple. Hitchcock with some thirty-five men from No. 2 Platoon, constituting the left detachment, was to move along the grass grown lane running N.N.W. until he reached the stream in the bottom of the valley between Terfyn and Newmarket. After crossing the stream he was to select the best method and line of advance open to him to launch an attack at 13.45 hours on the enemy in the Western and South-Western outskirts of Newmarket. The attack was to be pushed home.

Spencer with some 30 men (from Nos. 1 and 3 Platoons) formed the right detachment, ordered to follow the road from Terfyn towards Pen-y-Cefn-Uchaf Farm. He was to leave this road by a covered glade running in a North-Westerly direction to a river-crossing due east of the farm. Thence he was to advance in an East North-Easterly direction to deliver an attack on Newmarket from the direction of Pentremawr at 13.50 hours. Maclean with "E" Coy.'s Headquarters and the reserve (about 12 other ranks from No. 2 Platoon) were to move at 12.55 hours from Terfyn to Pen-y-Cefn-Uchaf Farm, "subsequent movement" depending upon "the development of the situation." This was in the event a wise provision.

The defending force from the Signals Training Centre at Prestatyn neglected to hold, and apparently even to observe, the excellent covered approaches exploited by the left and right detachments but sent a column of a dozen vehicles down the only practicable direct road, that running due south, from Newmarket to Terfyn. Owing to the delay in reaching the rendezvous, Spencer's party were not all clear of the road when this column approached Pen-y-Cefn-Uchaf. Spencer held the head of the opposing column until the little Headquarters reserve came up, when he succeeded in disengaging the bulk of his force and continuing on his appointed way. The reserve were then holding the road with a few riflemen while the remainder were making their way forward through the fields on either flank, but they became somewhat weary of firing upon an enemy who made no reply and were relieved when umpires arrived to sort out the tangle. It then transpired that the Signals had not fired or acted offensively because they had no blank ammunition left! Our folk who had scattered in ditches and hedges, suspected this mechanised army of having become too road-conscious and hugged the thought that perhaps after all we might be some use in modern warfare. Casualties were awarded to both sides. We scored two vehicles (one a wireless truck) and a dozen men, and thought this good measure for our loss of eight or nine men. The fight resumed, the road was deserted while our opponents tried to clear the farm buildings and hay-stacks of snipers. The process was costly and our opponents again lost rather more men than we. Forty or fifty of the mobile column's personnel and ten of the twelve vehicles were, however, unharmed; most of Spencer's party were well on their way to their objective and it was time for our outnumbered remnants to break off the engagement—if they could. Quietly they melted into the landscape and their enemy, unwilling apparently to move far from their vehicles, withdrew whence they had come.

Meanwhile Hitchcock's party, making excellent use of cover, had traversed nearly half their distance and crossed the stream without incident. Lce./Corporal Ebert sent to report this fact was intercepted and captured by the enemy during the mêlée at the farm but had the presence of mind to hide his message in the hedge by the roadside, where it was found a few minutes later by C.S.M. Coke who was with Headquarters and the advancing reserves. Pressing forward rather more hurriedly and less cautiously, because of their late start, than they originally planned to do the left party nevertheless were within 250 yards of Newmarket Village before they were observed. At this stage Hitchcock's narrative is graphic and interesting:—

"So far as my own party was concerned, having scouted the country pretty fully a day or so earlier, we were able to advance to within a hundred yards or so of the village with little or no opposition. At one point we ran into a section of the defence in the churchyard but their guns were all pointing the wrong way and by dodging amongst the tombstones we advanced right up to a couple of yards and cleaned up the lot (all round protection had hardly been thought of in those days). At this point we were only 200 yards from the centre of the village and I split the party in two, sending Wilson on a left flanking move round the back of some cottages whilst I took the rest along the main street. I ran into very heavy M.G. fire and had to admit being scuppered about 20 yards from the Mostyn Arms. Meanwhile Wilson had got round undetected to the road running north from Newmarket; collaring an enemy truck he compelled the driver to run his party right into the middle of the village where they filed out and after a hectic few minutes with the defenders were, I believe, given the verdict of having captured the whole shooting match.

"Two incidents in this exercise stand out quite vividly in my memory—the first is a picture of Wilson with the muzzle of his rifle jammed into a defender's navel with such force that had a bayonet been attached it would undoubtedly have projected a foot on the far side—what time the said defender let go a round of blank which burned clean through the sleeve of Wilson's overcoat, tunic and shirt, leaving a fairly severe burn and gash in his forearm. Within a few minutes however he was banging away on the piano in the local hall surrounded by the rest of the company.

"The other incident was the forcing of the Mostyn Arms on that *Sunday* morning. Sgt. Cowling and a couple of his squad made such a determined attack that they could only be appeased by a pint, whereas Frampton, whose instinct is normally infallible, found no more than a cup of tea. Although he never quite lived down the shame of this day he did retrieve his reputation to some extent a year or two later when, in the Llandudno 'do,' he was the only member of the party which attacked the Police Station to find his way to the canteen."

Spencer had divided his party into two sections, one composed of personnel from No. 1 Platoon under Sgt. R. A. G. O'Brien and the second of men from No. 3 Platoon under Sgt. Moolenaar. During the fight at the farm both parties had been engaged with the enemy, but Spencer had shewn considerable dexterity in drawing them out of the engagement when the reserves arrived and edging away to the north-east to accomplish his allotted task. He had, however, lost about a quarter of his force in the engagement, and the extrication of the remainder had not been easy. As a result, his two sections were unable to maintain touch. Spencer with the larger party, after crossing the stream in the bottom of the valley, took advantage of dead ground to his right flank to work up from the south to within about 150 yards of Newmarket without being seen and delivered his attack at 13.50 hours as ordered, securing a somewhat precarious lodgment with about a dozen men among the buildings and gardens on the south side of the village. O'Brien meantime had been having "a day out." It had started with active participation in the scrap at Pen-y-Cefn-Uchaf Farm from which he had, after a running fight, succeeded in leading most of his men to a crossing of the stream east of Pen-y-Cefn-Isaf. At this stage he considered his main task was to rejoin Spencer and so, avoiding a party of the enemy who were approaching the crossing from the north, he struck north-east up the slope towards Newmarket and made his way without serious opposition to the south-west corner of the village. Here he found a couple of attackers from Lawrence's parties and, assuming that the village was in our hands, sent Lce.-Corporal Byers to report at the Mostyn Arms where Maclean was to have established his headquarters if the village were captured. On being disillusioned he did not withdraw but established his small party of six under cover near the road junction north of the church whence he fired at all enemy movement in the village. At about 14.50 hours parts of the village were still in the defenders' hands and part occupied by the various attacking parties which were infiltrating from several directions. At this moment a sergeant of the Royal Artillery in charge of a lorry at the cross-roads, whose role in the action was far from clear, offered O'Brien a Lewis gun which was gratefully accepted and trained on the enemy on Gop Hill: shortly after this O'Brien and his party came unknowingly under fire from the enemy detachment still holding out in the Mostyn Arms and Maclean, considering their survival too incredible, withdrew the party from the action at about 15.15 hours.

Lawrence's personnel from "F" Coy. were to be "dropped" in the wood half a mile due east of Gwaenysgor at 14.00 hours, when they were to attack "with vigour from the north-east after first of all severing all communications from and to Sector Headquarters." At 14.00 hours Lawrence's force debouched from the wood in three parties. No. 1 Party of twelve men under Ker left from the northwest corner and, making use of the cover of the hedgerows, reached the cross-roads on the Gwaenysgor-Newmarket road about 500 yards south-east of the former place without opposition and, by 14.35 hours, had cut the telephone wires at this point. Here Ker's party captured three enemy motor cyclists and a staff car. The captured staff car, chauffered (under duress) by its original driver, was sent by Ker with a corporal and one man to Gop Farm, successfully passing all the defences. These two thoroughly searched Sector Headquarters at Gop Farm (at 14.55 hours), "interrogated the women and captured four men in the farm buildings. They successfully evaded a number of booby traps by refusing to enter rooms and court-yards by the obvious methods of access. Before being finally shot they claim to have demolished and set on fire the farm buildings." The remainder of No. 1 Party subsequently reached and occupied Gop Farm. At about 15.30 hours they were informed by an Umpire that, as the objective had been attained, the exercise might be considered over. Ker did not therefore take any steps to establish contact with the party which had attacked the observation post and was surprised to see preparations for a counter attack from the direction of the concrete pill-box to the south-west. The attack developed in force and was supported by another strong body from what proved to be advanced Sector Headquarters, with the result that his party was surrounded. It was subsequently understood that the counter-attack was "out of time."

No. 2 Party of twenty men under Selby left the wood from the south-west edge and, snaking along the hedgerow running parallel to the sunken road to Carn-y-Chain Farm, entered the wood on Gop Hill about 200 yards beyond and to the south of the farm, encountering strong opposition. The defenders, however, exposed themselves unduly and were awarded heavy casualties by the Umpires, and Selby's party were able to take up a position on the open ground east of the tumulus and immediately below the Gop Hill observation post. At this stage Selby received orders from Lawrence to re-organise and endeavour to seize Defence Headquarters in the vicinity of Gop Farm. The party cleared the brow of the hill but were then so outnumbered that they were declared out of action.

Party No. 3 was divided into two detachments: the first under Lawrence's personal leadership, the second, of fifteen men under Sgt. Robinson, to follow at a distance of 200 yards, formed his support troops. At zero hour Lawrence's party made an immediate capture of three lorries and a group sentry post in a clearing in the wood that had sheltered his "parachute" troops. After this initial success the party was by 14.10 hours making for the deep ditch and hedge to their west which runs parallel to the farm road to Carn-y-Chain, whence they reached a point about 100 yards from the northern end of Gop Hill Wood and came under fire from lorries parked on the farm track. A section detached to clear Carn-y-Chain Farm found and captured three lorries and a number of A.T.S. girls and troops unconcernedly at tea. Lawrence with characteristic intrepidity meanwhile launched a direct attack on Gop Hill Farm but was overwhelmed by a vigorous counter-attack from the wood; half his force was put out of action and he had to withdraw the remainder to cover. Lawrence was perhaps unfortunate at this stage as his supports under Sgt. Robinson had, in error, followed Selby's party and although they entered Gop Wood immediately south of Carn-y-Chain Farm and captured four stragglers they failed to locate Lawrence or come to his assistance until after the counter-attack had been delivered. Lawrence now led the remnants of his party to Carn-y-Chain Farm and picked up the supports under Robinson. Together they moved forward to the east edge of Gop Wood when the leading section ran into an ambush and the Lewis Gun Team and six men were made casualties. It was now 15.00 hours; in spite of local success no permanent dislodgment of the enemy from his Sector Headquarters or the observation post had been effected; contact had been established in Newmarket but possession of part of the village was still disputed and the position was confused; moreover, Lawrence's successes had been gained only at heavy cost.

Contact was, however, established with No. 2 Party and, with Selby advancing from the north-east and Lawrence from the south-east, the observation post was captured at 15.30 hours, but the attackers were now exhausted and disorganised and at 15.45 hours a strong counter-attack from the orchard and scrub surrounding Gop Farm overwhelmed the survivors.

This exercise had produced a deal of high speed fighting and more incidents of an unexpected character than usual. It was almost the only occasion on which the use of fifth column methods had been not only permitted but encouraged. Of this freedom we took considerable advantage. Three men who were detailed to act as fifth column cyclists in mufti moved with considerable freedom on the roads, and

Colonel Barton, C.B.E., M.C., takes the Salute

The Home Guard "Salutes the Soldier"

when stopped by a defending patrol were released on the display of a righteous indignation at being disturbed on a Sunday afternoon picnic. Another, Burn-Callender, also cycling in mufti, accompanied a Clergyman right into Newmarket and returned with much useful information. Perhaps, however, the most surprising adventure was that of a motor-cyclist in uniform who left the harbour at 14.00 hours and, chasing through all the positions, was admitted to Gop Farm, where he was able to take note of the general dispositions and was informed that the Operational Sector Headquarters had been transferred to the wood above the farm. He then made a complete circuit of the defences, returning through the village of Newmarket, where two motor despatch riders gave unsuccessful chase. He returned back to Lawrence with his information at 14.55 hours.

In a report to the Commander of the Left Sector Coastal Zone on the following day, Maclean gave an account of the dispositions of the Commanders of the detachments from "E" and "F" Coys. and summarised the lessons to be learned from the exercise thus:—

1. Individual Non-Commissioned Officers and men showed considerable skill in the use of ground, but it must still be insisted that every man is personally responsible for keeping out of sight, and must not relax his vigilance in this respect for one moment. The hedge that affords excellent cover almost invariably has a break somewhere at which the incautious exposes himself.

2. The injunction to withhold fire until the last possible moment was well justified as it led the enemy to advance without due caution in the presence of a foe whom he could not see or hear and consequently to present a perfect target.

3. In contrast with other exercises in which "E" Coy. has taken part the Company Commander issued no orders after 12.45 hours, leaving the development of operations to the officers and Section Commanders concerned. The experiment was successful and officers and non-commissioned officers made good use of their initiative, although in some instances somewhat slowly, but the passing of verbal messages quickly and accurately needs further practice.

4. The necessity for all-round defence must never be forgotten.

5. The particular lesson to be drawn from the incidents in the neighbourhood of PEN-Y-CEFN-UCHAF Farm is that all roads are dangerous avenues of approach in the presence of the enemy unless the front and flanks have been thoroughly explored, and protected. The subsidiary lesson is that Home Guards properly trained and properly led should be able to work round the flanks or rear of all but the most strongly held positions, and that they gain rather than lose in their effectiveness from working in small parties able

to make maximum movement unobserved and prepared to lie up in good hideouts for indefinite periods.

On the 15th November, Brigadier E. N. F. Hitchens, C.B.E., D.S.O., M.C., Commandant of the Signal Training Centre, who had acted as Chief Umpire during the first Exercise, presided over a Conference of all Umpires and Officers who had taken part in it. The discussion left us with the feeling that we had not done too badly: we did not know that our achievements had caused some concern, for our success in infiltration had shaken existing confidence in the local defence scheme. Brigadier Hitchins, accordingly, asked the Ministry companies to take part in a further exercise to test the defence, in which they would again furnish the air-borne enemy detachments. The exercise was fixed for 14th December, the Brigadier acting as Director on this occasion with Maclean as Assistant Director, and Colonel Bell as Chief Umpire. Lawrence was to command the attackers, with Capstick and Huskisson as his principal Lieutenants.

The area of operations was limited this time to the country around Newmarket, over which we were to work, and we were spared the untimely collisions with troops proceeding to adjacent areas which had been a feature of our first excursion.

If we now had the advantages of larger numbers and a better knowledge of the ground than before, the defence were conscious of our proficiency, which they had probably under-estimated previously, and were on their mettle.

The general background of the scheme followed that of the previous exercise; it was assumed that during the evening of the 13th December unopposed airborne landings had been made in various parts of North Wales and that by dawn on the morning of the 14th enemy troops (supplied from the Ministry Companies) were in concealed positions at the following points: —

    At Tan-yr-Allt 4 light tanks and 40 men under Hitchcock (Code name—COCKY).

    At Llanasa 40 men and a Heavy Machine Section of 2 guns under Looker (Code name—LUCKY).

    At Brynglas 2 light tanks and 40 men under Capstick (Code name—STICKY).

    These were the eastern group.

    At Gwaenysgor 2 light tanks and 40 men under Ker (Code name—KERRY).

    At Dyserth 4 light tanks and 40 men under Selby (Code name—SELBY).

    These were the western group.

The objective for the enemy force was the occupation of Newmarket and Gop Hill, so as to clear and cover the Abergele—Holywell road and render it available for a mechanised force to move eastwards along it by 14.30 hours.

TRAINING AND ORGANISATION—II

Lawrence's operation orders issued at midnight 13th/14th December added the information that the area Newmarket—Gop Hill—Gop Farm was a defended locality, of which Gop Farm was the normal advance headquarters, and that strong forces of up to 300 men armed with anti-tank rifles and heavy and light machine guns could be expected in the vicinity. Armoured anti-tank stops at the approaches to the West and South of Newmarket were to be anticipated.

Lawrence divided his forces into two groups. The westerly group under Huskisson comprised two parties. The easterly group Lawrence commanded personally; it comprised three parties. Huskisson was to develop the westerly attack from places of concealment at 11.00 hours and endeavour, by pressing it home, to draw the enemy forces into a close engagement so that the easterly attack to be launched later could exploit any weaknesses that had become apparent.

In this exercise, although we were on the whole remarkably successful, hardly anything went according to the time-table or plan and a special providence must have been watching to see that the contrariness of events did not frustrate individual enterprise and initiative. Lawrence's main attack from the east by COCKY and LUCKY was to synchronise with a subsidiary attack from the south by STICKY. The latter was dropped at the correct time and place and developed the attack at 11.00 hours according to plan. The main force, however, lost its way and was an hour late at its rendezvous. Huskisson put up such a good demonstration in the west and north, however, that most of the defence force was diverted to meet it and the operation was successful.

The action was full of incident, and if the troops were for the most part tired and weary at the end of the day, they could not make the complaint, which was sometimes heard at exercises, that they had stood and sat about for hours with nothing to do.

The forces on the extreme flanks had a considerable distance to cover: most of the ground was difficult, and from the vantage point of Gop Hill, whence the Director viewed most of the exercise, its development had the appearance of proceeding much more according to order and plan than was the case. SELBY in the west reached Mia Hall without serious incident, and thought they had scored considerably when their tanks were practically in Newmarket in the early stages of the fight, but here the Director intervened and, putting the leading tank out of action, sent the others back some distance to start again. The tank crews, which had run into Lewis gun fire only, felt they had been disposed of too easily and it was only a moderate compensation to them that the infantry of the party succeeded in shooting up, before they were observed, a whole platoon of defenders lining the wrong side of a hedge at Gop Farm. Huskisson, with LUCKY, had the time of his life and waged a continual battle from about 11.00 hours until about 14.30 hours when the action ceased. Some of the men in this party captured an enemy lorry and taking the defenders' steel helmets (for the attackers were in Field Service Caps) drove right into the yard at Gop Farm. Here again they felt they were hardly done by when the Umpires ordered them out. Undaunted they came back again from every quarter, and it was largely due to the continuous probing of the defences on the north and north-west by this party that so large a proportion of the defenders was drawn away and Lawrence's main attack, though delayed, could be pushed home. In the north-east and east, parties had the benefit of close acquaintance with the ground from the previous exercise, but here the going was at its heaviest and once again the attackers felt that the Umpires were almost too generous to the defence when they held up a party proceeding in well-spaced single file because of machine gun fire from 2,000 yards range. However, this was not an unmixed blessing for it gave them early intimation of the defenders' position, of which they were not slow to take advantage.

The easterly attack eventually forced its way into Newmarket. To Colonel Montgomery at Defence Headquarters near Gop Farm came a message that Newmarket had been taken. Throwing his cap on the table the Colonel exclaimed: "Well, if five Platoons cannot hold the place, two cannot retake it," and certainly they should not have been able to do so. But our party in the village were tired and perhaps confident that the day's work had been done. The Defence Commander threw his reserve into the battle, machine guns in motor-cycle sidecars swept round the outskirts of the town to come in behind the successful attackers while the two reserve platoons came down the hill to join in the battle. Before they had even realised that they were being counter-attacked, the victors of Newmarket were "in the bag," and Lawrence, Commander of the Paratroops, was among the prisoners! Here, to all intents and purposes, the battle might have ended, but, out of gear and timing as it was, the major surprise and success of the day was still to come. COCKY after being badly delayed on the journey, arrived on the fringe of the battle, grasped the situation and put in a left flanking attack, sweeping through the village to join with STICKY whose assault from the south broke into the defence at the same moment. Whether the Commanders of these two parties were more surprised at the successful concurrence of their attacks, or at being congratulated by the Brigadier on the "extraordinary" success of the timing which enabled their forces to join up at exactly the right moment, is not recorded!

It was after this exercise that we had another example of the kindly hospitality of the people of the country in which we were strangers. The imp that was in the clock that day chose to be freakish once more and delayed for some two hours half the transport that was to take the party home. The troops that had to wait for the delayed vehicles concentrated on the village institute where, as Moore afterwards put it, "a splendid lady supplied gallons of tea free which we carried over to the Institute, and a considerable number of men got a good cup of tea."

The concluding paragraphs of Maclean's report to the Director of this exercise are, perhaps, worthy of quotation: —

"*Consolidation.*—The most serious criticism of the exercise must be directed to the failure to consolidate a successful attack which had resulted in the capture of part of NEWMARKET. The attackers were hampered by the presence of troops that had been put out of action and who were impeding movement and preventing the Commanders on either side from assessing the true position correctly. This difficulty does not, however, excuse the attackers' delay in taking steps to consolidate their position. No scouts were pushed out to cover consolidation and when the defence (which had been unaware that only part of NEWMARKET had been captured) counter-attacked, the unprepared attacking force were wiped out by machine guns at close range.

"*Initiative.*—Probably the most important lesson for the rank and file is the importance of initiative. Many men (and some officers and N.C.O.s) appear to be under the impression that if there is anyone in the vicinity senior to themselves, they are absolved from any need to think for themselves and from all responsibility unless it be to carry out a direct order: (Their own safety is perhaps watched over by a beneficent providence and the defeat of the enemy is someone else's business.)"

The other exercise was the first of the full-scale invasion exercises, involving night operations, in which the Ministry Unit played an important part in attack. Two parties from "E" and two from "F" Coys. took part in the attack and spent a fairly strenuous night and day. After a morning's work and an afternoon's preparation, operations started at 18.30 on Saturday, April 25th, 1942, and continued almost without pause until 13.30 on Sunday, the 26th. (The newly formed mobile column was allotted a place in the defence scheme, transported to Llanrwst with great speed, and so effectively immobilised by the defensive strategy that they were seen no more).

The instructions to the attacking force were to inflict the maximum amount of damage, to fight to the extent to which this was involved in carrying out the demolition programme and then to lie up in the most effective cover available, surrendering when confronted with force sufficient to threaten annihilation—in fact to conform in conduct to that expected of air-borne raiders. The plan of attack was ambitious. Party No. 1 under Gair was to blow the bridge under which Dinerth Road passes, capture and hold the cross-roads at the top of Penrhynside Hill, clear the cross-roads where the Glanwydden road crosses the main Llandudno road, and return to the Little Orme to receive a landing party. Then they were to link up with a similar holding force under Spencer, whose first task had been to blow the bridge on the Llandudno-Deganwy road just south of the former, to destroy Llandudno Station, to occupy the cross-roads south of Nant-y-Gamar and finally to link up with the first party. (Had all this been done with success, the defending forces would have been denied access by road or rail to the eastern end of Llandudno Bay and the "Landing" would have been covered—at somewhat long range—from the hills). Meanwhile Party No. 3, under Richardson, was to have started their night out by demolishing the Pensarn railway bridge, and to have captured Llandudno Junction Station and Section H.Q. in the town, finally holding the cross-roads at Bryn Mair. The remaining party, under Hitchcock, was to start with an attack on Llandudno Police H.Q., demolish the telephone exchange, put the cable railway out of action and return to the Great Orme's Head to cover the landing from the other side of the bay. All this was to be directed and co-ordinated by H.Q. to be established in Llanrhos Vicarage.

What in fact happened, of course, no-one really knows in exact detail. The "fog of war" is at its thickest in night operations, and is even thicker on manoeuvres than in actual fighting because the dead rise and argue and fight again, the wounded recover suddenly and, like the Arab forces of Lawrence (of Arabia), troops retire for a cup of coffee in the heat of battle. (It is, incidentally, a pity that Milton in "Paradise Lost" did not give us a clearer lead on the technique of battle when both sides are vulnerable, but immortal). The Intelligence Diary, however, supplemented by personal narratives, shows the picture as it appeared at H.Q. and also from the slightly different aspect which it presented to those in the heat of battle.

The first entry in the Intelligence Diary records the capture of Llanrhos Vicarage by the H.Q. group, who settled down, with three "fifth column" despatch riders, to direct operations; this was completed by 19.45. Party No. 1, with which H.Q. was out of touch until midnight, crossed the valley after destroying their first objective and came into contact with the defending forces at Glan Wydden; they overcame them by weight of numbers, and victors and vanquished fraternised from 21.45 to 22.00, when they regrouped outside. By this time H.Q. was getting reports in from their motor-cyclists concerning the defence dispositions but were still out of touch with Party No. 2. These had been making progress: here is the account of Cessford, then Platoon Officer:—

"At last, 19.40 hours on Saturday, 25th April, found a tough party of some twenty volunteers from No. 2 Platoon 'F' Company under Lieutenant Richardson ranged in the vicinity of the abattoir at Mochdre and taking instructions from a zealous umpire. We knew we were in for a busy eighteen hours and our first objective proved to be Pydew, tucked above us on the ridge to the north of the Conway Road. The going was rough and trouble was expected from the start. Scouts and forward patrol advanced cautiously taking full advantage of the abundant cover. We sweated on, sure that the defence must be retiring to avoid combat.

"Close to our objective No. 1 Section went with Lieutenant Richardson by the main road, the Platoon Officer taking No. 2 Section in a left flanking approach to the village. No. 2 Section reached Pydew without incident.

"No. 1 Section was less fortunate. They ran straight on to the enemy who, flourishing his Air Raid Warden's armlet to indicate his belligerent status, called for the surrender of O.C. Platoon and his party. Toujours l'audace! The reply as reported to the writer must be omitted in deference to the susceptibilities of a large body of readers. Despite rumours to the contrary, the Warden was not buried near Pydew. By 21.30 hours the village was ours.

"Discipline was maintained despite the wiles of some local female fifth columnists. After a brief toilet performed with burnt cork and cocoa we moved off toward Marl Hall to keep our R.V. with the umpire, who chose a more convenient method of approach —by car, than scrambling through woods and down slopes. We missed a short cut down a fifty foot cliff by inches in the fading light. Had we made the short cut someone else would be writing this."

The third party are recorded in the Diary as having captured their first objectives, damaging the railway and bridge, by 22.00 hours. Almost simultaneously their attack on Llandudno station had developed. This was judged to have been successful, in spite of the great cost at which it inflicted heavy casualties on the defenders. Party No. 4 had captured the Police Station by 22.01 hours, but, proceeding to attack the gas works, had run into a very heavy crossfire: they were caught in an admirable defence plan, out-numbered and out-gunned. This is how it looked to a participant.

"We were whisked through to Llanrhos at 45 m.p.h. by army lorries. The drivers confided to us that they had a date with a couple of girls in Colwyn Bay at 8 o'clock. 20.00 hours was our zero time at Llanrhos, and the quick journey meant that we had to lie up in a copse for a quarter of an hour, watching the Llandudno Home Guard leisurely proceeding to the battle ground. An umpire (Major with car) soon arrived, but seemed a bit surprised that we had ideas of approaching a town otherwise than by road.

"Promptly at zero hour we set off across country from Vicarage Road for the hill-crest, using available cover to such good purpose that within thirty minutes we had half a dozen enemy signallers 'in the bag,' complete with lamps and signalling equipment. This included a pair of silk stockings.

"Our first objective was the Gasworks, and according to the umpires the attack was partially successful. We had lost quite a few men however. They became 'prisoners' in the Links Hotel before closing time."

From 22.15 H.Q. had been in contact with Parties 3 and 4: the diary records a thunder flash from the direction of the Little Orme at 23.45. That recorded the capture of the Penrhynside crossing by the first party; as the writer threw it he may now take up the narrative in the first person.

"Gair's party, proceeding along the lower road to Penrhynside, ran into light opposition at the approach to the village. This was overcome and we advanced, still along the bottom road, towards Old Penrhyn Hall, which, unknown to us, was defence H.Q. and stiff with reserves. Soon enough, however, we found out, and were heavily engaged. I found myself cut off from the main body, in the company of Baker and Verden, and we decided, as we had lost our leader but knew our objective, to attack it ourselves. We crept up the rough hillsides below the houses, stalked an isolated sergeant who seemed to be doing nothing in particular and tied him to a tree, and crept along the outside of the garden walls overhanging the precipice. Finally we worked our way, still on the 'cover' side of the wall, right up to the cross-roads. By an incredible piece of good luck a belated tram was coming up the hill, and, under cover of its noise, we made a final dash, landing 'grenades' from point blank range on the holding troops. We then sat to await our main body, who turned up, reduced to eleven in number, up the main road."

The second party, meanwhile, had been making progress. Here is Cessford's account of the next phase: —

"By 23.00 hours we were at our R.V. and the full moon was up in a cloudless sky. There we received our instructions to attack Llandudno Junction and moved off in battle order, No. 1 Section, with Lieutenant Richardson in charge, taking the Station Hotel Annexe as their objective, and the Platoon Officer with No. 2 Section making for the Railway Station.

"We advanced taking full advantage of the strong shadows provided by the moon and the wooded landscape. Our umpire was now foot-slogging with the infantry and providing a running commentary of advice on how it *should* be done. Approaching the built up area we took one prisoner whose only offence was being late for parade. We made him much later.

"The two parties separated, No. 1 Section to attack the Annexe, and No. 2 Section to the Station job. Our umpire continued with the Station party but was shortly afterwards lost down a side street as we made a detour to cross the bridge lying to the east of our objective. Our two advanced scouts were sent ahead and were shortly joined by O.C. Section and the remainder of his party. Trouble was expected at the bridge. A Section of three was disposed to give covering fire from the shadows and Corporal Wiglesworth, Lance/Corporal Hoare and O.C. Party crossed the bridge. When half way over a challenge came from the other side, a thunder flash was thrown among the defenders and the whole attacking party rushed across. Result, the usual argument with a party of three partisan defenders as to casualties.

"The Welsh defenders were appeased when, in the absence of an umpire, O.C. party, Wiglesworth and Hoare agreed to become casualties and the defenders in turn were written off. Lance/Corporal Elliott was briefed by the 'dead' officer and moved off with the remainder of the troops to attack the Station."

Elliott consequently takes up the story.

"The previous evening the Sergeant had, by means of a penny platform ticket, reconnoitred the objective and discovered a good approach.

"The first real action occurred when the party attempted to cross the bridge over the railway to the east of the station. The Lieutenant, Sergeant and five men had advanced on to the bridge, leaving five men, in charge of the Corporal, to cover their approach. As they got to the centre of the bridge pandemonium broke loose, with noises of machine guns, grenades, etc., and it was fairly obvious that a machine gun post was covering the bridge from the far side. In no time voices were being raised on the usual exercise argument 'Who's dead?' and so as to save further argument, the surviving Corporal and five men fixed bayonets and charged in true fashion. The enemy and the party's own 'dead' were so engrossed in argument that nobody witnessed the charge. However, as the Corporal passed through the enemy machine gun post, the 'dead' Lieutenant told him to carry on and do his best.

"Unfortunately none of the survivors knew one end of the station from the other. The Sergeant was 'dead' and so was his pennyworth of knowledge. Undaunted those five men and Corporal advanced to the objective—spirits high and as keen as hell, even though the whole town was against them. Wire fences, potato patches, cabbage patches and every other sort of obstacle they encountered and mastered until in the end there—twenty-five yards before them—stood the signal box. Their advance had been so quiet that the enemy had no knowledge of their presence. The Corporal detailed one man to throw the grenade and the whole squad was instructed to double to the other end of the station as soon as the explosion occurred.

"Up went the signal box in a glorious flash and away went the squad, and so did every other noise one could think of. Straight fire, cross fire—orders in Welsh—orders in every direction—the station was full of enemy. But that squad of five men and one Corporal had them taped. Right down the centre railway line stood a goods train—beautiful dark cover. The squad fired and threw grenades from the cover of that train until the enemy was running in circles and crying for peace and quietness.

"Their task accomplished, the five men and one Corporal left the station in peace and faced the town where enemy still lurked. The very first person they encountered was an umpire who suggested that they should have a crack at the enemy's Company H.Q. further down the road. The O.C. Company had established his H.Q. in a shop and put two sentries outside, but forgot about patrol and outlying piquets, so that for those five men and one Corporal who had busted a station in their stride, the task was simple.

"Down the road they went and before the two sentries could raise a cry they were 'dead.' What surprise registered on the face of the enemy O.C. Company when in walked those five men and one Corporal! The Corporal covered him with his '300' and said 'You are dead.' 'Never in your life,' said the enemy O.C. Company, as he unbuckled his revolver straps and produced that lethal weapon.

"The point was settled true and fair by a couple of umpires standing there. One turned to the enemy O.C. Company and said, 'This squad—five men and one Corporal—have busted your station through and through and to crown it all, they've busted *you.*' "

While this had been going on, the third party was recovering from its mauling at Llandudno station. A section from this party, however, had been successful in an attack on the Coy. H.Q. of a unit in defence. Here is the account of the Platoon Sergeant:

"At 23.45 hours we moved south-east, crossing the road between the old hospital and the gas works, and made our way south along the mountain side to make contact with you at Cwm-Howard. Approaching the cross roads we ran into the enemy, and lost Sergeant O'Brien. In an endeavour to contact you, on the way to Cwm-Howard, we moved to the main road and stayed there. I judged it would be impossible for the small party to make their way through the village and thought we should attempt to deal with an enemy signalling post. We made our way east and then south-east along a lane and got to these grounds. There was motor car activity and we stopped an umpire's car and then entered the grounds, avoiding the sentries. It seemed an important post from the disposition of the sentries and we made our way carefully to the north-east point of the enclosure. We noticed motor cars, and eventually an umpire and one other man appeared. This man spoke to the sentry and we then dealt with both and proceeded along the rear of the building to find the post or headquarters. On the way we were met by several startled men but they gave us no real trouble, and after investigating some rooms in vain, we burst upon the officer commanding 'C' Company with his staff, and captured the lot. The umpire agreed that the building could be regarded as destroyed, that we had seized confidential papers and that headquarters of this Company would be out of action for one hour.

"While I personally dealt with the Company Commander, Corporal Grant and two men were beating off an attack outside. I collected my party outside and by making use of cover we moved to the south fence and got across the spiked railings without losing anyone. The short action was spirited and exciting, but only lasted approximately 5-10 minutes.

"It was only due to good team work that we succeeded, and I think the Company Commander should know that we were not aided, as he thought, by fifth columnists, but that his signalling light gave away his position.

"I felt very pleased indeed at the manner in which the men in my small party—some of them were much older than myself—bore the fatigue of the operations, and were never backward in surmounting any obstacle, be it mountain or barbed fence or spiked railing.

The team, if I may say so, did particularly good work in the attack on the Company Headquarters, when at various stages we must have accounted for almost twenty men."

Meanwhile, No. 4 Party had attacked the Llandudno telephone exchange. In the words of their O.C.: —

"A small party of eight arrived to within 10 yards of the back entrance without being detected, under cover of two flanking parties, who were liquidated. The small party mentioned opened fire on three men at the back entrance with a Sten gun; the umpire then told the party to stay put. Otherwise I am confident we could have forced an entrance before defence measures could have been taken. By the time the umpires had finished investigations, however, the doors were lined with defenders. We were awarded three men in the building, but were unsuccessful so far as material damage was concerned."

This brings the story to midnight, when a brief halt was called, and food and rest were "issued" in infinitesimal quantities. Casualties, prisoners, wounded and those who were just trying to find some tea got a little mixed, and one party at least, who sought hospitality, were taken prisoner. Henceforward the record gets more difficult to interpret as parties became scattered and intelligence personnel got more tired.

Consequently it is probable that a more coherent narrative is likely to result from following separately the fortunes of each party.

The first, under Gair, made a long detour over the golf links to attack the Llandudno-Glan Wydden cross roads from the east. Unfortunately this was marred by the only serious accident of the exercise: Corbett, jumping down from a wall, made a bad landing and broke both ankles. This cost the Unit a member who was remarkable for the time and energy which he found for the Home Guard among his very many other pre-occupations. The crossing was cleared: contact with the enemy was again made at Old Penrhyn Hall, and after a short rest in cover, the first light of dawn saw the party fighting their way up through the woods behind Penrhynside and over the downs into Holland, where a defending unit held the school. Thence they worked their way, picking up a group from the third party, to the top of the hill overlooking the main road from the north, due south of the Little Orme. There they lay in the frosty grass, in admirable cover and gradually thawing out, until finally they went down to a last assault on the defence H.Q. at Penrhyn Old Hall.

Let Cessford speak for the second party.

"We were joined by Lieutenant Richardson and No. 1 Section as they were ejected from the Annexe, having enjoyed a measure of grudging hospitality from the military garrison whose defences had been over-run, despite a preliminary *faux-pas* caused by an indiscreet army boot contacting a bucket as the owner of the boot dropped over the wall into the grounds.

"The problem of rest looms large at 02.00 hours on a somewhat wintry morning. We now decided to be more typical huns and to attack a first aid post which looked hospitable. The attack was a complete success, as the defence was weak and our boys were dirty and desperate. Soon stretchers were laid down, blankets provided and our commando in repose, lulled to sleep or desperation by the snores of an erstwhile casualty whose sausage roll must have laid rather heavily on his unsoldierly digestion.

"Reveille came two hours later. The F.A.P. staff, among whom was a sprinkling of attractive St. John's Nurses, provided us with tea. We ate some of our pack rations, and by 04.45, washed and refreshed, we were again on our way.

"Before leaving the Junction we reported to Major Lawrence at H.Q. by telephone, then on to our next objective. We reached this, after a three mile march, about 06.00 hours, and realising that we were rather early for the scheduled attacks on this important road junction, we placed our party under cover. Lieutenant Richardson and his Platoon Officer emerged on to the road to carry out a preliminary reconnaissance. The stillness of the morning air could be felt. It was broken by that slang American expression, 'stick 'em up,' which came from the scrub on the opposite side of the road. The two officers agreed that they were several kinds of fool, but the battle was now joined.

"Our commando opened fire briskly and deployed towards a neighbouring hen run. A Sergeant from the fifth Caerns., who commanded the defence approached; it was agreed that we would disengage and renew the battle at 07.00 hours by which time one or two well fed umpires would be on the job.

"At 07.00 hours the struggle was resumed, about 15 all ranks against 120 defenders. By 07.50 we were within 50 yards of the cross roads and still waging a lively battle. The umpires were satisfied, gave the decision to the defenders, and we arrived at the local H.Q. as prisoners.

"Soon the umpires found another assignment for us. By now Corporal Elliott had picked us up with his five men. They had had a lively time at Llandudno Junction. They were given the decision at the Station, had captured a Company H.Q. and had rested there for a time during the night, making their way across country to the scene of our fight at the cross roads, to arrive there just too late to muck in with the platoon. They had enjoyed their party. Now we were reinforced and ready for anything and set off about 10.00 hours to relieve Lieutenant Hitchcock, who was besieged in Deganwy Station which he had captured some time before.

"We gained our objective after a spirited action in the hills where we liquidated a section placed there to delay our advance.

We reached the station soon after without incident. Once there we relieved the garrison of some of the guard duties and played hide and seek round the railway wagons in a siding with a party of Royal Signals who were apparently not strong enough to come in and make a fight for it.

"At 11.30 we got word to stand down. This ended a most memorable exercise full of incident, training lessons and fun. The staff work had been good. But then, we were in the attack. Defence, as we learned many times to our cost, was not so funny. Our main lesson in defence was how to be cheerful though bored."

The stories of the third party, and of the H.Q. group, run together, and may be reconstructed from the intelligence diary. Several attempts to link up the two parties failed: finally a junction was effected at 04.00. Several attacks, the final successful one led by an escaped prisoner, were made on H.Q., which was finally evacuated. By 08.05 the third party were lying up on the Little Orme, according to plan, and finally the H.Q. Group fought their way to Penrhynside in time for the end of the exercise.

The fourth party had meanwhile been active. Here is the account of one of its members.

"Our third objective, at midnight, was the P.O. This was adjacent to the Police Station, and being warned of our approach, the defenders gave us a rough time. We got a few men into the Post Office and the umpires called the affair off—a kindly enemy inviting us to their H.Q. for hot cocoa. Objective No. 4, Crosville Garage, enabled us to use the cover of the football ground and neighbouring allotments for most of the way without incident, and a final 100 yards sprint on the lee side of the last tram, took us to our objective. The defence was taken by surprise but maintained we were under heavy L.G. fire for the last 100 yards. A tour of the defence lay-out by the umpires found the L.G. in question to be an imaginary one. It would have been there if the gun team had turned up. We got the verdict and were ordered on to No. 5 objective—a Platoon H.Q. Via allotments we got within twenty yards of the H.Q. when a burst of fire showed our presence was discovered. The reason for this was that a Section Commander on our right flank, finding that the only course open to him was to crawl across a splendid onion bed, as a good gardener, promptly ordered his men to 'close on the road on the right' rather than damage the onions.

"Objective No. 6 was a pillbox on the promenade. The moon gave us deep shadow cover, and, by using only the men with rubber soled shoes, the first that pillbox knew about us was a thunderflash through the window. The defence came out at the double.

Apparently this satisfied our umpire because he ordered us two hours' rest.

"But there was no rest. An urgent message came to reinforce Major Lawrence at Llanrhos Vicarage. We were sent straight into action against a force out to capture the Major and his small H.Q. This attack was beaten off and prisoners taken.

"We had now been on the move for eight hours, and by the time we got to the Town Hall were nearly 'all in.' We were given two hours' rest. Ten minutes of this had been enjoyed when an umpire whom we had not previously run across ordered us out of the town. He informed us that he had come to the conclusion that we knew too much about the place. 'May we get to Deganwy?' we asked. 'Go anywhere you like as long as it is not in this town,' was the reply. Reluctantly we left that hall and any chance of sleep. Many had 'gone off' as they hit the floor, but fell in again on the command, 'Stand to.'

"Lieutenant Hitchcock led us across the cricket ground and after a bit of scouting we captured a military Car Park. This may not have been cricket, but the Car Park had an armed guard, and the guard was caught napping.

"We then crossed the sand dunes to a beach defence post, complete with Lyon lights, barbed wire, etc. Admittedly it was just before dawn and possibly the sentry was fed up at having had no excitement all night. Anyhow scouts reported he was inside the wire but 'nodding.' It was found possible, therefore, for Lieutenant Hitchcock and Sergeant Stock to get through the wire and rush the post with Sten guns. 'What the hell?' exclaimed the surprised Sergeant of the guard. 'Heil Hitler,' replied Lieutenant Hitchcock.

'Where's my sentry?' said the Sergeant as he rushed out of the dug-out and set about his sentry in the choicest possible language.

"According to the umpire accompanying us, the Deganwy enemy had an advanced post at the road junction by the West Shore Bathing Pool and this was to be our next objective. But our carefully planned attack was wasted—the post was found to be unoccupied.

"On we went to Deganwy—a Co. H.Q.—and actually took the Castle Hotel which was the local defenders' H.Q. But, after a consultation of umpires, we were informed that, being so numerically inferior to the *force inside the hotel,* we must get out again. (The bar was closed anyhow). We had not to go far this time.

"The Railway Station was held by a small squad whom we attacked and took and, in spite of several counter-attacks, we held on there until the umpires called off the exercise in the early afternoon."

This is the story of the exercise—or rather a series of stories about it. It has been included at such length, partly because one exercise had to be described in some detail in order to round off the picture of Home Guard work at this time, and partly because of the manner in which it illustrates the stage which organisation had reached. The resulting reflection was far from discreditable. After some eighteen months of spare time training, carried out for part of the time without proper equipment or resources, a complicated military operation had been carried through with some success. Mistakes had been made, but the intelligence organisation had held the operation together as a coherent whole, and all branches of the Unit, Headquarters, Signals and plain ordinary Infantry had come through a strenuous and testing exercise without any signs of disintegration. At about 2 o'clock in the afternoon, operations concluded. As we trooped home, tired, stiff, hungry and soaked in perspiration, the general feeling was one of satisfaction. We had pitted our strength and endurance against darkness, fatigue, and physical obstacles; tested our metal against that of our fellows, and emerged successful. It was a good feeling.

CHAPTER 5.

TRAINING AND ORGANISATION III.

The Ministry of Food Wing: Directed Men: 1st June, 1942, to 31st December, 1942.

"Freedom . . . is the recognition of necessity."

Frederich Engels.

The most marked characteristic of this period in the development of the Ministry Unit is the increasing emphasis on organisation, resulting from the change in the function of the Home Guard. Shortly before the wing was founded compulsion, or, as it was termed, "direction," came into operation, and with it the character of the Home Guard underwent a subtle but definite change. The old Home Guard was prepared, if necessary, in each district to stand alone and defend its territory until relieved, if ever, by troops of the Regular Army. Emphasis, therefore, was upon the efficiency of the Local Force, and upon its capacity to operate individually if cut off from supplies and from the Military Authorities. With the changing pattern of the war, compulsory service in the Home Guard was introduced in circumstances which rendered it the function of the Guard to operate as a junior but closely controlled partner of the Regular Army, undertaking garrison duties and local defence in support of the expected invasion of the continent. The new Home Guard had, therefore, of necessity to accept a stricter and more complete degree of administrative control from the War Office.

These changes had taken place during the last of the period covered by the previous chapter; it was indeed in February, 1942, that compulsory service in the Home Guard was introduced. But it was only, roughly speaking, during the period in which the Ministry of Food Wing was inaugurated that this change reflected itself in the organisation of the Unit. Consequently, the focus of interest changes, as between the last chapter and this, from exercises in the field to organisation.

Orders issued by Maclean to the Ministry of Food Unit Home Guard foreshadowed the change. The eighth issue of these Orders, on the 15th May, 1942, for the first time was headed Ministry of Food Wing, and began, under the heading "Organisation," "As from the 1st June, 1942, 'E,' 'F' and 'G' Companies of the 1st Denbighshire Battalion will form what will be known as the Ministry of Food Wing. This wing will be commanded by Major L. F. C. Maclean, O.B.E., C.St.J., who will establish his own Headquarters at the Ministry of Food. For operations this wing will come under Left Sub-Sector of the Coastal Sector. For administration it will remain under the 1st Denbighshire Battalion as heretofore." The new "G" Company was commanded by Moore, with Cessford as Second-in-Command. Sherman was appointed as Wing Training Officer, Bowles as Intelligence Officer, and Sharp as O.C. Wing

TRAINING AND ORGANISATION—III

Quartermaster Stores. The new "G" Company was organised on approximately the same lines as the Headquarters Company of a Battalion. It was divided into five platoons, and the layout was as follows: No. 1 platoon, Headquarters, consisted of four sections, of which the first was composed of administrative, headquarters, and orderly room staff, the second of wing intelligence, war diary writers, guides, rousers, and traffic police, the third of the wing training staff and headquarters guard, and the fourth of wing quartermasters, storemen, cooks, cleaners, and loaders. The second platoon consisted of three machine gun sections, and one section of loaders. The third platoon was the signals platoon, of which the first section was the headquarters signalling unit, while Nos. 2, 3 and 4 were the Company signalling sections appointed to each of the three Companies complete with telephone orderlies, dispatch riders, and runners. The fourth, or transport platoon, consisted of two sections operating vehicles, one concerned with workshops and maintenance, and one in reserve. The fifth platoon was mobile, the first section being responsible for reconnaissance, the second being a rifle section and the third a light automatic gun section, while the fourth consisted of bombers. Platoons 2 and 3, machine guns and signals, although operating separately for training were administered as one platoon and came under the command of Lt. Holt for discipline. The mobile platoon was so organised that each section was capable of division into two, thus permitting the formation of two mobile columns each comprising all the necessary elements.

Although the Ministry Unit was not yet a Battalion, it is clear from this layout how completely it had become an effectively independent unit. The background against which this change had taken place must now be set out. ACI.151/1942 laid down the conditions under which separate units might in special circumstances be organised —"Certain Government Departments, Railway Companies, Public Utility Undertakings, and Factories of National Importance are permitted to form special Home Guard sub-units in which their employees may be enrolled primarily for the protection of their undertakings. These sub-units, however, will normally form part of the local Home Guard Battalion, and their employment in their special tasks will be co-ordinated with local defence schemes by the Military Commanders concerned." This was published in the Ministry of Food Unit Orders on the 17th February, 1942, and clearly foreshadowed the organisation of the separate Ministry of Food Unit. At the same time considerable change had been introduced into the general atmosphere of the Home Guard by the issue of the new Home Guard Regulations (S.R. & O. 1942/91) under which compulsory enrolment was applied in areas designated by the Army Council and the Ministry of Labour and National Service on the recommendation of the Commander-in-Chief of Home Forces. The Ministry of Labour and National Service became responsible for the selection of men (British subjects between the ages of 18 and 51) to be enrolled and for directing them to join the unit where they were required. It was not proposed that they should exercise this power of direction in the case of Civil Servants without the concurrence of the employing Ministry, but it was understood that exemption from service would be granted only in cases where the continuation of the employee's civil duties was clearly essential even in conditions of great emergency. The direction of men into the Home Guard, therefore, meant that necessarily the Establishment Division came to play a more important part in the organisation of the Home Guard. Already a scheme had been operated under which members of the Home Guard had been divided into two categories; those who in the event of national emergency would be released for operational duties with the Home Guard, and those who would be required to remain in order to carry out their civilian duties with the Ministry, until the last stand was made on the doorstep of Colwyn Bay Hotel. Consequently, we find Office Memorandum 614, issued on the 12th February, 1942, setting out formally for the first time the way in which it was proposed that the responsibility of Ministry of Food Home Guards should be divided as between their military and civilian duties. "During the period in which the platoon or other part of the Home Guard to which he belongs is mustered for the purpose of resisting an actual or apprehended invasion a member of the Home Guard may be required to serve continuously and to live away from home. Members will, therefore, be divided into categories 'A' and 'B' according to whether they will be in the circumstances then prevailing:—

"(a) available immediately for full time military service, or

"(b) available only at a later stage because of indispensable pre-occupation with essential civil duties, but having to report within 48 hours, when they will be told according to the operational situation at the time whether to parade for military duty or to continue their civil duties for a further period.

The decision as to whether any officer of the Ministry of Food who is in the Home Guard should be included in list 'A' or list 'B' rests with the Ministry, and not with the Commander of his Unit."

It was clear that henceforward the organisation of the Ministry of Food Home Guard Unit must be dovetailed pretty closely into that of the Ministry as a whole. At the same time, two further steps were taken regularising and rendering more formal the status of the Home Guard. Regimental numbers were issued to all members of the Guard, and in addition identity cards had to be stamped with the insignia of the Home Guard Unit to which their holders were attached. (In point of fact only one stamping machine was issued to the whole of the Ministry of Food Wing; this moved around from platoon to platoon and necessarily all members of each platoon were not on parade when the stamp turned up. It is extremely doubtful if this laudable attempt to divide the sheep from the goats was ever in effect brought to a satisfactory conclusion. Several casual attenders at Home Guard parades got their cards stamped on the only occasion in months on which they attended, while many keen and regular members of the unit were never branded at all).

Closely associated also with the introduction of compulsion and with the stipulation of a minimum period of training, which by force of law Home Guards must put in each month, was the introduction of proficiency badges. Obviously if training and operational duties were to become compulsory, there was a very strong case to be made out for demanding different periods of training for the proficient and for the novices, particularly in view of the fact that so many of the latter were somewhat reluctant conscripts, while so many of the former were competent old soldiers who had been undertaking strenuous training for some eighteen months. Consequently, before the end of 1941 when it was apparent to those in a position to anticipate the flow of events that compulsion was coming, schemes had been set on foot at War Office level for holding examinations and awarding proficiency badges to those whose training had reached a satisfactory minimum level. The first of these tests after a short period of intensive refresher courses was held early in 1942, and a very large proportion of the entrants passed and were awarded small lozenged shape badges, the receipt of which exasperated their owners owing to the enormous number of different places on their uniform in which they were told to display it week by week. It moved up and down the arm and from right arm to left until in most cases it was left off altogether. The level demanded of examinees was not very high; owing to the fact that the last of the proficiency tests was held before many of the directed men had passed into the Home Guard its main function was to distinguish between the volunteers and the conscripts.

One of the principal changes resulting from the more regularised and official status of the Home Guard was the increasing amount of administrative work demanded of Company and Platoon Commanders, and, indeed, of anyone in the Home Guard who could be given forms to fill in.[1] Shortly afterwards the War Office sanctioned the appointment of full time Adjutants seconded from the Regular Army, and on the 10th August, 1942, Captain R. D. Green, M.C., was appointed Adjutant to No. 1 Battalion. His duties were mainly connected with training and he also supervised a great deal of the work of administration. However, the extent to which the change increased the administrative duties of responsible officers is shown very clearly in the twenty-ninth issue of Ministry of Food Wing Home Guard Orders on the 2nd December, 1942, where it is stated that "In some cases officers commanding Home Guard Companies are not giving sufficient attention

---

(1) The warning leaflets flutter thick,
 Upon the heedless Germans,
 Poor chaps! Like us, they have to stick,
 Interminable sermons!

to the training of officers and men owing to most of their available time being taken up by office duties in connection with administration. Although the O.C. Company is responsible for all matters appertaining to his Company he must make full use of decentralisation to his subordinate officers in order that they may lighten the burden of administrative work and thus free him for training. The bulk of the administrative work should be undertaken on his behalf by the Second-in-Command of the Company assisted by the Company Quartermaster whose appointment is authorised by Command Home Guard Order 787/42. Each Company is also allowed a storeman clerk. The Second-in-Command of the Company aided by the Quartermaster should be made responsible to the officer commanding the Company for the recording of clothing and equipment, accounts, transport, feeding, and medical arrangements on mustering and ammunition, and for the claiming of subsistence and travel allowances."

It is fairly clear from the evidence quoted above how closely by this time the Home Guard had become dovetailed into the Regular Army organisation, and how completely its nature had changed from the days in which it was intended to operate as an emergency defence service guarding isolated points against the invader. It follows, therefore, logically if somewhat paradoxically, that as the organisation of the Home Guard became more rigid its defence plans should become more fluid and its strategy closer to that of an army in the field than to that of an isolated group holding on to a cross roads or other defensible position. Consequently, we find one of the earliest of the Unit's Orders, before indeed the wing was founded, dated May 28th, 1942, announcing in the following terms a demonstration of "THE NEW BATTLE DRILL." "A demonstration of the New Battle Drill will be given at Penrhos College grounds on Monday, the 8th June, 1942, at 20.15 hours. No. 1 Platoon 'F' Company will provide the demonstration section under Sgt. H. Jefferson assisted by Lance Sergeant C. Cowling. All officers, warrant officers, quartermaster-sergeants, platoon sergeants, and sergeants, are requested to attend." Not only did these attend; so did the C.O.s of neighbouring regular units as well as officers from our parent Battalion. It was the first chance they had had to see the drill, and months in advance of the official H.G.I. laying it down!

Jefferson and Cowling had been away to a course where the new battle drill had been shown to them, and had come back brimming over with enthusiasm. Battle drill was to dominate the training of the Home Guard for a long time to come. It consisted, as all will remember, of a formalised parade ground version of the technique of attack which had been found to be most effective in the field under modern conditions and with contemporary weapons. The central idea was that this drill should be thoroughly learnt on the barrack square before the section attempted to put it into practice tactically; every movement represented an action on the battle field. It was intended that movements should be carried out as in squad drill, smartness and precision of movement being insisted upon. Fire was represented by men standing to attention, troops on all other occasions standing at ease. In general the enemy was represented by a red flag in the middle of the parade ground. The section, divided into riflemen, bombers, and automatic weapon section, advanced and were then informed by the instructor that they were under fire. Thereupon the section halted, shouting at the top of their voices, "down, crawl, observe, fire." The idea of this was to assist troops to memorise the essential movements involved in avoiding and replying to enemy fire; taking cover, moving from the point where first observed, and then opening a carefully calculated fire. The subsequent movements of the drill were those of a right or left flanking attack, in which automatic weapons covered the advance of riflemen and bombers alternately, culminating in a bayonet charge and re-organisation on the farther side of the enemy position. Unfortunately, however, the ingenuity displayed by those responsible for the introduction of this drill was somewhat overdone. In the first place both the movements and the incantations were over-systematised. Consequently, at short intervals the script had to be rewritten, and even so there was indeed some remaining danger that troops trained on this basis might have found themselves so overcome by the series of catch words and movements they had to memorise as to overshadow in their minds the field conditions which the parade ground rehearsal was intended to simulate. Anyhow, one of the rank and file of the Home Guard has recorded the way in which it looked to him.

"BAR GROUP OVER THERE !"

(A Ballade of Variety)

Monotony's our portion. Cheerful change
  Rarely beguiles us here at Colwyn Bay.
We do not ever feel that rich and strange
  Adventure will befall us on our way.
Nothing will change—we know th*.t*, come what may.
Nothing will change ? Admitted, one thing will :
  For every week some sad squad will display
Another version of the Battle Drill.

The Fates seem impotent to rearrange
  Our lives to colour chunks with more than grey.
Even a puppy bitten by the mange
  Exhibits spots comparatively gay.
We never go a-tumbling in the hay ;
What was routine remains *our* routine still—
  One sole variety the week's display :
Another version of the Battle Drill.

Garments ? Our last year's suit is this year's range ;
  Diet ? Alas! potatoes all the way ;
Billet ? *We'll* never leave the Welsh for "Grange" ;
  And as for work—*that* never seems like play.
So long, sad day succeeds to long, sad day,
Till Sunday, when we stagger up the hill

> To stage the week's Variety Display:
> Another version of the Battle Drill.
>
> ### L'ENVOI
>
> Sergeant! In my *damned dreams* I hear you say:
> "To-morrow we shall march up Ruddy Hill,
> And round its peaks we'll practise all the day
> *Another* version of the Battle Drill!"
>
> A.F.E.

This change in battle training was accompanied by a very welcome addition to the arms of the Home Guard. In 1943 the Sten gun appeared, a light, ungainly, unfinished but efficient sub-machine gun, which for all its Woolworth appearance was to prove both accurate and effective. It had been produced partly as a new automatic weapon for the British Army, partly as a means of arming the guerrilla formations operating behind the enemy lines in occupied countries, for which purpose it was designed to take ammunition identical with that employed by the standard German sub-machine gun, so that captured ammunition could be utilised by the patriots. Its issue to the British Home Guard, where fairly soon most Officers and N.C.O.s were so equipped, was both welcome and stimulating. Unlike the early special weapons with which the Home Guard had been issued, it was efficient and workmanlike, and did not bring to light any inferiority complex among its possessors. Moreover, its action was not altogether unlike that of a garden hose, and seeing that the bulk of Officers and N.C.O.s of the Home Guard, particularly the Ministry Unit, was drawn from those who in peace would be the proud cultivators of suburban gardens, it was a doubly appropriate weapon with which to practise on Sunday mornings.

During the same period another new weapon was also made available—the Blacker Bombard, or Spigot Mortar. Unlike the Northover Projector, the Spigot Mortar, although unorthodox in design was extremely accurate and effective, and had indeed been put to very good use by the defenders of Stalingrad, delivery to whom had for a time precluded its supply to the Home Guard. The only drawback to the Spigot Mortar in training was that, as a dummy shell filled with sand or concrete was necessarily employed for target practice, this projectile tended to bury itself yards deep in the sandy soil of Coed Coch, and therefore after every discharge a squad of gunners had to dig like terriers in order to get their ammunition back. It was, however, an heartening acquisition, and both the mortar and the sub-machine gun showed the Home Guard that at last they were being taken very seriously indeed.

A further instance of the change in Home Guard organisation during this period was the increasing importance laid upon the part which the Home Guard might play in civil defence. During the great air attack on Great Britain in 1940 the Home Guard had indeed played a prominent part in civil defence—cordoning off bombed areas, and undertaking rescue and demolition work. This, however, had in all cases been undertaken on the initiative of local Home Guard Commanders, who had naturally reacted to the emergency conditions in the same way as had the Commanders of those regular troops who had similarly taken part in defensive measures. With the new importance of the Home Guard in air defence, however, and with the intended replacement of the Forces released from garrisoning Great Britain to invade the continent, it was necessary to organise and train Home Guards for work in civil defence. Consequently, during the autumn of 1942 instructions were issued that, while weapon training must in all cases take priority over civil defence training, proficient Home Guards must be prepared to undertake training for fire fighting, demolition work, and the like. In Colwyn Bay the local organisation of the National Fire Service placed its resources at the disposal of the Ministry Unit, and a great deal of work was done in training members of the Ministry Unit as fire fighters. (A pressure hose is an unwieldy instrument in unpractised hands, and the proportion of Officers and N.C.O.s, as opposed to other ranks, who became the victims of accidental immersion was surprisingly high!)

Meanwhile, as Captain Sherman's narrative in Chapter 3 showed, it had been necessary to institute special courses for the "new intake," caused by the direction of men into the Ministry Unit. These had been put through a moderately strenuous training, being expected to attend on Sunday mornings, and on Tuesday and Thursday evenings, the courses covering squad and arms drill, guard duties, and weapon training, particular attention being given to the use and care of the rifle, bayonet fighting, and to the use of the hand grenade.

By this time also it had become necessary, in order to avoid endless repetition as well as to increase the efficiency of the Unit, to provide instruction for the proficient members of the Unit relating to new aspects of military duties. Perusal of Battalion Orders during this period shows that the number of courses open to Officers and N.C.O.s of the Home Guard was rapidly increasing and that normally Home Guards returning from these courses became instructors to their fellows. For example, in June, 1942, a course was held at Wrexham on the interrogation of prisoners of war, to which German speaking members of the Home Guard were invited. At this course the technique of interrogation, at least in the preliminary stages which the Home Guard would undertake in the field, was thoroughly instilled into the students together with the technique of handling reluctant and recalcitrant prisoners. In August a travelling instruction unit held an area course for Intelligence Officers and N.C.O.s in the County Secondary School at Colwyn Bay. Among the items staged at this school was an exhibition of the way in which not to run a Battalion intelligence room, which besides being instructive, was as good a piece of pure comedy as ever was produced on a British stage. In addition, special courses were held at Wrexham, Altcar, and elsewhere for officers and other ranks, dealing with the delicate but offensive art of umpiring, chemical warfare, first aid, weapon training technique for

N.C.O.s, and the use of the anti-tank mines which were by this time in the course of issue to Home Guard Units. To and from all these courses a constant stream of officers and men moved, and from them sprang a steady flow of instruction to all ranks in the Ministry Unit.

The points characteristic of this period in the history of the Ministry Unit are, it must be repeated, the change in organisation and the change in the temper of the Home Guard, both in Colwyn Bay and throughout the country. Numerous exercises were held and the level of efficiency reached by the Ministry Unit continued to improve. They are, however, incidental during this period, rather than the dominating feature, as in the time covered by the previous chapter. From June to December, 1942, the Ministry of Food Unit was building up its own organisation and assimilating new intake in preparation for the change that was shortly to take place; it was developing specialist units of all kinds, which will be dealt with in a later chapter, and recruiting armourers, clerks, cooks, cyclists, guides, loaders, orderlies, scouts, stretcher bearers, telephone operators, traffic police and weapon training officers. It was, in short, preparing to become an independent unit closely based, as were at the time all Home Guard Battalions to an increasing extent, upon the Battalion organisation of the Regular Army.

On the 31st December, 1942, Maclean issued the last Order of the Ministry of Food Wing. "Under authority War Office letter 20/HG/267/HG.1. dated the 9th December, 1942, approval is given for the formation of a new Home Guard Battalion to be known as 11 Denbighshire Battalion Home Guard, and to be formed out of the Ministry of Food Unit now with the 1 Denbighshire Battalion Home Guard. The ceiling for the new Battalion will be 1,050. The date of formation of 11 Denbighshire Battalion Home Guard will be 1st January, 1943. No further Ministry of Food Wing Orders will be issued."

CHAPTER 6.

Training and Organisation IV.

The 11th Battalion Denbighshire Home Guard: The Wing takes Flight

"Evolution . . . is a change from an indefinite, incoherent homogeneity to a definite, coherent heterogeneity."

Herbert Spencer.

From the 1st January, 1943, the Ministry of Food Wing became the 11th Denbighshire Battalion. As indicated in the course of the last chapter, the change was in the title of the unit rather than in the nature of the organisation; the command had become well established, the cadres had been built up, and a Headquarters unit suitable for a Battalion was already in existence. Some inter-change of officers took place, and some new officers, particularly specialists, were appointed. From this stage onwards it is difficult to present a simultaneous picture of the whole of the Battalion's activities at any one time, owing to their increasing range and capacity. Accordingly, subsequent chapters will deal with the work of the specialist units of the Battalion, such as signals, intelligence, and catering, and with the training in the field centred upon Pentre Foelas. This chapter is mainly concerned with the organisation and public activities of the Battalion.

Before developing this theme, however, a few words on the origin of the Battalion would not be misplaced. It had been decided upon a considerable time in advance, indeed, upon the withdrawal of the Signals holding unit of 1,200 men, but various obstacles had had to be overcome before its foundation was possible. The impetus came from above, and from outside the Ministry. The number of officers was according to establishment, but recruitment did not come up to expectations and the Battalion was never up to full strength. The position was very largely saved by the older and unfit men who were invited to take a hand and whose response was wonderful.

The first Orders of the new Battalion were issued over Maclean's signature on January 26th, 1943. The personnel in "E," "F" and "G" Coys. of the 1st Denbighshire Battalion Home Guard were transformed into "A" or the Administrative Coy., "B" Coy. and "C" Coy. of the 11th Battalion. The Battalion Specialists Officers were appointed in the same Orders; Dr. Edgar Morison as Medical Officer, Sherman as Training Officer, Sharp as Quartermaster, Bowles as Intelligence Officer, and Polfrey as Catering Officer. Subsequent Orders completed the appointments of the Specialists. Wheatley became Chemical Warfare Officer on February 13th, and was succeeded by Essex-Lopresti on the 2nd September. On March 24th, Buddin became Transport Officer, and on the following day Captain C. W. Hunt, of The Leicestershire Regiment, joined the Battalion as Adjutant. On the 13th of the following month Sgt. R. H. Johnson as Mustering N.C.O. took over from the Battalion Intelligence Officer responsibility for the administrative work of the mustering scheme; he was followed successively by Sgt. Weaver and Sgt. Trevor.

Battalion Orders dated June 23rd recorded the appointment of F. C. Baker as Ammunition Officer, and also recorded the establishment of the Women's Service Unit. This had already been effectively co-operating with the Ministry Home Guard and the announcement was to the effect that it had now been recognised by the War Office, with an establishment of ninety. It was to be led by Miss L. Bridgman, with Miss A. E. French and Miss E. Corbet-Owen as Sub-Leaders. The organisation was divided into six sections, Administrative, Communications, Intelligence, Catering, Guides, and Transport. Its subsequent development and experiences are recorded elsewhere. On August 11th Captain A. F. G. Hewett, M.C., R.A., took over A. and Q. duties at Battalion Headquarters, thus relieving Sharp who had been rendering valuable service to the Battalion as acting Quartermaster from the 1st January. The Battalion Commander's appreciation of his services was recorded in the same Orders.

The new "D" Company was authorised by Cambrian Sub-District on the 2nd December, 1943, and appeared for the first time in Battalion Orders No. 38, 1943. It was announced that in future "A" Company would be known as the Headquarters Company of the Battalion (instead of its earlier title of the Administrative Company), and that the present "B" and "C" Companies of the Battalion were to be recruited exclusively from Home Guards in (i.) or "A" category, which it will be remembered consisted of those free to take part in active operations as soon as the Home Guard was mustered. All category (ii.), or "B," personnel in "B" and "C" Companies were transferred to the new "D" Company which Captain J. C. W. Holt was to command. On the 15th December, 1943, an Intelligence Reconnaissance Section, consisting of one Sergeant and two Corporals and five men was set up. This section was to be responsible to Battalion Headquarters, and to work directly under the Intelligence Officer. Its duty was to seek and obtain information during operations, and it was intended to round off the intelligence organisation of the Battalion. This concludes the record of the major changes in organisation resulting from the establishment of the Battalion.

The Orders of the new Battalion, however, published on February 17th, 1943, set up a Battalion Finance Committee to advise the Commanding Officer in regard to proposals for expenditure from the Battalion imprest or training funds. It was composed of Cessford, Holt and Sharp, with Capstick as Chairman, and it was announced that Sgt. B. W. Brixey, F.C.A., Sergeant in charge of Battalion accounts, would attend meetings of the Finance Committee in an advisory capacity. This notice provides opportunity to draw attention to one phase of devoted service, for which the Battalion is greatly indebted to a small group of men. For a long time it had been necessary to maintain some form of financial organisation to look after the accounts of the Ministry of Food Unit, the task being a difficult one, particularly in the early days when no one knew from what sources funds were to be raised for Home Guard purposes, nor upon what objects expenditure was justifiable. Holliday, one of the pioneers, and the original Platoon Commander of "E" Coy., had acted from approximately September, 1940, as Finance Officer responsible to the 1st Battalion Denbighshire Home Guard for the payment of cash subsistence to outlying and inlying piquets. The original catering arrangements, it must be remembered, had aimed at supplying hot food and drink to men on duty, but supplies had been irregular; the position had been far from satisfactory (see some of the comments recorded in Chapter II.), and eventually both for the Penmaen Head and the Colwyn Bay Station guards cash subsistence allowances were paid to all those who chose to claim them, as from the 2nd December, 1942.

The subsequent arrangements, including the manning of the observation post on the Golf Course, the telephone piquets at Artillery House, and the beach patrols covering the railway and the beach from Penrhos Old Sanatorium, were organised in the same way. This involved a great deal of monotonous and uninteresting work, and Holliday combined with it two other equally onerous tasks. He acted as treasurer to the Ministry of Food Home Guard general fund, and was thus concerned with the organisation of the dances, the first of which was held on the 20th February, 1941, in order to raise funds which in those early days were expended in supplementing the inadequate equipment officially provided. Maps, sandbags, signals gear, film exhibitions, and even lectures were financed out of the cash raised from these social activities and administered by the Finance Officer. In addition he also acted as treasurer to the C.O.'s fund which was financed by individual subscriptions. Its original purpose was to institute a transport section, which saw the light of day at the end of 1942 under Moore, and subsequently became part of the Headquarters Coy. of the Battalion. These duties were taken over by Brixey as from the 20th October, 1942, by which time they had been reduced to a certain extent to routine, but had grown considerably in volume. From the 1st January, 1943, throughout the whole period of the Ministry Battalion, Brixey, who was later appointed to a commission as Battalion Quartermaster, became responsible for controlling the official Territorial Army Association Funds which became the direct responsibility of the Battalion, upon its formation, and he had of course to undertake the organisation of the Battalion's finances in the light of its new status. This included setting up a skeleton organisation to deal with Battalion finances in the case of a muster. Had a general muster taken place, the duty of the Finance Officer of the Battalion, never at any time a sinecure, would have become extremely arduous as the attached footnote indicates.[1]

As the activities of the Battalion increased in scope a Dance and Social Committee was instituted, to reinforce general funds, and to organise social events under the chairmanship of Lieut. Wilson, the proceeds of dances being allocated between the C.O.'s fund (still mainly concerned with financing the transport section), and the provision of such cooking facilities and other general amenities as could not be otherwise obtained. Later, when U.S. forces began to arrive, the social committee undertook the establishment of "contacts" with our allies, and a very successful concert was organised to welcome them, among other forms of hospitality. It might here be mentioned that our visitors provided interested spectators at many of our exercises, and that a party attended the exercises centring upon the farm of Cefn-Garw which was staged from the Pentre Foelas camp. Incidentally, while mentioning the additional administrative work caused by the organisation of the Battalion, attention should be drawn to the work put in at this time by Sharp and Ball, in the first phase of the Battalion, before the assignment of a regular Adjutant and A. and Q.

(1) Office Memorandum No. 614 (Circular D.E.C. No. 195) of 12/2/42, described the arrangements whereby Civil Servants who were members of Home Guard Units became liable for "mustering" in the event of an actual or apprehended invasion :—

1. It is not expected that the period during which the platoon or other part of the Home Guard may be mustered will last beyond a limited period. It has accordingly been decided

(a) that no "mustered" Civil Servant shall receive less favourable treatment as regards civil pay than he would have received had he been called up for service with H.M. Forces ;

(b) that all Civil Servants who have received an order to muster, including temporary employees not directly and continuously employed since March 3rd, 1939, who would not be qualified to receive balance of civil pay if called up for military service in the ordinary course, shall be eligible to receive their civil pay after muster for a period of 6 weeks. Further instructions under this head will be issued if they should be needed.

2. Civil pay for the purpose of this Circular will consist of the basic salary or wages of the post held by the officer at the date of mustering, together with bonus (if any) as appropriate. Army rates of pay as such are not payable to the Home Guard, and so long as Civil Servants are in receipt of their Civil emoluments compensation from Home Guard sources for loss of earnings will accordingly not be payable.

3. In order to secure approximately equal financial treatment as between Home Guard and non-Home Guard Civil Servants, however, members who have been working well defined periods of paid overtime may receive an allowance in lieu of overtime based on the average of the 12 weeks prior to mustering.

TRAINING AND ORGANISATION—IV

Not only did the institution of the Battalion involve a great deal of work for those upon whose devoted shoulders it fell; it also improved the sartorial standards of the Battalion. Immediately upon the formation of the 11th Battalion, the Commanding Officer wrote to the Officer commanding the Depot Party of the Royal Welch Fusiliers, expressing the appreciation by all ranks of the Battalion of the honour accorded to them in sharing the badge of the Royal Welch Fusiliers and that Regiment's great tradition, and expressing the hope that, in a relatively minor capacity, the members of the 11th Battalion might maintain its dignity. The following reply was received:—

"I have to acknowledge with very great pleasure receipt of your letter dated the 26th February, 1943, regarding the formation of the 11th Battalion Denbighshire Home Guard. Your very kind appreciation of the honour of wearing the badge of the Royal Welch Fusiliers is much esteemed, and will be brought to the notice of the Colonel of the Regiment without delay. You are probably aware that his Majesty the King, Colonel-in-Chief, Royal Welch Fusiliers, has also approved of Officers and Warrant Officers of Battalions of the Home Guard who wear the badge of the Royal Welch Fusiliers wearing the flash of the Royal Welch Fusiliers. This further privilege will, we feel, be jealously safeguarded by those concerned in your Battalion."

As a result Officers and Warrant Officers proceeded to decorate their battle dress tunics with black pendants, designed when they were originally adopted by the Royal Welch Fusiliers to prevent the wigs and pigtails of the troops from soiling the collars of their uniforms.

The new status of the Battalion, too, meant that to an increasing extent, as was indeed the case at this time with the Home Guard all over the country, the Battalion, which was now properly dressed, decorated, and trained, was invited to take part in ceremonial parades. The Battalion took part in a "Wings for Victory" Parade on the 1st May, 1943, being ninth in order of procession of a long column, including regular troops and Civil Defence units, of which the salute was taken at Eirias Park by the Lord-Lieutenant of the County. "A" and "C" Coys. took part in this parade under the leadership of Captain Cessford.

Much more impressive and memorable, however, was the parade which took place on the occasion of the third anniversary of the formation of the Home Guard. By direction of the Prime Minister, ceremonial parades in celebration of this anniversary were held all over the country on Sunday, 16th May, and were followed by displays of skill at arms, fieldcraft and battle drill, and demonstrations of interest to the general public. The day was indeed the first occasion on which the nation had shown any signs of public rejoicing over the existence of the Home Guard. His Majesty the King very gracefully complimented the Home Guard by permitting a guard from the 1st

G

Battalion of the County of London Home Guard to take over duties as Palace Guard. He moreover expressed the nation's gratitude in the following words:—

"On this, the third anniversary of the formation of the Home Guard, I, as your Colonel-in-Chief, would like you to know how greatly I appreciate the regularity with which, in spite of many difficulties, you keep up your attendance at parades and how gratified I am by the high standard of proficiency to which you have attained.

"It must, I am sure, be encouraging to you to know that the value of your training has been so clearly felt by those who have left to join the Regular Army.

"Many of you now take your place side by side with my Regular Army in the anti-aircraft and coastal defences, and as that Army passes more and more to the offensive so will your responsibility for the defence of this country grow heavier.

"The importance of your role will therefore inevitably continue to increase.

"The Home Guard has built up a tradition of service and devotion to duty. I am confident that the coming year will add to that tradition and to the debt that my people owe to you."

A message was also received from Lieutenant-General E. C. A. Schreiber, C.B., D.S.O., General Officer Commanding-in-Chief, Western Command:—

"On this third anniversary of the inception of the Home Guard, I want to congratulate all ranks on their achievements during the last three years.

"I think that the birth of the L.D.V. and its growth into the Home Guard has been one of the most inspiring episodes in our long island story. In those early days, Britain, left all alone to face the victorious might of Germany assembled a few miles from her shores, called on her people to keep her soil inviolate. Three times the number of men asked for came forward, almost in a night, to join the L.D.V. I firmly believe that one of the reasons why invasion was not then attempted was the realisation by the Germans that they would be fought relentlessly from every building and hedgerow throughout the length and breadth of Britain.

"Since those days the organisation, the training and the equipment of the Home Guard have improved out of all recognition. One thing, I know, remains the same—the fighting spirit. I want all ranks to know how much I appreciate their devotion to duty in giving up their spare hours during these three long years to make themselves efficient defenders of their country, and I thank them for it.

Ministry of Food Platoon, 2nd City of London (Civil Service) Battalion.

Inspection of Guard of Honour by Major-General Wilson, C.B., D.S.O., O.B.E., Colonel of the Royal Welch Fusiliers

"The Home Guard may well feel proud of its effort of the last three years. May it crown its achievement by striving to increase its efficiency in the future. In this way, the Home Guard will continue to keep our country safe and thus release our maximum offensive power for operations overseas.

"I am intensely proud of the Home Guard in the 309 battalions under my command, and have great faith in all ranks. I therefore send them my best wishes for the future in the sure knowledge that they will maintain the great tradition they have created and remain steadfast to the end—that is until complete victory has been won."

In Colwyn Bay the Ministry of Food Battalion did their best to justify these high opinions by turning out in strength for the anniversary parade. Headed by the Band of the 35th S.T. Regiment, Royal Artillery, and led by Major Capstick, they paraded past the Saluting Base at the War Memorial, where the salute was taken by Col. J. S. Barton, who was accompanied on the Saluting Base by Maclean. The parade was notable for the fact that for the first time the Women's section, under the leadership of Miss French, marched with the men and impressed the spectators by the spirit and precision of their marching. At the conclusion of the parade a series of demonstrations took place, designed to exhibit to the population of Colwyn Bay the level which the training of their visitors had reached. On the beach the newly digested battle drill was demonstrated, together with a running commentary by loud speaker. There was also a demonstration of all weapons used by the Home Guard—at each stand instructors were present who explained and answered the questions of the public regarding the characteristics of the various weapons, and their method of operation. Practice demonstrations of firing live ammunition were also given, particular interest being roused by a display of firing at moving targets by machine guns. It is not recorded that anyone told the public exactly what the Home Guard thought of the Northover Projector or risked setting inquisitive members of the public on fire by firing S.I.P. grenades. Demonstrations of the use of radio communication were also given, and moreover, for the enlightenment of local landladies, a demonstration of field cooking was given in Eirias Park. These demonstrations were shared with the 1st Battalion, which had also taken part in the parade, and the result was certainly to impress upon the general public the efficiency of the new fourth branch of His Majesty's Armed Forces.

Soon after, on the 30th June, 1943, Battalion Orders announced the impending visit of Major-General N. Wilson, C.B., D.S.O., O.B.E., Colonel of the Royal Welch Fusiliers, and also that the Battalion would furnish a Guard of Honour to welcome him. (Incidentally, the same Orders also record the resignation of Major C. Huskisson, D.S.O., M.C., of the command of "C" Coy. and the rank of Major, upon grounds of ill-health. There can have been very few resignations from the Ministry Unit which have been so much regretted by the rank and file, although in this case, fortunately, Huskisson's withdrawal from active Home Guard life was temporary and partial only). Major-General Wilson duly came and was sufficiently impressed to authorise Col. Shennan, the Home Guard Commander of the Conway Valley Sector, to write to Maclean in the following terms: —

"I feel I must congratulate you on the really first class turnout of your men. It certainly was a parade to be proud of—and especially when we reflect that it is all voluntary—unpaid—and the work behind it is all done by busy men who are doing a first class job of work for the country in a Ministry which has a very difficult task and is performing it supremely well. If their fighting training —which I have not yet had an opportunity of seeing—is as good as their drill, God help the Boche if he comes here."[1]

On the 12th of November, 1943, Lord Woolton left the Ministry of Food to take up those wider responsibilities with which his name was later associated: he had been a pillar of strength to the Home Guard in their early days of difficulty, and indeed remained so. The new Minister, Colonel The Rt. Hon. J. J. Llewellin, C.B.E., M.C., M.P., who spent the whole of the last war with his regiment and nearly all the time in France, was to prove as good a friend. His first visit was on the 7th of January, 1944, when he attended the Auxiliaries' birthday party, and took the opportunity of becoming enrolled as a member of the Battalion. On his subsequent visits to Colwyn Bay, he missed no opportunity of making contact with the Home Guard: if there was no parade for him to attend, he would visit H.Q., dine with some of the Officers, or attend whatever social function Home Guards or Auxiliaries happened to be holding.

The end of the year saw hopes renewed for a termination of the war in 1944. It was clear that, whether the war was to end in 1944 or not, its tempo would be accelerated and, therefore, that it behoved the Home Guard to be prepared for anything. The mood of the rank and file was well interpreted by Maclean in a Special Order issued on the last day of December, 1943 : —

"The New Year will see the launching of the combined offensive against the enemy's European fortress, and the supreme effort to secure his speedy surrender. We know enough of his military skill and resource to realise that our attack will inevitably call forth every possible effort to dislocate our offensive if, indeed, it is not anticipated.

"We must, therefore, regard it as certain that the opening of operations on the Western Fronts will synchronise with offensive action against this country, in which this district may be involved.

(1) The same point has been put rather more briefly by a Home Guard poet :—
    The Germans dared not cross the sea
      Our quarrel to discuss.
    For that I thank the L.D.V.,
    Since history surely will agree,
    That, though they weren't afraid of me—
    They were afraid of US.
                                        A.F.E.

TRAINING AND ORGANISATION—IV

This will be the critical—the decisive hour when courage, determination and past technical training will be the key to success.

"The Civil Defence Services and the whole nation in the stern days of 1940, so conducted themselves that their steadfastness will be remembered long after their generation has passed away. If the testing time should come for the Home Guard, no less efficiency and determination will be expected. In the New Year, therefore, all ranks should make a supreme effort to put the finishing touch to their training which will ensure that if called to action in the field, their achievement may be second to none. So may we deserve New Year happiness and ensure future security."

Before the great day came, however, a loss was experienced by the whole of the Western Command when Lieutenant-General Schreiber relinquished the appointment of G.O.C. He also in his farewell message paid a graceful tribute to the Home Guard:—

"During the eighteen months I have been in Western Command, my one object has been to instil and maintain a sense of urgency and the fighting spirit throughout the troops under my command. I have looked upon the Regular Army and the Home Guard as one, both having the same aim in view—to prepare themselves for the day of battle. This preparation entails intense training and a high sense of duty, which is the essence of discipline.

"On relinquishing command, I wish to convey to all ranks my very great appreciation of their loyal co-operation and devotion to duty.

"The prolonged period of preparation for battle is a heavy strain on keenness and discipline but the enthusiasm that I have found throughout the length and breadth of the Command has been a continual source of inspiration and encouragement to me. I thank you.

"It is with great regret that I leave the Command, and I wish all ranks God-speed and victory in the near future."

Also, before the great day, in April, 1944, the "Salute the Soldier" Savings Campaign reached its local climax, and the Battalion, in conjunction with the 1st Battalion, took part in a series of displays, including machine gun firing, demonstrations of battle drill, sten gun shooting, bayonet fighting, and E.Y. rifle demonstrations. Incidentally, the P.O. unit, under Lieut. G. Glover, took a prominent part in this parade. Since the formation of the Battalion, they had frequently trained with the Ministry Home Guard, in whose operational area they were included, and were of the greatest value to the signals section in their training. Again the public showed considerable enthusiasm for the display.

Shortly before D-Day, in May, once more the anniversary of the Home Guard came round, and once more the King expressed the gratitude of the nation:—

"The fourth anniversary of the Home Guard falls in a year when the duties assigned to you have a very special importance.

"To the tasks which lie ahead the Home Guard will be enabled to make a full contribution. I know that your greatly improved efficiency, armament, and leadership render you fit in every way for the discharge of these tasks.

"The burden of training and duty dependent as it is on the needs of war, cannot fail to fall with greater weight on some than on others. To that great number of you who combine proficiency and enthusiasm in Home Guard work with responsible work of National importance in civil life, I would send a special message of thanks and encouragement.

"To all of you I would like to express my appreciation of your past service, and my confidence that you will continue to carry on in the same high spirit of patriotism that you have always shown, until the day of victory."

On the 28th May, Major General Viscount Bridgeman, C.B., D.S.O., M.C., Director General Home Guard, visited the Battalion and met its Senior Officers. He also saw "B" Coy. engaged in a tactical exercise against an "enemy" force provided by the 1st Bn. Denbighshire Home Guard. At its conclusion he complimented those who had been responsible for organising the exercise, and those who had taken part.

Finally, the day towards which all our work and training and aspirations had been directed dawned upon the invasion of France. Battalion Orders were clear and precise concerning the impending responsibilities of the Home Guard. "With the opening of the second front enemy reprisals against this country become more probable. Operation orders covering the tactical tasks allotted to the Battalion have already been issued to those concerned. It is, however, possible that aerial attack in the vicinity of Colwyn Bay may occur without the Battalion being engaged in military operations against the enemy. In order that maximum assistance shall be rendered to the Civil Defence Services when needed. . . . " There follows precise and practical instructions concerning the duties which the Home Guard were to undertake should attempted reprisals either by aircraft or by the landing of troops be attempted by the enemy. We know now that none such were designed nor were indeed possible in view of the diversion of German aircraft-producing resources to the flying bomb. Consequently, after a short lull, the ordinary training of the Battalion continued, its centre of interest changing after the end of June to the camp at Pentre Foelas, of which more in a subsequent chapter. Once more, however, before Standing Down, the Ministry Battalion was to preen its feathers for an official display. On the 8th July, Col. Llewellin again visited the Unit, witnessed a tactical exercise, took tea in the field at the hands of the catering section, presented the Platoon Proficiency Cup to its proud winners and expressed his satisfaction with the appearance and performance of the officers and men of the Unit. At the end of the day, Maclean announced that while there was no such official appointment as "Honorary Colonel" in the Home Guard, it was the intention of the Battalion to regard him as such, and that he was content to let it be so. Finally, this record of the focal points of the Battalion organisation is concluded by a quotation from Battalion Orders, 6th September, 1944: "There will be no compulsory training parades after Sunday, 10th September, 1944, and no Duty Platoon will be furnished after Saturday, 9th September, 1944."

This record, unfortunately, cannot hope to deal with the many Home Guard detachments of Ministry personnel which were organised from the staff of various Divisional and Local Offices, the most notable of which was perhaps the complete Platoon of the 34th Battalion (Birmingham) Home Guard, which was recruited from the personnel of the Local Food Office at Birmingham and, in the early stages, was commanded by the then Food Executive Officer, Mr. J. P. Eames. The story of the Ministry Battalion's organisation in Colwyn Bay would not, however, be complete without reference to the development which the London Unit was undergoing at the same time. The Ministry Unit formed with such enthusiasm at Great Westminster House in May of 1940 had been rudely broken up by the transfer of the bulk of the personnel to Colwyn Bay. The dissolution of the remnants was completed by the insistence of the Treasury on the return of the ten rifles which had been placed at their disposal, a decision which consorted oddly with the completion of the defence works at the entrance to the building upon which Maclean and Lawrence had been at such pains to secure expert advice. The little group of Home Guards, however, who remained in the London Offices of the Ministry, had no alternative but to seek membership of other Units in order to continue their service, and the Ministry building, for the protection of which they had officially been gathered together, became a strong point deprived of its garrison.

By the latter part of 1941, however, the size of the staff at the Ministry Headquarters at Portman Court indicated that a Home Guard unit should be formed. The proposal had the warm support of the Minister and the Secretary. Accordingly the formation of a Platoon was put in hand in December, 1941. Mr. Howard Marshall was offered the command of the Platoon and Dr. (as he was then) J. C. Drummond, who transferred from the 1st City of London Battalion, was appointed Second in Command.

The Platoon came into being early in 1942, as Number 6 Platoon of "E" Company of the 2nd City of London (Civil Service) Battalion, commanded by Lt.-Col. P. M. Walker, M.C., with its Headquarters at Somerset House, W.C.2. The Battalion was affiliated to the Royal Fusiliers Regiment. At this time "E" Company, which had its Headquarters at Berkeley Square House, W.1, was commanded by Major Gibson Graham, M.C., and subsequently commanded by Major R. B. L. Hill, M.B.E., M.C.

About the beginning of June, 1942, most of the members responded to the appeal for transfers to the Home Guard A.A. Units, then being constituted. On the 26th August a large part of the Platoon was transferred to the Anti-Aircraft Wing, 1st County of London Battalion Home Guard. They were among the first Home Guards to man the A.A. Defences in London, and their keenness and efficiency won high praise. Thus the O.C. 101 (County of London) Home Guard Mixed "Z" A.A. Battery in writing in the middle of 1943 to ask for further volunteers for the A.A. Command, said, "The nucleus of this Unit consists of your Berkeley House Company, who have turned out an extremely fine body and have been the backbone of this Unit, the majority of them now being officers or N.C.O.s; I would greatly welcome transfers of the same calibre."

As a result of this transfer the Ministry of Food Unit was reduced to seven men and could no longer function as a Platoon. With effect from the 28th September, 1942, the residue of No. 6 Platoon was therefore posted as No. 3 Section of No. 1 (H.Q.) Platoon of "E" Company. This Platoon was commanded by Lieut. (subsequently Captain) G. V. Hole, the Company Adjutant, and Dr. J. C. Drummond, Mr. Howard Marshall having been appointed Battalion Press Liaison Officer on the 14th August, 1942. It will be remembered that he subsequently went to North Africa as a commentator for the B.B.C.

Strenuous efforts were made to rebuild the strength of the Ministry of Food Section. Chiefly as a result of the return from Colwyn Bay to London of members of the Ministry who were trained Home Guards, the numbers increased and, at the beginning of June, 1943, it was possible to form a second section from the Ministry of Food personnel.

At the end of June, Dr. Drummond was promoted to Lieutenant and Platoon Commander, Sgt. R. A. G. O'Brien being later promoted to 2nd/Lieut. as Second-in-Command; and at the beginning of the following September the Ministry of Food Unit was sufficiently strong to be reconstituted as No. 6 Platoon of "E" Company. The Platoon immediately began specialised training as the Sub-Artillery Platoon of "E" Company. The Platoon Officers and one Sergeant had recently taken courses at Purfleet in the Smith Gun and Spigot Mortar and had qualified as instructors. Besides these weapons (one Smith Gun and two Spigot Mortars) the Platoon was allotted a Boys Anti-Tank Rifle and a Lewis Gun.

During the winter 1943/44 each Section in the Platoon specialised in the use of one of these weapons, whilst every member learnt at least how to handle all of them. This was in addition to ordinary infantry training. The Platoon was given an important role in "E" Company's operational scheme and in all exercises. Shortly before the standing down of the Home Guard, the Platoon was also given charge of two Vickers Machine Guns, in the use of which the Officers and N.C.O.s were being instructed by the Battalion Adjutant. Owing to the Order to stand down this course was not completed.

In Company Orders dated 5th January, 1944, the Officer Commanding "E" Company offered the Company's congratulations to the Commander of No. 6 Platoon on the Knighthood which had been bestowed upon him in the New Year's Honours List.

The Platoon was on duty at Battalion Headquarters on the night of 15/16th June, 1944, when the first serious flying bomb attack was made on London. On another occasion a section of the Platoon was called out to render assistance after a flying bomb had exploded in the vicinity of Battalion Headquarters.

Meanwhile, both in London and Colwyn Bay the normal routine of training had continued. With the slackening of new intake, however, the general increase in the level of proficiency, the change over to the new operational area surrounding Pentre Foelas, and the development of the Specialist branches, interest in the training programme moves over to the training of the specialists, and to training in the field at Pentre Foelas. Subsequent chapters deal in detail with both of these aspects.

Perusal of Battalion Orders shows that the War Office policy of opening Regular Army training courses to officers and men of the Home Guard was becoming increasingly important; the idea that an inferior type of training was adequate for the Home Guard had been abandoned with the acceptance of the change in the role the Home Guard must play. The special Home Guard training schools which continued to operate were taken very seriously.

Consequently, as an illustration of the calibre of Home Guard training during this period, we may quote the experience of one Home Guard of many who went to Burwash—the S.E. Divisional School of Fieldcraft. Incidentally, the Commandant was Major Langdon Davies, M.B.E., the unorthodox lecturer, "despised and rejected of all men," over paying the expenses of whose visit the unit had had so much trouble in 1941.

"To those of us who went to the Southern Command School of Fieldcraft one week-end in the autumn of 1943, the phrase 'The Enemy is in Burwash' will at some time in the future recur, and what memories will that revive! How many of us will remember the wait for transport at Burwash Station, and the tentative schemes to get back to what we were told was the only pub in the village. Those ideas were very quickly knocked on the head when we did arrive at the school. Before we had got down from the trucks, or had had time to realise where we were, it was 'Fall in and pay attention,' and we found ourselves listening to a recital of the School 'Standing Orders,' barked at us by a very efficient Sergeant-Major. And so I suppose we can say the week-end of instruction began, and what a week-end it was! None of us had much idea of what we were in for when we had signified our willingness to attend, and now we were on the job the theory seemed to be 'Keep the troops going at something or other and they won't have time to realise that they are being run off their feet, neither will they have any inclination to slack.' We hadn't time even to think about slacking.

Dumped down in messes for a meal that was prepared and waiting for us, the Adjutant came along, and, as we ate, fired at us more rules and regulations, divided us into sections and informed us of various things that we must or must not do, and most of all impressed upon us that 'The Enemy is in Burwash.' As our place of abode for the week-end was under direct observation from Burwash, all our actions both on and off parade must be governed by that one paramount consideration 'Keep under cover at all times, carry your arms and ammo whenever you move, no lights after dark, not even smoking outside, no loud talking!' (No one who ever attended that school could possibly have had any inclination to sing, but all the same singing was prohibited).

"Before we had finished eating, it was time for the first parade, sitting, perhaps a little crowded but in comparative comfort, to be lectured to with the aid of lantern slides on camouflage and art of concealment. The proceedings had of course been opened by the usual introductory talk, which included amongst other things how we were to be allocated jobs to do in addition to attending parades, exercises, and lectures. We were cheered by the information that there would be a limited amount of liquid refreshment available and promised that we should even be allowed time to drink it. We were organised in sections in which erstwhile Adjutants and Coy. Commanders were reduced to the ranks, and became liable for various duties from ration orderly to latrine attendant. When the lecture was finished, and we had got through folding blankets, and building a bivouac, we were allowed our freedom to get a bottle of beer and relax.

"It was now getting on toward 10 p.m.; we found that our relaxation included settling the place where we were to sleep, making up a bed and preparing vegetables for the main meal of the following day. Who can ever forget that dimly lit garage, with a concrete floor running with water and a crowd of Home Guards attempting to peel spuds and drink beer out of pint bottles, with an occasional reminder from the Sergeant-Major that lights out was at 10.30. Relaxation!!!

"That first night we were allowed the luxury of sleeping in the house, because, as the Adjutant regretted, there wasn't really time for us to construct bivouacs for use on the first night. We were up before it was really light and went outside to wash and shave under somewhat primitive conditions, to be told a little later on that we had wasted time in attempting to shave; 'Didn't we realise that under observation from the enemy such a proceeding was unnecessary and might be highly dangerous! Get a move on; you will now be shown your camp site and you can get on with making your bivouac and cooking your breakfast'!! Now we started to attempt to put into practice some of the things that the lecturer of the previous night had tried to instil into us.

"The holes were dug, groundsheets laced together, and some sort of cover erected. Sticks no thicker than a finger should have been gathered for the fires and gathered without noise—but were they? It was a merciful act to boil water for us because otherwise there would have been no tea to drink, but we did fry bacon and eggs. (Yes, genuine new laid eggs). We were just patting ourselves on the back on having achieved some sort of breakfast when it was 'Come along, get these lines cleaned up and get on parade'—we did—chewing as we went.

"We found that the scene of operations was to be about two miles from our place of abode and, 'not forgetting the Enemy was in Burwash' were to move there accordingly. We got there and were the recipients of some rather sarcastic comments on our ideas of movement under observation, from the School Commandant, whose acquaintance we now made for the first time. Lectures, practical demonstrations and exercises, all with the design of improving our knowledge of fieldcraft, followed with sometimes bewildering rapidity. We were allowed a break during the morning, with time to buy a bun and a cup of cocoa and to inspect the Commandant's rabbits. Mid-day a snack lunch was provided and then on into the afternoon with more demonstrations, exercises and instruction.

"Back to camp, and joy of joys, cook your own dinner. We had found a certain amount of difficulty in frying bacon in the morning but the problem of boiling a dixie full of potatoes under the same conditions was up another street entirely. Did we scratch and blow and curse that fire? The camp cooks, presumably out of previous experience and possibly with the idea of saving us all from starvation, had undertaken to provide cooked meat and sweets. Our responsibility was vegetables. The meat arrived on time but the spuds refused to boil and to say the least the dinner we cooked for ourselves was makeshift. I remember turning out for the evening parade with a half boiled potato in my hand.

"Lectures went on until about 9.30 and then, as we poor unhardened sedentary workers were to sleep out for the night (the temperature was already below freezing point and a thick white frost lay on our groundsheet roof), we were provided with hot cocoa to help us sleep comfortably. Some angel in disguise produced a bottle, and personally, although I've always claimed that whisky and tea mixed spoiled both drinks, the contents of that bottle certainly didn't spoil the cocoa. And so to bed, of which the less said the better. With a few minor interruptions, like changing the camp guard, an air raid warning and noises which, in spite of the silence ban, did occur at intervals, the dawn eventually came. The Commandant, being a very wise man, had decided that messing arrangements for this our second and last day should be taken out of our 'incapable hands, and in consequence we were adequately fed.

"Sunday followed much the same routine of crowded instruction, details of which will probably not be of interest now.

"Mid-afternoon it was decided we had had enough, so back to camp we went in our own time, and this last time we went down the road like ordinary human beings, without the 'Enemy in Burwash.' Did we learn anything and did we derive any benefit from what was to describe it mildly a very hectic week-end? That is a question which only individuals who went through the mill can answer. I think that they will all agree that the School and the way it was organised was a credit to the Home Guard. The Commandant and his whole staff with the exception of the Adjutant and Sergeant-Major were Home Guardsmen, and I myself have both in this war and the 1914-1918 business had my share of schools and courses and never have I struck one so well organised; with real interest crowded into every minute of the time, and this, mark you, with facilities cut to the bone and in many cases improvised on the spot. Never have I experienced one that I would rather go through again."

Shortly after the formation of this Battalion the only really serious accident in which a party of troops of the unit was involved took place. On Sunday, 10th January, 1943, No. 11 Platoon of "C" Company was scheduled to do an exercise somewhere beyond the golf course on the hill, and about thirty men piled into an army lorry at Penrhos, in full battle dress with rifles, machine guns, grenades, mines, and live ammunition. It was a high lorry with seats either side; about twenty were seated and ten standing. The account of one of the "victims" follows.

"The driver was a regular from a nearby camp and he was in a hurry. He came along Lansdowne Road too fast and at the turning to the left into King's Drive cut the corner too fine and went into a skid. When the back wheels struck the opposite pavement the lorry teetered over and threw the standing men off balance with the result that the lorry went over broadside on to the road. It was quite a sensation for the men inside.

"The driver shewed presence of mind in shutting the petrol off and clambered out of his cabin to lend assistance in the rear. The debussing took place in an orderly fashion but at a somewhat slower pace than normal. When everyone was out the lorry was heaved back on to its wheels again and casualties reckoned up. There was only one rather serious case. Cpl. Forster was unconscious from severe blows on the nose, jaw and ear and was taken into a private house nearby. Later he had eleven stitches and several weeks rest to put him right. A less serious case was Cpl. Midwood who was bleeding copiously from a face wound and also needed stitching up. Others escaped with bruises and were prepared to continue the exercise on foot or with an alternative conveyance, but the officer in charge—Lieut. J. Roberts—decided to dismiss the parade after commending the Platoon for its orderly behaviour. The Platoon was never fond of army lorries after this incident."

Colonel Llewellin presenting the Inter-Platoon Challenge Cup to Sergt. Clark and Sergt. Harris, representing No. 10 Platoon and No. 12 Platoon, joint winners

Demonstration on the Spigot Mortar

"Cookhouse"

Col. Shennan, Mr. A. Grieg, Major H. M. Pemberton, Lieutenant Polfry, Colonel Barton and the Commanding Officer inspecting Field Kitchens

CHAPTER 7.

THE SPECIALIST SERVICES.

"When God made the world he took the wind and said : 'Be a man,' and he made the Bedouin. He then shot an arrow into the air and said : 'Be a camel,' and the camel came into being. From a lump of clay he made the donkey. And then, as an after-thought, and to help the Bedouin, he created the cultivator and the town-dweller from the dung of the donkey."—*Arab Proverb.*

The attitude of the fighting man of the desert to his specialist and supply services is indicated by the proverb quoted above. It is the traditional attitude of plain ordinary infantry, as much of the poetry, quotable and unquotable, of the last war indicates.[1]

It is, however, the existence of specialist services and the central direction which they make possible which creates the essential difference between an Army or a Regiment, and a guerilla band. The Home Guard of the earliest days, of the L.D.V. Period, was essentially designed as a body of guerrilla troops. Their function was to stand and fight, with local direction and employing local resources; to move at their own discretion, if they must, but to operate upon their own responsibility and as an independent unit. Such defence, although the defenders might move from place to place, was essentially static; mobile defence calls not only for movement but for direction and co-ordinated mobility. For that purpose, therefore, it is necessary for any organised fighting force to have some, at least, of the specialist services, which were built up inside the 11th Battalion. They may be outlined as follows.

In the first place comes the organisation of Military Intelligence. Before a fighting force can operate as a coherent whole, its Commander must be able to depend upon a steady flow of information from the fighting units, from which he can construct a picture of the whole operation, and the relevant details of which he can pass on to Higher Command, so that they too can paint their larger picture. And, in addition, there must be a fund of local knowledge; there must be, somewhere within the unit, a depository of information concerning every lane and highway, water and petrol supplies, the location of such defence positions as prepared mine-fields; all the data essential for the rapid and successful movement of troops about a battle-field. This also is the work of an Intelligence Unit, although it may, in some cases, be delegated to a separate Guides organisation.

The second prerequisite for effective military organisation is an effective signalling service, which can transmit the information which Intelligence and Guides collect, and which can also relay the decisions of the Higher Command, built up upon this basis. The

---

(1) For example :
 "(If I were fierce and bald and short of breath
 I'd live with scarlet majors at the base,
 And speed grim heroes up the line to death . . . ."
 Siegfried Sassoon.

Signals unit of the present day must be competent to handle all modern means of communication, including wireless, and should be able not only to operate but also to repair and improvise methods of communication.

Thirdly, a Home Guard unit needs one piece of machinery which is absent in the Regular Army. That is its rousing organisation. There is very much more work than is apparent to the outsider involved in building up and maintaining an organisation whereby hundreds and hundreds of men, scattered often over thinly populated areas, can be roused and mustered in a short space of time; its successful operation involves a great deal of painful, painstaking, and un-glorious donkey-work, checking changes of address, and doing all the essential clerical work involved.

Fourthly, it is necessary, particularly under modern conditions, for transport to be organised, in order that men, food, and ammunition may be moved rapidly from place to place, as the changing situation demands. This does not only involve the possession and operation of vehicles, it also necessitates the building up of a body of reserve drivers, amassing information about the location of vehicles which might be requisitioned in an emergency, and building up, in co-operation with the Intelligence and Guides sections, detailed road knowledge covering the area of operations.

Fifthly, any military body, however loose its organisation may be, must have a quartermaster, and the appropriate quartermaster's organisation for handling stores. (It is also essential to have someone for the rank and file to grumble at, which is another of the traditional functions of the quartermaster). Something like a "Q" organisation, however, existed from the earliest days of the unit, and it has therefore already been dealt with.

Sixthly, although all soldiers engaged in mobile warfare should be able to forage and provide for themselves, it not only adds to the amenities of warfare, but also to the efficiency of a fighting force, if its feeding is properly organised. A Catering branch in any armed force not only sets the fitter and more active men free to concentrate on the work of patrolling and fighting, but it also, in the nature of things, is able to provide very great assistance in the sphere of morale.

Seventhly, it is an essential part of the tactics of modern warfare to be able to concentrate overwhelming fire, when necessary, upon a narrow front. In a body, such as the Home Guard, mainly composed of riflemen and tommy-gunners, this can either be done by accumulating men at one point, or by using some form of artillery. This normally is under the direct control of the Commander of the Battalion, in order that it may be directed to whatever part of the fighting front demands its presence. Consequently, most modern armies maintain some kind of artillery, or sub-artillery, under the direct control of the Commander of an Infantry Battalion. For example, there was normally an Artillery unit in each of the German Infantry Battalions. In the Ministry of Food Home Guard, the role of artillery was played

THE SPECIALIST SERVICES 99

by the Machine-gun section. (The Unit indeed for a short time owned three two-pounder anti-tank guns, offered to it in the autumn of 1942, delivered on 12th September, 1944, and returned in grease, as received, on 16th October, 1944!)

Eighthly, from the outset of this war, our British shortage of manpower has rendered it necessary for us to call upon our womenfolk to take part in military service. As the Regular Army enjoys the assistance of the A.T.S., so the Ministry Battalion of the Home Guard built up its own body of Women Auxiliaries, who served in one capacity or another, in almost every phase of Home Guard life except the machine-gun section. (It is, perhaps, not correct to say that the Battalion organised them. They organised themselves, and would not rest content until they were given a great deal of work to do).

Ninthly, a medical service is necessary for reasons which become more obvious the nearer to action the unit moves. Although remote from the immediate dangers of war, the Ministry Battalion had its medical unit ready for emergencies.

Finally, one of the least pleasant aspects of modern warfare has made necessary a Chemical Warfare Officer, and a small specialist staff, responsible for the training of troops in anti-gas measures, and for the inspection, overhaul, and replacement of respirators and other forms of protective clothing.

All these specialist services were in existence at the time of the Stand-down, and before proceeding to describe them one by one, a tribute must here be paid to the energy and devotion with which all were served. In the majority of cases, the specialists had to turn out for most of the ordinary parades and, without exception, they played their part in guards and patrols, during the period in which the Home Guard was active in defence. In addition, however, the very nature of the duties which they undertook voluntarily—and service in the specialist units was all voluntary—involved them in a very great deal of extra time and work. During the last two years of the Home Guard there can have been hardly a single night when some devoted members of the specialist branches were not staying up late, drawing maps, cleaning motor cars, compiling menus, de-coking motor bicycles, or doing any one of the innumerable tasks with which their devotion had saddled them.

The "I" organisation of a Battalion may be regarded as its nerve system. At one extreme it is in touch with the Higher Command, and on the other with its own and neighbouring units and services. The Battalion depends upon its Intelligence organisation that it can maintain co-ordinated action, play an appropriate part in the Sector military plan, and maintain effective contact between its own Headquarters and its fighting units. (Indeed, in one sense, the entire Home Guard may be regarded as part of the Intelligence Service of the Regular Army. Particularly, in the earlier days of the Home Guard, when the threat of invasion was imminent, and when it was apparent that if invasion came it would be accompanied by the landing of many scattered airborne forces, the task of obtaining and reporting information about the enemy wherever he might appear was regarded as one of its most valuable tasks). Cessford put in an enormous amount of pioneer work and got intelligence taken seriously. Bowles, who later became Battalion Intelligence Officer, worked as hard at development as Cessford had at the foundations.

The organisation of the Battalion "I" section centred upon the Battalion Intelligence Officer, who was responsible to the C.O. and to Sector Intelligence. He was responsible, not only for the separate Company organisations, but for the Battalion Reconnaissance section, consisting of three N.C.O.s and three privates, which was under his direct control. Each Company, except the Headquarters Company, had a Company Intelligence Officer and N.C.O., and one or more men, at the discretion of the Company Commander. In each platoon an Intelligence N.C.O., normally a lance-corporal, formed the nerve-end of the whole system.

In addition, the Headquarters Reconnaissance Section and the Coy. "I" Sections had writers attached who were employed on message and log writing, and upon such essential office work as must be conducted in the field. One of the results of the North African campaign was to prove the necessity for some kind of skeleton mobile office organisation, and portable equipment was therefore provided which could, if necessary, be carried into action by the staff.

The Platoon "I" N.C.O. was referred to as the "nerve end" of the intelligence system. Nerve ends have to be sensitive; these particular nerve ends had in addition to be tough. It was the duty of the Platoon "I" N.C.O. not only to provide necessary information for his own platoon, and to be a store of local and Battalion information; he had also to collect information in the field, to act as a message writer and to attempt to maintain contact with the Coy. Intelligence Officer. This meant that in nearly all cases he had also to become platoon scout; in addition to being platoon scout, he had the thankless task of attempting to persuade his Platoon Officer to spare runners in order to pass information back, just at those exacting moments in the life of a platoon on manoeuvres when runners can least be spared. Consequently, he frequently became, in addition, platoon runner. The result was that, in general, the Platoon Intelligence N.C.O. became the instrument wherewith the platoon found its way, particularly on dark nights, tested the depths of brooks, the bearing capacity of ice and bogs, the powers of resistance of thorn hedges, the height of banks of nettles, the scalability of mountains; he in fact tended to become platoon whipping boy. (It is not recorded on any occasion that the Platoon Intelligence N.C.O. was required to test in advance the quality of the beer when an exercise concluded, as usual, in the immediate neighbourhood of licensed premises, nor even the purity of the local water supply on hot days, but nearly everything else tended to be tried out on him).

In much the same way the Headquarters Reconnaissance Section had to undertake the task of establishing contact with Units of the Battalion upon manoeuvres when, as not infrequently happened, they got lost, and also of establishing contact with the enemy, who were usually much easier to find.

Training in map reading, field sketching, compass work, and reconnaissance patrol work was, of course, carried on by every platoon and section; this was taken much more seriously in the training of the intelligence staff who, indeed, during the intensified training preceding the award of proficiency badges, undertook a considerable share of this specialised training. Particular attention was paid to night work and camouflage, and all training was continually directed to the end of achieving unseen motion, resulting in the collection of intelligence and a satisfactory withdrawal from observation points. In addition it was necessary for the rudiments of message writing to be understood by the rank and file generally, in order that information might be conveyed about the Battalion with little loss of time and as high a degree of precision as was possible. In this work of training, again the intelligence staff played their part and, of course, themselves underwent intensified training. The art of military message writing is a simple but exacting one. It consists in memorising a very definite hard and fast set of rules (hard and fast that is at any one time, as War Office instructions tend to vary with distressing frequency) which are designed to ensure that only standard abbreviations and a completely rigid terminology are employed. All message writing is based on the assumption that sooner or later it is going to be transmitted by a signaller, and that the signaller is mentally deficient, and that, as transmitted by him, it is going to be delivered to a harassed O.C. who is, as a result of his manifold anxieties, in not much better shape. Consequently, while words must not be wasted, any term which can possibly be misunderstood must be avoided and words must invariably be written in full unless the standard abbreviation is known. Even full stops must have a circle around them, presumably on the assumption that flies cannot draw rings around fly spots.

From the early autumn of 1943 a great deal of intensified training was undertaken by the Intelligence Section. Following a fine performance at a Western Command Intelligence Course three of the "I" personnel, Head, Richardson and Emmanuel, were appointed to extra-regimental posts as interrogation officers. By this time the section was reasonably proficient and lectures as such were discontinued, but paper and, particularly, out-of-door exercises based on the training lectures, were substituted. Noiseless movement was carefully practised under all kinds of conditions, camouflage was studied in all its aspects, and interesting experiments in the possibility of moving unobserved in full moonlight took place. Interest among the Intelligence Section was maintained at a very high level, which was evidenced by the extensive use made of the small library of training booklets which the Battalion Intelligence Officer succeeded in accumulating.

As pointed out in the introductory chapter, the Ministry Battalion was unlike the ordinary Home Guard Unit in that it was operating not on its own ground but two hundred miles away, in a part of North Wales where English was not always spoken, nor at times even understood. The Battalion area consisted of some 12 square miles on the Northern coast line, and some 37 square miles on the edge of the Denbigh Moors, straddling the main Holyhead road and centred upon Pentre Foelas. This, particularly the addition of the second area, imposed a considerable amount of work on the Headquarters Reconnaissance Section, and also upon the Transport and Dispatch Rider Sections which co-operated with them. The Company Intelligence Sections were, of course, responsible for knowing their own Company areas, both in Colwyn Bay and on the Moors and the adjacent areas, and most of the staff took steps to build up a very considerable body of local knowledge. The Headquarters Reconnaissance Section, however, needed to know not only the coastal locality and the garrison area at Pentre Foelas; it had to have an exhaustive knowledge of the intervening country. As D-Day approached, and in preparation for any possible retaliatory measures the enemy might spring on this country, all intelligence work was speeded up. The men of the Headquarters Reconnaissance Section went over every road, track and main path in the Pentre Foelas area, and with the assistance of Company Intelligence Officers and their sections, the whole of both areas was carefully surveyed from a military standpoint, and a complete system of observation points and standing patrol posts with the necessary communications was planned. This involved a great deal of map making, charting, and gazetting, over which not only several devoted members of the section spent very long hours, but in which also the Women's Section assisted with great distinction. For a period of six or seven weeks in early 1944, the Headquarters Reconnaissance Section, with two of our men who were attached to Intelligence at Sector, worked continuously every Sunday. On two occasions cars had to be manhandled out of snow drifts, and on one, four of the section found it necessary to go up to the 1,700 ft. mark, forcing their way through thigh-deep snow drifts. Nevertheless, the survey work was carried out through snow, sunshine, sleet, and everything that the North Wales climate could bring out of the bag. As part of the survey it should also be recorded that, with the co-operation of the D.R.s, all the alternative routes between the Battalion Headquarters and the garrison area at Pentre Foelas were mapped, in order to anticipate any difficulties that might arise from the blocking of the narrow and vulnerable main roads approaching the garrison area. Although in addition to arms and equipment the Intelligence Section only carried a map and a writing pad into action, their life was far from sedentary! Throughout, their work was carried out in close co-operation with the Transport and D.R. Sections, without which their job would have been impossible. It would equally have been impossible, or at least doubly difficult, without the wholehearted assistance of Lieut. Roberts of the

2nd Denbigh. Home Guard, whose unrivalled knowledge of the whole area, stock of local information and tireless service as guide over the remoter parts of the Battalion area were constantly under requisition.

No account of the section would be complete without individual mention of Lieut. F. W. C. Herbert. Badly wounded in the last war, Herbert struggled under severe physical disabilities to carry out the duties of Platoon Sergeant in the original No. 5 Platoon. When Companies were permitted to appoint Intelligence Officers, Herbert became the I.O. of "B" Company and proved himself of inestimable value to the Company and to the Battalion. An expert cartographer, he produced a series of map enlargements of both Colwyn Bay and Pentre Foelas areas and supervised the creation of a large relief map of the Colwyn Bay area, which was quite remarkable in the accuracy of the detail it contained. His last work was the provision of the Company's fighting book which became the standard and example for other Companies to emulate.

One amusing and extremely profitable incident, not so much in the work of the Intelligence Section as in the intelligence training of the Battalion, relates to the visit of the "revue" staged by the Intelligence Section of the 5th Caerns. Under the leadership of Lieut. Johnson, three cameo sketches for the stage were produced, illustrating various aspects of security and intelligence work. These proved so popular in the Caernarvonshire area that the Company went on tour, and presented to the 11th Denbighshire Battalion at the Drill Hall, three sketches: "The Quartermaster's Office," "Careless Talk," and "The Intelligence Room." Not only was the standard of acting high, but in all cases the moral was put over with force and wit; the first sketch dealt with the right method of checking identity cards, the second with security in general, as the title denotes, and the third, which was an ambitious production in two acts, demonstrated firstly how an intelligence room should not be run and, secondly, the correct method. It would be interesting to know whether this was the germ of the similar two-act sketch subsequently presented as part of the training programme of the Travelling Intelligence School organised by Western Command.

Closely connected with the Intelligence Section are the Signallers. Intelligence which cannot be transmitted, or which is wrongly transmitted, is useless, and if the Intelligence Section provided the nerve ends and certain of the lobes of the brain of the Battalion, it was the Signals Section which provided the actual nerves along which information and instructions flowed to and fro. Not only were their functions complementary, but a considerable amount of mutual training was undertaken, and certainly the intelligence staff enjoyed the privilege of being able to play from time to time with their colleagues' wireless sets. Mention might certainly have been made earlier of the admirable work put in by Field in the pioneer days of the section: in this he was ably seconded by Nutting, Firth, Holt and Marwood: the two latter in turn became Signals Officer after Field had resigned.

In common with the experience of other specialist sections in the L.D.V. and early days of the Home Guard, training equipment from official sources for the Signals Section was conspicuous by its absence. From strangely diverse sources a few morse flags and sundry pairs of semaphore flags were collected and training began in earnest in the autumn of 1940 with three parades each week. The ex-signallers of the last war soon found that, apart from the form of individual letters of the alphabet under both codes which had not altered during the interim, abbreviations and procedure had changed, in some cases substantially. With the acquisition of one or two morse keys increased rates of transmission were achieved, and the resulting enthusiasm and efficiency attracted additional members to the Signals Section.

By a lucky chance, a unit of the Royal Corps of Signals was located in our vicinity and, by the courtesy of their Commanding Officer, the unit's training equipment and the services of two of their N.C.O.s, voluntarily given during week-day evenings, were placed at our disposal. This marked a big step forward, particularly in the direction of wireless telegraphy, in which field the Section had had no opportunity hitherto of making progress. The departure of our friends in the Royal Corps of Signals was greatly regretted but was followed by the arrival of a unit of the Royal Artillery, whose members and training equipment proved equally useful to us. As a result a large percentage of the signallers were reasonably good wireless operators by the time our own wireless sets eventually came to hand. Actually it was as late as June, 1943, before we received five wireless sets. The type issued was the No. 38 set, which is easily recognised by the throat microphone, and at one time was often referred to as the Commando set. This enabled the signallers to assist in many exercises with varying degrees of success, and gave them much needed experience under practical conditions. Immediately after the wireless sets were issued a night exercise was held in which two Coys. of the Battalion took part, and the Signallers were afforded the first opportunity of putting their training into practice by maintaining wireless communication between Pwllycrochan Hotel and Bryn Euryn Huts. Most of the night was spent in endeavouring to obtain wireless communication, but for some unexplained reason their efforts were not rewarded although there appeared to be nothing wrong with the wireless sets when used again a few days later. Failure was probably due to poor conditions on this particular night, the usual type of weather being experienced, and to the unsuitable nature of the ground, which has been found considerably to affect wireless communication on other occasions, particularly with such short range sets.

Concurrently with the progress in wireless signalling, all members of the Section were given a course of instruction on the departmental telephone switchboards, thanks to the courtesy and assistance of the G.P.O., the local telephone Superintendent and a few of the operators with whose voices our official duties so often bring us into contact.

This phase of signals activity proved invaluable on a number of exercises in and about the town.

A week-end course at the North Wales District School of Signals, Chester, in 1942, which was attended by the majority of the Section, demonstrated very clearly that, by H.G. standards, the Section had attained a high degree of efficiency in all fields of signalling, an impression which was confirmed in 1944 when the Signal Platoon secured seventh place, with a total marking of 80½%, in a collective test embracing all H.G. Units throughout the Mid-West District. In July, 1942, the Signal Section became No. 3 Platoon of the newly-formed "G" Company, and in January, 1943, became No. 3 Platoon in "H.Q." Company, of the 11th Denbigh Battalion.

From its inception the Signal Platoon had an efficient D.R. Section which increased in size and importance as service motor cycles began to be supplied. The D.R. Section suffered at first from "teething" troubles, as it was found that the two W.D. motor cycles originally issued were entirely inadequate to permit of organised training on a sufficiently large scale. Further difficulty was also experienced owing to the fact that several members of the Battalion appeared to have the impression that the motor cycles were issued for anything but D.R. training, and some tact and patience were required before they learned to think otherwise. The number of motor cycles was eventually increased to six and the Section was then enabled to develop quite considerably, also to proceed with an organised training programme. During 1944 the D.R.s of the Battalion were entrusted with the duty of carrying out the regular Despatch Rider Letter Service on each fourth Sunday, thus easing the burden on their opposite numbers in the Regular Forces.

In 1943 a number of communication exercises were held to test the operational efficiency of the H.Q. Staffs of formations and units and of the intelligence and signals personnel. For one of these exercises (24/25 July, 1943), Maclean was detailed to command the Sub-District in the absence on leave of Colonel F. Latham, D.S.O., the regular officer in command. While Maclean was at Bettws-y-Coed for this purpose Moore took command at Battalion Battle H.Q. at Pentre Foelas.

During 1944 a Section of Women Auxiliaries was attached to the Signal Platoon for training. Instruction was given in Phonograms and Signal Office Procedure, and there is little doubt that they would have proved to be a valuable asset in helping to maintain communication in an emergency.

The volume of work which fell upon both the Intelligence and the Signals Section was largely due to the fact that the Battalion was responsible for two areas, separated by a considerable distance. This alone would indicate the importance which should be laid upon the Transport Section of the Battalion. It never was, and was not intended to be, responsible for the transportation of the whole Battalion to any place in which the exigencies of war might necessitate its use. It would clearly have been wasteful if transport had remained permanently at the disposal of Home Guard Units all over the country on the assumption that it might possibly be wanted. Consequently, for most of the actual transportation which took place, the Battalion made use either of lorries borrowed from the Regular Army or of buses hired from commercial operators. In the former case the military atmosphere was maintained, but relations with the local forces did not tend to be improved, because in general the drivers would otherwise have been off duty. (The Home Guard trained while the Regular Army rested or walked about the streets contemplating adding to its responsibilities). Ordinary buses on the other hand were not designed to carry full cargoes of armed men over mountain roads. And so, not infrequently, the Battalion had to get out on the steepest parts of a hill, after a tough day in the field, and even on occasion had to push. On one occasion indeed, a night exercise came to an untimely end because the "airborne troops" who were due to land at nightfall in the hills above Colwyn Bay found that their "troop-carrying aeroplane" broke down disastrously getting up a hill! But, although responsibility for the operational transport wherever it might go was not the work of the Battalion Transport Officer and his staff, he still had the more onerous task of cajoling transport out of the Military Authorities and securing adequate bus accommodation. This was another of the dull, painstaking jobs which had to be done behind the scenes, of which life in the Home Guard produced so many. Its difficulty was evidenced too by the fact that there were occasions on which exercises involving the transport of personnel had to be cancelled because no transport was available either on requisition from the army or from civilian sources. With regard to the Transport Platoon itself and its operations, the words of the Transport Battalion Officer perhaps carry more weight than those of a mere passenger. Here, therefore, is his account.

"It has been stated that the Transport Platoon came into existence when a certain Sergeant (who shall be nameless) decided to dissociate himself from the endeavours of the Home Guard to out-do the reputation of the legendary army of a certain Duke of York. Be that as it may, there were nevertheless some very good reasons for its formation. It has become painfully obvious to us all that wherever there is an 'army' there is always plenty of 'fetch and carry' and particularly so, when that little bit of 'army' is stationed at sea level while most of its strong points are situated on top of steep hills. The call for mechanical means to transport ammunition, rations, weapons (and quartermaster!) up those hills cannot be ignored.

"In the early days of the Unit, transport was more or less a domestic matter for each platoon, which relied upon the personal disregard of damage shown by its members who volunteered to use their own cars for such purposes. When, however, the unit grew to three company dimensions, and at the same time petrol restrictions resulted in many cars being laid up, the need for organised transport became evident.

"Thus it was that three pioneers, Fryatt, Buddin and Acock, two of whom had previous experience with a Territorial Armoured Car Company, took on the job of producing a Transport Platoon, with little other assets than enthusiasm and an enviable faith in their ability to beg, borrow or scrounge. The Colonel undertook, and what is more laudable, achieved, the equally onerous task of providing the financial means, as well as the difficult job of obtaining from the authorities the necessary car licences and petrol.

"The original vehicle backbone was provided by four of the Battalion's unsung heroes, deserving of honourable mention, if not special medals, namely Colonel Maclean, Major Lawrence, Private E. B. Anderson and Sergeant Rayner, who placed their cars at the sole disposal of the Platoon and at the tender mercies of its drivers. The next addition to the fleet came in the nature of a gift from Sergeant Fairclough of a 20 h.p. Vauxhall saloon, which proved to be the greatest boon of all. Taking full advantage of the concession which allowed unrestricted treatment, its beautiful saloon body was stripped and a wooden truck body was built on behind the cab. The 'Vauxy' in due course became a well-known spectacle in Colwyn Bay and district, the sight of which was sufficient to revive many memories in the minds of the veterans of the Platoon. These were the days (and nights) when the infantry platoons were either completely ignorant of the existence of 'Transport' or registered disbelief that in the gloom of Pwllycrochan garage, relieved by one dismal lamp, was being enacted a drama literally poignant with blood, sweat and almost tears, as a small body of men worked and experimented with blunt saws on green wood and with a handful of ill-assorted tools, to produce a truck capable of carrying ten fully equipped men or one ton of material, which with a minimum of attention or replacements was to serve the Battalion for a period of more than three years.

"Under such conditions the work went on and the Vauxhall was launched on the road. The cars and the truck were in ever increasing demand by Platoon Officers, training officers and quartermasters, who each wished to use them at the same time with increasing degrees of priority. It was essential to expand the scope of the platoon. In a relatively short space of time our fleet grew in size to ten cars and three trucks, with a corresponding increase in personnel reluctantly released from the infantry. The history of the Vauxhall has been related but brief mention of the other trucks is deserved. They consisted of a 7 h.p. Triumph bought by the Machine Gunners and a 20 h.p. Buick purchased by the C.O.'s Fund. Both were transformed into trucks by the members of the Platoon from a very limited supply of new wood, much scrap material, plenty of ingenuity and many hours of hard labour. The Triumph was not very successful, the engine proving too small for its new purpose and it was later used as an instruction vehicle by the Auxiliaries. The Buick, on the other hand, was tremendous in every respect. Converted to take 12 fully equipped men it was capable of more than ever was allotted to it, but it had an insatiable thirst for petrol which caused it to be kept mainly 'in reserve.' By this time the Workshop had been reorganised and fully justified its name. A complete lighting circuit had been installed, woodwork and metal work benches erected, a forge fitted up and equipped with an adequate set of tools. All these essential improvements had been carried out with no outside assistance and within the limited after-office hours.

"The Platoon now functioned in two sections, a Driving Section and a Maintenance Section. Buddin looked after the organisation, Fryatt the garage work and Acock was the liaison between the two. At a later date a section of Women Drivers and Clerks was posted from the Women Auxiliaries and became a valuable and integral part of the Platoon in its expanded duties. Particularly in spring and summer, calls upon Transport became thick and fast. The duties carried out by drivers were frequent and at times vehicles were in use every night of the week and at week-ends. Duties were of all descriptions from the normal carrying of rations, stores and personnel, to co-operating with other platoons in training exercises. The times at which vehicles were called out varied as much as the duties themselves, but seldom was difficulty encountered in providing the necessary transport, be it during the lunch hour, early morning or in the small hours of the night. The Platoon did yeoman service during the period of the camp and exercises at Coed Coch, and was at the disposal of the infantry during the summer evenings at the Mochdre Range. The extension of the Battalion territory at Pentre Foelas placed added responsibilities upon the resources of the drivers and vehicles but still the only limitations on our ability to assist the Battalion in its work, so far as our vehicles were capable of coping with it, was the careful watch which had to be kept on the available supply of petrol.

"In addition to these ordinary driving duties, this section of the Platoon was responsible for keeping check upon the 20 commercial lorries, earmarked for use in the event of an emergency, and in the organisation of a Transport Office which could be set up at a moment's notice to control cars, lorries or buses. Much thought and practice were expended in perfecting a foolproof machine to ensure a smooth organisation. Although happily no call to 'action stations' was ever received, should the occasion have arisen the Platoon was indeed ready to face all aspects of this problem. The services of the Women Auxiliaries were exceedingly useful in this part of the work and to a great extent the responsibility for the success of the scheme depended upon them, in so far as their duties included the maintenance of records, movements and inspection of vehicles.

"All our own Work."—The Runabout

Colonel Llewellin meets the Auxiliaries

"With the many calls upon the vehicles little opportunity was afforded to the drivers to give more than a merely superficial scrutiny to their cars or trucks. The maintenance section was therefore relied upon to inspect and set at rights any running defects which became apparent. The type of work which the cars were asked to do was quite different from that for which they were intended and as a result the strain was heavy. The attention of the Garage staff was therefore in constant demand. They did not, however, confine themselves to attention to repairs of this kind alone and were always willing to undertake major overhauls and replacements. Some astoundingly good work came out of the Workshop and the section is justifiably proud of its successful efforts to keep the vehicles on the road.

"In spite of so many calls upon them, the members of the Platoon found time to keep up to date in the subjects of those proficiency tests which did not call for specialised infantry training, to carry out firing practices on the ranges, develop convoy driving, to obtain a detailed knowledge of the roads within the Battalion Sector and to study co-operation with fighting platoons.

"To the ordinary footslogger Transport Platoon might have appeared to be in the nature of a 'cushy' job, but it is possible that these few paragraphs may be sufficient to shed some light on certain aspects which were not always apparent. The opportunities to show off' what could be accomplished by the Platoon as a unit were few and far between but one instance may be quoted which at last impressed the infantry of its value. 'C' Company had been warned to parade at Penrhos College at 18.30 hours for an exercise in attack. The Company Commander called for as much transport as possible to be available, and Transport Platoon 'laid on' eight private cars together with the Vauxhall and Buick trucks—a total passenger capacity of 46. 'C' Company received its orders at 18.30 hours precisely. These had to be digested, junior commanders instructed and men detailed before the Company could start to move. Even so, the arrangements went so smoothly that, although the total Company strength (that night) of 90 had to be carried in two lots, the whole force was deposited at its appointed place by 19.00 hours. The Company Commander was enabled to have his attacking force actually in fighting position within 40 minutes of zero hour, from sea level to a front about a mile and a half from his headquarters and high up above the Pwllycrochan Woods. His opponent didn't stand an earthly.

"That was the sort of job for which the Transport Platoon had been formed and they literally 'delivered the goods.'

The Transport Platoon certainly did, in the opinion of the Battalion in general, deliver the goods, but one word must be said about the triumph of engineering represented by the home made trucks. Unfortunately, the bolts with which they were held together protruded from ½in. to 1in. through the unpadded sides and when travelling fast over rutty roads were liable to punch holes in the occupants. (The Transport Officer when present rode on the driver's seat at the smooth end of the bolts). All the same, many of the Battalion, the writer included, after reconnaissance or surveying work in the hills, have been more than grateful for the ride home.

The Battalion in common with all Home Guard Units was not, however, like the Regular Army, always ready to go into action. Normally it was engaged in its daily tasks or its nightly relaxations, and indeed usually a quite appreciable portion of it was away from Colwyn Bay. The mustering scheme, therefore, and those responsible for its operation, rank high among those specialist services which were essential to the life of the Battalion. Bowles, not content with being Battalion Intelligence Officer, which involved enough work for any reasonable man, also had the rousing scheme under his wing. His description of it, therefore, which follows is almost certainly as lucid a statement as is possible of a piece of machinery with which the rank and file of the Battalion only came into contact in moments of distraction and irritation, i.e., when changing a billet or being called out in the middle of the night.

"The fundamental duty of a Home Guard Unit, and one perhaps more urgent for Battalions on a sea-board or in rural areas, to attack and destroy any enemy troops landed from the sea or air as quickly as possible, called for an effective scheme for rapid muster as an essential part of its organisation. The normal Home Guard Unit, moreover, was designed to fight on its own door-step. The 11th Battalion Denbigh was an outstanding exception to the rule, as the Battalion personnel had been evacuated from London, and other provincial towns, with the Ministry of Food, and were billeted in Colwyn Bay and the adjacent neighbourhoods. Broadly the platoons of the Battalion were organised on an office basis, each of the larger office buildings occupied by the Ministry in Colwyn Bay having its own platoon or platoons. During the office hours the transmission of an order to muster merely entailed a telephone call from Battalion Headquarters to the various offices. A muster after office hours presented an intricate problem, as the use of an audible signal remained impracticable until D-Day, when it became possible for the public 'Alert' signal to be used for mustering the Battalion. To ensure an approximately complete muster two factors ruled out anything but a scheme based on a house-to-house call. These factors were, first, the extended area within which the members of the Unit were living, from Llanddulas and Llysfaen in the East to Glan Conway, Llandudno Junction and Llandudno in the West—an area of about seventeen square miles—and, second, the large number of changed addresses notified to the Battalion each week. It was noticeable that just before Easter each year a substantial number of men moved from the centre of the town, to return again in the Autumn after the holiday season had finished. Changes were so frequent, especially at the beginning of the holiday season, when as many as a hundred have been registered in one week, that without special arrangements to meet the difficulty any scheme for mustering would have broken down.

"As a first step a number of the men, representing a cross section of the billeted personnel, were asked how long it would take them to be ready to leave their billets fully equipped, if called when asleep at night. With the exception of one man who estimated 25 minutes the answer was the same for all, 20 minutes. An enlargement of Colwyn Bay Town Plan, 11 inches to the mile, was made by Cpl. D. J. Mudie, from the 14 Bn. City of Glasgow Home Guard, who served with this Battalion for a few weeks before joining the Army. The address of every man in the Battalion was plotted on this plan, and on subsidiary plans of the outer areas. From this data it was estimated that an average allowance of 30 minutes per man, from the time of call to reporting for duty at the respective Company rendezvous, was necessary. On that basis it was estimated that the whole Battalion could be completely mustered in 2 hours 50 minutes. Later, on test, the estimate proved to be about correct, although a substantial proportion of the strength could be paraded for action considerably under that time. A further consideration in planning the scheme was that, as far as possible, no Officer or N.C.O. was to be employed on the duty of what became known as 'rousing.'

"The organisation of the mustering scheme was based on the division of the Borough of Colwyn Bay and neighbouring districts into a number of areas each under an Area Controller, the size of each area being determined by the number of men billeted within the neighbourhood. The built-up districts of Old Colwyn, Colwyn Bay, Rhos, Penrhyn Bay and Mochdre, were divided into eight areas; Llysfaen, Llanddulas, Glan Conway, Llandudno Junction with Deganwy, and Llandudno, were classified as Outer Areas, for which it was necessary to modify the general plan. The Areas were again divided into two, three or four Districts, each under a Deputy Area Controller. Finally the Districts were divided into beats, each covering the billets of not more than eight men, one of whom was appointed as 'Rouser' for the beat. In practice, the average beat comprised the billets of five to six men only.

"In addition, two Chief Controllers were appointed. The most important duty of the Chief Controllers was to attend at Battalion Headquarters during the mustering of the Battalion and to report to the Duty Officer any breakdown during the call-out, beyond their powers or authority to put right. They were also responsible for the control of the large amount of clerical work involved in maintaining the scheme. This required a staff of about eight people, four Home Guardsmen and four or more women clerks, who worked on Sunday mornings and Wednesday evenings during the greater part of the year. Tribute should here be paid to the first party of women clerks, who were all volunteers from the Ministry's Enforcement Branch. They were not members of any Women's organisation connected with the Home Guard; none existed at that time. These women were content to carry on behind the scenes to contribute to the success of the work. Their work was excellently done.

"The actual working of the scheme was in itself, quite simple. All troops knew from their Company Standing Orders their places of rendezvous. Upon the receipt at Battalion Headquarters of the order to muster, the Telephone Orderlies, who were on duty at Headquarters at nights and week-ends when the H.Q. staff were away, verified the authenticity of the order. They then transmitted the order by telephone to the Battalion H.Q. Officers, the two Chief Controllers and the Area Controllers, and by messenger to the dispatch rider N.C.O., who would report to Headquarters to be available to deal with any hitches which might arise. The chain of transmission was then taken up by the Area Controllers from their billets, by telephone to their Deputies in all Districts. Finally, each Deputy Controller conveyed the order in person to the 'rousers' in his District. The use of the telephone for the final transmission to the 'Rousers' was found to be impracticable.

"The unwisdom of relying completely on the Telephone Service for the initial transmission of so vital an order was foreseen, and had that service failed through enemy action or from other causes, it would then have become the duty of the dispatch rider at Headquarters, assisted by cyclists, to carry the Mustering Order to the Chief and Area Controllers and the Battalion H.Q. Officers. On the occasion of a test muster, telephone contact could not be made with one or two Areas. The dispatch rider who, in accordance with the Standing Orders had been called by messenger, demonstrated that the provision made to meet the situation would work efficiently.

"Owing to the large number of the Battalion personnel who were liable to be away from Colwyn Bay for shorter or longer periods on official business or from other causes, it was arranged for each member of the mustering staff to hand over his duties to his 'next man' when absent. By this means all posts in the plan were duplicated. Upon examination it had been found that the lack of a similar provision was a major cause of the partial failure of early muster exercises. The mustering exercise already mentioned, was arranged to test the efficiency of the plan and the mustering staff. The muster was carried through down to the 'Rousers' who were instructed to walk their beats without actually knocking up their men. A time estimate of ten minutes was allowed for 'knocking up' each man. This was also to cover the time occupied by the Rouser walking from billet to billet.

"This test proved that an immediate muster of from 80% to 85% of the Battalion strength would have been secured, and that proportion of the strength would have mustered well within the original estimate of 2 hours 50 minutes. It also reflected the con-

THE SPECIALIST SERVICES

sistent and conscientious work put in on this extra duty by the members of the mustering staff. To test the scheme fully particular care was taken to ensure that no advance rumours of a pending muster leaked out! The Commanding Officer and the Battalion Intelligence Officer who was responsible for the scheme, the Mustering and Battalion Intelligence N.C.O.s, together with two Senior Local National Fire Service Officers who had arranged for the use of a Sub-fire Station as a report post, and the Sub-station Officer, were the only persons 'in the know.' The signed order to muster was handed over to the Headquarters Orderlies at precisely 22.00 hours. There had been no general muster for many months prior to the test. The orderlies got to work on the unexpected order with quiet efficiency. There was a hitch on the first call. Contact could not be made. A second and successful call was put through in routine order. 'Who are you, please?' In clear and measured words the orderly read the order, 'This is Battalion Headquarters speaking—the order is EXERCISE —,' to receive the prompt query, 'What, NOT TO-NIGHT?' "

Shortly before D-Day orders were issued for the partial muster of the Battalion on the public "alert" being sounded and for the complete muster in the event of enemy attack on the town or neighbourhood by air.

When Napoleon said that an army marched on its stomach, he was enunciating a profound truth, which is not disproved by the apparent contradiction that modern lorry-borne infantry does the exact reverse. The Battalion Catering Officer, and his staff, formed an essential part of the Battalion organisation, and while always necessary were popular nearly all the time. Their functions became particularly important when the Battalion got itself properly organised and started to spend considerable stretches of time in camp, first at Coed Coch and then at Pentre Foelas.

A catering officer, Polfrey, was nominated in 1942 and his appointment was confirmed in January, 1943. At the time of his nomination the catering officer found that cooking duties were being carried out independently by each Company and without any co-ordination from Battalion Headquarters. It was decided to set up a Cooks Section in the Headquarters Company, and several men were transferred as a nucleus. Privates Meyer, Duckworth, Foulkes, and Gavin were made Lance Corporals and Corporal Dry was later promoted Sergeant. Sergeant Dry eventually left the Battalion and was replaced by Sergeant Waite from "D" Company. During 1942, 1943 and 1944 the Cooks Section carried out catering duties for all field operations and exercises, which meant duty during most week-ends from April to October! Since there was no "official" issue of cooking utensils to the Home Guard the 11th Denbigh were, at the beginning, much handicapped by the lack of equipment. We began with five dixies for about seven hundred men! In due course the Battalion acquired its own Catering Stores, catering equipment and reserve supplies of food. The unofficial equipment was purchased from Battalion funds while certain additional "official" equipment was borrowed from other units. The difficulties which arose from the dearth of male cooks (it was seldom possible to get more than three on parade for any week-end) were alleviated on the advent of the Women's Unit. It should go on record that the success which the catering section achieved during 1943/44 was largely due to the help it received from the Women's Unit, certain individual members of which attended practically every operational exercise at which catering services were required. The women were willing, unselfish, cheerful and apparently tireless.

Catering operations were carried out under varied conditions. Cooking was done in the hills (Coed Coch), in the streets (Pentre Foelas), in ditches (Bryn Euryn), on the beaches (Morfa), and in the rain at the standing camp at Pentre Foelas. The co-operation of the Adjutant, the Officer i/c A and Q, the Transport Officer and the Battalion's suppliers of foodstuffs was always available. The constant zeal and cheerfulness of Sergeant Waite (who was awarded the B.E.M. for his services in connection with Battalion Catering duties) and of Private Stembridge, were a byword.

Sergeant Waite, and his male and female assistants, by common consent cooked like angels. Unfortunately, angels live in eternity, and not in time, and therefore there were occasions when the Home Guard, earthbound by their bodily passions, showed some signs of discontent when waiting for their dinners. But by sheer force of character Waite overcame all difficulties: a man who has been an army cook for most of a period of twenty-three years' service, and has preserved both his life and his integrity, has little to fear.

In the opinion of the Catering Officer his chief function was to remonstrate with O's.C. Companies for failing to give adequate notice of exercises, to explain why officers, including and especially the C.O., who turned up on exercises without mess tins and cutlery, could not be fed (the C.O. improved towards the end!) and to moan and moan for more cooks, which he never got.

There is also a story about a meat ration for one of the earlier exercises, but this is one of those subjects which, like some diseases, certain bodily functions, and the Establishment Divisions of departments of the Civil Service, are not discussed between gentlemen except towards the concluding stages of a regimental dinner.

The feeding of the Home Guard comes into this story from another angle as well. This is the history of the Ministry of Food Home Guard and not of the Ministry of Food and therefore it is not the place to tell the whole story. But it was, in the main, officials of the Ministry of Food who were active in the Home Guard Unit and who, indeed, held the highest positions within it, who were concerned in most of the steps which were taken, in consultation with the War Office, to finalise the provisions which were made for feeding the Home Guard in the field had it become necessary.

As was described in Chapter 2, the earlier arrangements for feeding the Ministry Unit on duty were chaotic, and they no doubt only reproduced conditions existing elsewhere. Instructions in due course were issued covering the position of Units built round the defence of a works or similar undertaking, which based their feeding arrangements on canteen facilities already available. In the case of the Ministry Home Guard, given a choice between drawing food from the canteen and accepting money payment, a very large proportion of the Ministry Unit, for reasons best known to themselves, voted for the magnificent sum of 3s. per night. No doubt in other parts of Great Britain a similar choice had to be made.

In Western Command, in which we were stationed, Major General Dickinson, D.A. and Q.M.G., and Sir Thomas Jones, the Ministry's Chief Divisional Food Officer in the Command, had early put their heads together to see that the best was made of the facilities provided under the current regulations and both attended meetings of Home Guard Commanding Officers in June, 1941, at Chester, Shrewsbury, Caernarvon and other centres at which the arrangements were explained in detail and questions answered. In November of that year, Maclean, in his capacity as the Principal Assistant Secretary in the Ministry responsible for the rationing procedure and also for catering establishments, gave evidence before Lord Bridgeman's War Office Committee on the feeding and subsistence of the Home Guard.

The outstanding problem, however, was what to do in order to feed the Home Guard should it be called up. Not unnaturally this was considered to be part of the responsibility of the War Office, but the War Office, true to their tradition of regarding the Home Guard as civilians whenever administratively convenient, put the ball back in the Ministry of Food court and suggested that special allocations might be made on a civilian basis. This is not the place to give the whole story in detail, but a great deal of work was done in laying down plans for providing emergency rations to bridge the gap between leaving civilian life and being fitted into the feeding arrangements of a fighting army; and, moreover, arrangements were made covering the supply of suitable quantities of food to Home Guard troops under canvas in summer camps or training with the Army on special courses.

In all this the personnel of the Ministry of Food Home Guard Unit played a prominent part, and the success of the final scheme would have largely depended, had it been put into operation, on the experience and understanding they derived from their dual responsibility.

The Machine-gun section, or its embryo, appeared very early in the development of the Ministry Home Guard. It will be recollected that on the occasion of the second Inspection carried out by the Minister a machine-gun section was already operating as a separate unit.

It commenced with the arrival of a Browning medium-heavy machine-gun towards the middle of the Autumn in 1940. A sergeant of the Cheshires turned up and delivered a course of lectures to a small, but select, band of N.C.O.s. These, armed with the required information, dispersed back to their units, leaving Sergeant Lowe with the task of building up a gun-team from a group of eight volunteers. The group, however, were all enthusiasts and progress was rapid. Soon a new gun arrived. With their training at a fairly advanced stage, and armed with their new gun, the section took part in an exercise in defence, in which they acquitted themselves very well against an attacking platoon. Indeed, so well did they acquit themselves that they managed to convert to enthusiasm for the machine-gun another gun-team from the attacking platoon, who applied for transfer, and gave Sergeant Lowe material from which a second full gun-team, complete with reserves, could be built up. It was now considered that the section was large enough to form a platoon, together with the Signals, and it continued to operate as a half-platoon until the attachment of both the Signallers and Machine-gunners to the Headquarters Platoon, upon its re-organisation.

Subsequently, another machine-gun, this time a Vickers, arrived, and with it Lance-Corporal Mitchell, who was attached to the local unit of the Royal Corps of Signals, as a machine-gun instructor, who put the section through a course of training in the new weapon. By this time, the principal problem of a heavy machine-gun section—lack of transport—had been solved by the enterprise and devotion of a group of the members of the section. It must be remembered that a medium-heavy machine-gun is a fairly solid piece of ironmongery. The tripod weighs 56 lbs., and the gun approximately 30 lbs. (These weights have inscribed themselves indelibly on the memory—and on other portions of the anatomy—of the writer. On one occasion, having captured a heavy machine-gun in the course of manoeuvres, and having very foolishly allowed his prisoners to be taken away, he found himself, at the cessation of the Exercise, confronted with the task of bringing in his captured machine-gun across half a mile of very rough country). The story of one enthusiastic member of the section describes how the transport difficulty was overcome.

"At that time the Machine Gun Section was under the command of Sergeant Lowe and, as new recruits, we received a warm welcome. We quickly found that the principal pastime of the members was jig-saw puzzles. The puzzles took the form of a Browning medium machine-gun and the game was to break the gun into as many pieces as possible and re-assemble it against the clock. The technical term for this game is stripping and to add difficulty to the operation we used to blindfold the player, so that he had to re-assemble the gun in complete darkness using only his sense of touch.

"At this time the Machine Gun Unit enjoyed an almost complete autocracy. We soon came to the conclusion that this was because the powers that be had found it impossible to fit us into their plans, but we were content with the position and did not enquire too deeply into the reasons. We were in the pleasant position of being quite independent of the Transport Officer as we had enough transport of our own. It must be admitted that there was some lack of standardisation in our transport. At the top of the list was the car owned by Burn-Callander who was then, I think, a Corporal. It had an excellent boot at the back which would hold two guns and a front seat which would hold Corporal Burn-Callander and even then could usually squeeze in two or three other passengers, and so far as I recall, all survived this ill-treatment with no lasting ill-effect. At that time Burn-Callander alone shared with the guns the distinction of being quartered at Penrhos College and this had a certain advantage for other members of the Platoon who, turning up at the last minute, usually found that Burn-Callander had single handed loaded his car with all the equipment and was ready for the 'right away.'

"At the other end of the convoy came the transport owned by Huntley and myself. Huntley's little Austin could have come straight out of a Walt Disney film. It consisted of an engine, four wheels, some string and very little else but nevertheless did yeoman service in conveying Huntley and his intrepid passenger of the day to the appointed destination and back again. My contribution was a 1932 8 h.p. Singer which had already done more work than a car ought to have been asked to do but which nevertheless still had plenty of useful life. I think it only let us down on two occasions and these defaults could be attributed to the over optimism of its owner in assessing the ability of the battery to discharge continuously without any help from the dynamo, and it was just an unfortunate coincidence that the same team had the job of pushing it home on both those occasions.

"Then came the cessation of the basic ration and the inflation of the Platoon and our days of transport independence were over.

"It fell to my lot to be in charge of the Gun Team which featured in the incident which has since become legendary in the Machine Gun Platoon. The occasion was an exercise in which the Home Guard collaborated with the Regulars and I was instructed to take one gun and report to a Regular Officer at his Headquarters in a farm opposite the Rhos Golf Course on the Llandudno Road. There was the usual delay in moving off and on this occasion it appeared to have been due to the inadequate distribution of a last minute order, to the effect that for the purpose of confusing the enemy Penrhos College would be called Rydal and Rydal would be called Penrhos. This involved the hasty re-transfer of equipment, rations and men. Being now dependent on outside help for transport we had some difficulty in reaching the rendezvous, but after some delay a small car was provided which was just sufficient to take two men and the gun, leaving the rest of the party to follow in transport provided by the Crosville Motor Company. This was a source of considerable indignation to certain members of the party who conducted a long correspondence, which for all I know may still be going on, regarding the iniquity of being obliged to spend their own pence on transport and being refused re-imbursement by the Military Authorities. Apparently they should have requisitioned the bus and so have avoided all these financial difficulties.

"The party having re-assembled at its destination I reported to the Regular Officer in accordance with my instructions and was taken by him to the point he had selected as the site for the gun. This proved to be about 10ft. from the ground in the branches of a small tree. With due regard for military discipline I pointed out to the officer that we had had no previous training in mounting a heavy machine gun in the branches of a small tree and that with only a few thin and rotten planks, and a hazy knowledge of the law of contributory negligence, I felt it unwise to experiment with the project, particularly as it was rapidly getting dark. The officer did not press the point and said it would be equally satisfactory from his point of view if we mounted the gun on the ground at the foot of the tree. This we did and the rest of the night passed without incident. At the time we felt that the moral to be drawn was that it would be unfortunate indeed if we should have to go into action under the command of officers who had no knowledge of machine guns, but in retrospect I am by no means convinced that the officer's action was as stupid as it then appeared. He probably knew what we subsequently discovered, namely, that the regular inhabitant of the field we had so rudely invaded was a large bull. The bull turned out to be quite friendly and even to show an interest in the amount of force needed to overturn the gun, but we townsmen felt a certain security in the proximity of this tree and the little stone-built enclosure which surrounded it."

The Anti-Gas training of the Battalion was successively in the hands of Wheatley and Essex-Lopresti. Future research may reveal why the Nazis, who made preparations for gas warfare on a very extensive scale, refrained from using that weapon. One thing is certain; neither the Geneva Convention of 1928 nor humanitarianism would have deterred them if they could have derived any appreciable advantage from its employment. It may be that the true reason for their abstention was our preparedness. They liberated Chlorine against our armies with disastrous effects in 1915, but then the element of surprise was present, and we were totally unready for the attack. In this war, our fighting services were issued with excellent defensive equipment and were well drilled in its use.

Gas has a powerful psychological effect upon untrained personnel. The unknown inspires dread; now our armies know too much about gas to be frightened by it. Every regular serving man has experienced tear and nose gases in the gas chamber; he encountered Phosgene; Mustard gas was applied to his skin, and he was able to test for himself the efficacy of his anti-gas equipment. Gas might have had a considerable nuisance value, but the casualty risk was insignificant. If equal protection could be given to the fighting man against other weapons this might well have been a relatively bloodless war. It is therefore reasonable to guess that the Germans, knowing this, directed their energy to the employment of weapons producing a higher casualty rate.

The threat of chemical warfare must not be written off as a total loss to the enemy. Preparedness was not achieved without cost to the British. A large number of research chemists had to be unceasingly employed in experiments and tests. Gas Schools had been set up in different parts of the country where considerable staffs were engaged week in and week out. Specialist officers and men were detailed from every unit for strenuous initial and refresher training courses. These specialists returned to their units, and training programmes made provision for the instruction and drilling of personnel in anti-gas measures. If the man-hours involved in all this could be computed, the diversion of energy from battle training would be seen to reach staggering proportions. In addition huge factories and quantities of materials, including precious rubber, were devoted to producing the equipment.

The Home Guard probably found the burden of anti-gas training heavier than the regular services. We had had to cover much of the ground of the regular infantry, and the time at our disposal was filched from our meagre leisure hours. Specialist officers and N.C.O.s attended Courses at Army Gas Schools; junior leaders were trained in each platoon, and training and instruction went on under their guidance. As a result the unit attained a high degree of proficiency, and probably enjoyed the immunity which this provides. Had a gas attack developed, therefore, there is little doubt that they would have provided a very valuable local "stiffening."

Total war involves the civilian population as well as the fighting forces, and the effect of a gas attack on civilian morale would be the more serious because these have not had the advantages of training and experience which the fighter has "enjoyed." Therefore we may find consolation for our unproductive labour if it has helped to avert from the home front one of the major beastlinesses of war. It may well be that our preparedness contributed to this immunity.

The services of the medical staff of the Battalion were fortunately never called for to support them in action, but there is little doubt that they would have been more than equal to their task had they been called upon. They operated very much in the background of necessity, but their work cannot pass unrecognised. The basis of medical arrangements was co-operation with the Civil Defence Services. The Home Guard was responsible for immediate first aid treatment of casualties and for their care until they reached the Civil Defence Casualty organisation; after that they were to be the sole responsibility of the Civil Defence Authorities. The points at which the "handing over" was to take place were the casualty collecting posts, set up on a platoon basis. If possible, a Civil Defence first aid point was to be chosen as the Home Guard casualty collecting post.

As far as Colwyn Bay was concerned the position was clear though it is doubtful whether the Civil Defence Services were adequate to deal with more than a very small number of casualties. At Pentre Foelas, however, the situation was obscure. The Civil Defence Services in that area were naturally almost non-existent and there seemed to be good grounds for opening a Home Guard Regimental Aid Post. (These Regimental Aid Posts were authorised for outlying districts, and were to contain medical and surgical equipment under the charge of a Home Guard Medical Officer). Actually no Regimental Aid Post was ever authorised for Pentre Foelas, partly, no doubt, because of the difficulty of finding a doctor who would be able to take charge of the post in the case of a muster. Officially the medical personnel of the Battalion consisted of the Medical Officer and a Medical Orderly Sergeant at Battalion Headquarters, one Medical Orderly Corporal and eight stretcher bearers for each Platoon of approximately 100 men.

The official issue of medical equipment for each platoon was not ungenerous, including—2 Stretchers, 6 Blankets, 2 Pillows, 2 Stretcher Slings, 2 Water Bottles and Carriers, 1 Haversack containing Shell Dressings, 1 First Aid Outfit containing dressings of various sizes, 1 set of wood splints, 8 armlets S.B. and a small number of bandages for practice.

The Medical Officer of No. 1 Battalion was Major Lynch. On the formation of No. 11, Dr. E. Morison, of Brompton Avenue, was appointed Medical Officer and retained this position until his resignation on health grounds in 1944. After an interval during which the Battalion had no Medical Officer, Dr. W. B. Martin was appointed to the position and held it until the "stand down." Dr. Morison was very keen but his age and health would not allow him to do anything very active. He did good work lecturing on first aid, but most of the training was of necessity left to the Sergeant and Corporals. Dr. Martin's appointment came too late for the Battalion to have got to know him well before the "stand down." Sergeant Hughes of the Ministry of Food was Medical Orderly Sergeant of No. 1 Battalion and on the formation of No. 11 he elected to stay with No. 1. Tyack was appointed Medical Orderly Sergeant of No. 11 from the start and remained in that position throughout its history. One of the most difficult tasks was to collect and keep together sufficient men to form even a skeleton organisation. Home Guard regulations forbade the recruiting of men for medical duties only, and all stretcher bearers had to be trained as ordinary Home Guards first. Every platoon was desperately short of men and there was some reluctance on the part of Platoon Commanders to allocate them to specialist jobs. Moreover the men, although keen enough when on the job, found that either their Home Guard duties were increased by taking on stretcher bearer duties, or they dropped behind their comrades in general battle

International Gallery

The Adjutant explains the "War"

THE SPECIALIST SERVICES

efficiency. So, the medical personnel never approached more than about 50% of the strength laid down, at one time falling to fewer than 20 for the whole Battalion. Training new stretcher bearers in stretcher bearing and elementary first aid was the main work, accompanied by revision courses and practices for trained men and lectures and demonstrations for all Home Guard personnel, co-operation with troops in field exercises, and the provision of first aid services at rifle and bombing ranges and camps at Coed Coch and Pentre Foelas, which brought reality in to the training. Most of the training was done at Pwllycrochan Hotel under Tyack and his staff; they did wonders under adverse conditions.

As previously stated, Home Guard medical services were only intended to carry out immediate first aid on the field, and to transport casualties to the Civil Casualty Post. They therefore concentrated on elementary treatment and transport under adverse conditions such as enemy fire, rough country, etc. In this they were helped by the experience of the Royal Army Medical Corps in North Africa and other places and learned to improvise with a good deal of proficiency, working wonders with the casualty's own webbing equipment, haversack, rifle, bayonet, handkerchief and even bootlaces!

Meanwhile there was another sort of emergency they had to be prepared to deal with—a real accident such as a No. 68 grenade being put into the cup the wrong way round or a cook upsetting a dixie of boiling water over himself. The War Office never seemed to consider the possibility of accidents such as these and the official equipment was woefully inadequate to deal with them. Equipment would have enabled them to deal after a fashion with a severed limb—but not with a blistered heel! A grant was therefore made out of the Commanding Officer's Fund to purchase such things as elastoplast, dettol and cottonwool.

At this point the narrative may be continued by Tyack.

"Although the Battalion medical personnel dealt with a large number of minor injuries we were fortunate in having no really serious cases. It is true that accidents sometimes happened when no trained men or equipment were available but this was usually not our fault. The officer concerned had omitted to make the necessary arrangements! (I was usually the last person to be notified of an impending exercise—sometimes only the day before).

"The Pentre Foelas camp was our most ambitious attempt at providing medical services. In this we were fortunate in having the assistance of the Ministry of Food Nursing Division (St. John's), who provided personnel and additional equipment. These girls had undertaken to help the Home Guard if called upon, and while they had paraded on such occasions as 'Wings for Victory' Week there had been few opportunities of using them. (A notable exception was an exercise when they manned the post at Pwllycrochan). They were extremely valuable at Pentre Foelas, particularly as there were a large number of Women Auxiliaries attending the camp. Most of the St. John's girls later became Auxiliaries but their enrolment was too late for them to be engaged in many exercises as such.

"During 1944 several Medical Orderly Corporals and I were able to attend week-end courses at the Camp Reception Centre, Park Hale Camp, under Major Pearce. Demonstrations were given by Royal Army Medical Corps personnel and lectures by Major Pearce and others. These courses were very helpful and more of our men would have attended if there had been vacancies.

"Two inter-Battalion stretcher bearer competitions were held during the life of No. 11 Denbighshire. The first was held at Rhyl on the 7th November, 1943, and was regarded as a little unsatisfactory by those who took part. The second was held at Crows Nest Farm, Sychnant, on the 28th May, 1944. This was well organised and General Viscount Bridgeman paid us a visit during its progress. No. 11 put up a good show and came second (1 Denbighshire was first) by a small margin. The team consisted of Corporal E. W. Alcock, Privates G. Little and L. S. Barker, of 'B' Company, Private H. Handforth of 'C' Company, and Private H. A. Clark of 'D' Company."

Finally, we come to the last but not the least important of the Specialist branches of the Battalion—the Women Auxiliaries. This body may have been "specialised" by nature, but they de-specialised themselves to the extent that they took part in almost every phase of Battalion work with the exception of actual infantry training. Here is the account of their leader, Miss Bridgman.

"In September, 1942, when the achievements of the Russian Women were making headlines, a member of the staff of the Ministry of Food circulated a round-robin for the names of women interested in forming a Women's Home Guard. A hundred and thirty names were soon added to the list. On the 1st December, Major Lawrence addressed a large gathering at Colwyn Bay Hotel, outlining the many ways in which women could be of service to the Home Guard. We became affiliated to the Women's Home Defence under the chairmanship of Dr. Edith Summerskill, M.P., and with the help of the Officers of the Men's Home Guard, a syllabus of training was drawn up which included lectures on the following subjects:—

."The Object and Role of Women's Defence Unit: Role and Organisation of the Ministry Home Guard Unit: Secrecy: Discipline: Military Vocabulary (official): Arms. and Equipment of Home Guard: General Knowledge of the Area: Visual Training: Map Reading: Anti-Gas Drill: First Aid: Squad and Section Drill.

"At the end of this Course, members who had attended 75% of the lectures were enrolled and given the badge of the Women's Home Defence Unit. In April, 1943, we were officially recognised by the War Office with a 'ceiling' of 90, and as the Women's Service Unit we worked in six Sections, Administrative, Catering, Communications, Guides, Intelligence and Transport. A Leader, 3 Sub-Leaders and 6 Section Leaders were appointed.

"The Administrative Section undertook many various clerical duties, typing letters, accounts, etc., for the Home Guard Offices. They also helped a great deal with the Rousing Scheme. (After the stand down they continued to render sterling service to H.Q., including a lot of work on this book).

"The Catering Section, as their name implies, worked as Cooks under Lieut. Polfrey and Sgt. Waite. This work, needless to say, was that most appreciated by the men. A Section of Cooks was out every week-end when the men were on Exercises or at Camp. Night Exercises were also made more enjoyable for the men by the fact that the Women's Section were preparing hot drinks and meals for them. The Section had a good idea of what was expected of them before the week-end camps started, as they had been going out every time there was a Sunday exercise at Pentre Foelas. Lieut. Polfrey had got them all dishing up by numbers, peeling onions with the minimum of tears and tackling the grease up to their elbows with true army gusto. Gone were all the housewives' principles and labour saving comforts; stacks of potato peeling and eyeing became just one of the natural habits of the Section.

"The Communications Section trained in Phonograms, Signals Office Procedure, Morse and Wireless (Portable Wireless Set, Commando No. 38) and at the time of the 'Stand Down', the Section was becoming proficient in the reading of morse signals by lamp. On the night of 17/18th June, 1944, the Section participated in an inter-company exercise, operating communications at Colwyn Bay Hotel.

"The Guides Section was trained to know every inch of the locality and the Intelligence Section compiled a gazetteer of all the villages and places of interest in the area from the appropriate ordnance maps. This entailed weeks and months of tedious work, picking out each minute village and marking the appropriate Grid reference. (It has now been handed over to Sub-District H.Q. for the use of the regular forces). These two Sections then combined and trained together in panorama sketching, making maps and also a model of Pentre Foelas. The men had completed a scale model of Colwyn Bay, so the Auxiliaries were given a similar job, but this time of Pentre Foelas. This meant a great deal of work in tracing and enlarging sections of the map of the operational area and then making a model therefrom. Roads and rivers were marked and the model woods, made of painted pieces of sponge, placed in their appropriate positions. This would have been invaluable in working out a plan of campaign had the occasion arisen.

"The Transport Section was under the direction of Lieut. Buddin, the Battalion Transport Officer. The Lieutenant, rather at a loss

K

to know what to do with the Section, never having had so many women on his hands at one time before, immediately instituted a series of lectures as the easiest way out of the difficulty. These were given over a number of months by a member of the Workshop staff, during which time we were instructed in the many and varied peculiar things that might (and knowing our cars, did) happen beneath the bonnet. We were also 'allowed' to go to the garage on Sunday mornings, to get used to hearing the type of language one might expect to hear when cars went wrong. This was useful training, because it saved the men stopping work to count ten or turning round and saying, 'Sorry, my dear, didn't see you,' which was what happened when we first went there. When this first series of lectures finished (much to the relief of the lecturers who had never had female pupils before) we began our mixed parades, and were very proud of the fact that we were the only section that paraded with the male Home Guard. The girls were allowed to take out the cars. They did such jobs as carrying stores, picking up troops on a Sunday morning, and taking troops out to view the area from the Bryn-y-Maen district. By this time, most of the lectures had finished and we seemed to have more spare time, so we asked Lieut. Buddin what he thought of the idea of our cleaning the cars once a week. 'Fine,' he said, 'the boys will be pleased' (which, of course, was a typically masculine retort). Our cleaning job was greater than we first thought—we found that the inside of the cars looked as if they had never been touched. We brushed and shook and cleaned and polished, and at last the cars began to look as if someone owned them. Then the Section aspired to greater things. We wanted to paint the truck. At first we met with quite a lot of opposition, but after this had been worn down, we started. The Lieutenant, who was quite sure we would have to call for help, was there with his chief henchman, watching, rather sceptically, how we went about it. This was not at all to our liking, so we set them to work opening tins of paint. Tin opening, unfortunately, did not keep them busy for long, so we were forced to listen to their caustic remarks, in spite of which they had to admit we had done a good job of work. The Transport Section really felt they had been accepted when the Colonel asked to have one of them to drive him around.

"On 7th January, 1944, the Auxiliaries celebrated their first birthday. We were fortunate in coinciding with our new Minister's first official visit to Colwyn Bay, so Colonel Llewellin, accompanied by Sir John Bodinnar and Mr. Damerell, was the guest of honour. We were able to give him his first introduction to the Battalion. During the celebrations our birthday cake was cut with fitting ritual by Colonel and Mrs. Maclean. Afterwards Mrs. Maclean was formally presented with a badge and nominated an honorary member of the Unit, in which capacity she worked hard for the Auxiliaries and willingly tackled all jobs from peeling potatoes with the rest of us at camp to acting as orderly to the Deputy Controller of A.T.S. at the Stand Down Parade.

"In August, 1944, a Nursing Section was formed of members of St. John's Ambulance, and this Section was always on duty during visits to Pentre Foelas and other exercises.

"The Auxiliaries spent many week-ends in camp and where possible their training was combined with that of the men and included observation marches, first aid, tent pitching, mess tin cooking and acting as runners in tactical exercises. Two week-ends the Auxiliaries spent entirely on their own in camp.

"The War Office having deemed a uniform unnecessary for our work we decided to provide our own, as we found cooking, and cleaning cars, taking a heavy toll of our civilian clothes. We raised funds by running a dance, and through gifts from interested officials of the Ministry of Food, and by the generosity of the men members of the Home Guard, we collected enough money and coupons to purchase 26 civilian battle dresses and fifty black berets. For our flash we chose the Ministry of Food sign encircled with our new name 'Home Guard Auxiliaries.' This uniform caused quite a sensation in the Press reporting on the Stand Down Parade and we received a request from the Director of the Imperial War Museum that we send a specimen uniform to the Museum for exhibition there.

"The Auxiliaries paraded with the Battalion at the Home Guard Birthday Celebrations in 1943, at the Stand-Down Parade in December, 1944, and at the Victory Parade in 1945. They were inspected by the Minister of Food, Colonel Llewellin, in July, 1944. At the Stand-Down Parade we had the honour of being inspected and addressed by Controller A. Chitty, O.B.E., D.D.A.T.S., Western Command. The Controller expressed her gratification at the turn-out and sent the following letter to the Unit:—

"May I send you my congratulations on a splendid parade yesterday, and on months of good work. I do think you who joined in the work of the Home Guard have set an example of willing service given without any thought of self and given in addition to other work.

"It was very nice of you to ask me to inspect you yesterday—it was a privilege which I very much appreciated."

"The Colonel also expressed his congratulations on the Stand-Down parade in the following words:—

"Just a line to congratulate you on the excellent turnout of the Women Auxiliaries on Sunday. They looked smart, marched well and earned praises from the crowds of onlookers, praises that were very well merited. I am glad to see that you have got very excellent publicity in the 'Daily Express' and, I believe, reference in other papers.

"The Women Auxiliaries should have the satisfaction of knowing that they made a marked contribution to the public's appreciation of our Final Ceremonial Parade and I am glad to think they were prominently associated with us on this occasion."

"One other event must be mentioned. Our Unit had been formed when Dr. Edith Summerskill founded the Women's Home Defence Force and stimulated women all over the country to take their places beside the men in defence of their homes, in spite of Ministerial discouragement and official obstruction, and before approval for the employment of women with the Home Guard had been wrested from an unwilling War Office. It was therefore a great occasion when, on her first visit to Colwyn Bay after her appointment as Parliamentary Secretary to the Ministry of Food, Dr. Summerskill was the guest of the Auxiliaries at dinner and delivered an inspiring and memorable address.

"Through the very loyal backing of the Colonel and the willing co-operation of the Officers and men of the Battalion, we feel that our efforts to help the Home Guard have been well worth while."

This account of the Women's Auxiliaries' work, however, cannot be allowed to stand without some expression of the gratitude felt by the men of the Battalion for the comradeship and assistance of the Women's Unit. Particularly, there should be placed on record the gratitude of all who attended the Pentre Foelas camp for the work put in by the Transport and Cooks Sections in relieving men for the more interesting and exacting work of actual military training. If it had not been for the assistance of the Women's Section on these occasions much more of the short time available to the Home Guard for training in camp would have been spent in doing the thousand and one odd jobs involved in feeding troops, and the help of the Women's Unit was a factor which contributed very largely to the success of the camps.

One more word, too, should be said, a word for the loyal wives of the men of the Battalion. They did not parade, they wore no uniforms, they received no recognition. But, often after a week's work in the house or the office, they spent solitary Sundays digging the allotment or struggling with the difficulties of boarding house homes, while their husbands were in training. Without their help, effort and sympathy, the unit could not have carried on.

This concludes the account of the Specialist Sections of the Ministry Battalion. Between them they accounted for a not inconsiderable proportion of the strength of the Battalion; to them was due the fact that the infantry of the Ministry Unit were able to work up their training and organisation to the level which was reached. Many of them were unknown to their comrades, and laboured obscurely without praise or reward. Many of them were unfit men who could not otherwise have served and whose service none could have demanded. Their record of anonymous and devoted service is typical of the best that the Home Guard found in the national character during the years of trial.

THE SPECIALIST SERVICES

So much for specialists inside the Battalion—it is perhaps fitting before concluding this chapter to refer to the Specialists whom we supplied to higher formations. F. Taylor, who, from "C" Company Training Officer, went to Sector H.Q. as "G" Staff Officer with the rank of Major and was subsequently appointed Lieut.-Colonel Commanding the 1st Caernarvon H.G.; Bingham, who was selected as Transport Officer at Sector H.Q. with the rank of Captain; Head, Richardson and Emmanuel, already referred to, who were appointed Interrogation Officers, and the several Officers, N.C.O.s and Specialists who either remained with No. 1 Battalion to carry on the work they were already doing when the Ministry Battalion was formed or who subsequently were selected for duty elsewhere.

CHAPTER 8.

THE BATTALION IN THE FIELD.

"They shall march forth and examine which is the best place in the city for a camp, selecting a site from which they can at once control any disobedience to the law within the city, and repel all attacks from without if the enemy comes upon them like a wolf upon the fold. Let them make their camp, offer sacrifices to the proper gods, and then make arrangements for sleeping."

Plato. The Republic. Tr. Lindsay

The previous chapter justified the existence of the specialist services within the Battalion by explaining the manner in which they contributed towards the centrally controlled mobility which is essential for a modern fighting force. In its last phase the Ministry Battalion was indeed a mobile unit. An earlier chapter dealt with training in the field in so far as exercises were concerned, but its interest was concentrated upon and its examples were chosen from an earlier period in the development of the Battalion, when it is doubtful whether the organisation would have stood prolonged operation away from the Battalion's base. At that time the Defence Plan in which the Home Guard figured was still predominantly a static one. By the time, however, that preparations for "D" Day were in advanced progress the plan had changed and the role which the Home Guard was expected to fulfil was a double one; it had to be prepared to stand and defend key points, but at the same time to move its men as and when they were required as part of the general campaign against a possible landing designed to frustrate our plans of invasion. For example, the duties of the Ministry Home Guard were at the last intended to be twofold. Had a German landing on the Welsh Coast taken place, with the intention, which it would undoubtedly have had, of penetration eastward to vulnerable industrial areas, the duties of the Ministry unit would have been divided. During the first phase, when the threat was imminent but the place where the blow would fall uncertain, their energies would have been concentrated upon guarding the site of the Ministry in Colwyn Bay. But in the second phase, when a landing had been accomplished and a drive to the east commenced, it was intended that the bulk of the unit should move up to the Pentre Foelas area and straddle the Holyhead Road, thus denying to the enemy the use of one of the major west/east highways.

This implied, therefore, that from early 1943 when the new duties of the Ministry unit were made known to them, an increasing proportion of the time of the unit had to be spent in and around the Pentre Foelas area. This change in the training area of the Battalion brought with it new problems and new opportunities which will be discussed below. Pentre Foelas, however, was not the only area away from Colwyn Bay in which the Ministry had trained and camped. For a long time its training programme was concentrated upon the range equipped and erected in the first place by the 1st Denbighshires at Coed Coch, and by way of introduction to the story of the Battalion's activities at Pentre Foelas some account of the former training ground is appropriate. From very soon after the affiliation of the Ministry unit to the 1st Denbighshire visits to the Coed Coch range had taken place. Its advantages as a training ground were undoubted, particularly at that stage in the development of the unit's training. In the first place the range is located some five or six miles from Colwyn Bay (a useful marching distance) and the part of the Coed Coch estate which had been put at the disposal of the Home Guard for training purposes constituted a deep coombe, heavily wooded on the western side, running southward from the Glan Conway—Bettws-yn-Rhos Road for some one and a half miles into the hills above the valley of the River Dulas. A clear stream, drinkable for all but the squeamish, runs through the bottom of the valley, which is in some places somewhat muddy; the sides of the coombe were steep and covered in bracken where they were not wooded, and with the exception of some deserted cottages which were used as the basis of the camps which subsequently took place, the upper part of the valley was completely uninhabited. It was, therefore, while weapon training still dominated the Battalion's training programme, an admirable venue. Training with live bombs and live ammunition could take place without risk to any but sheep and Home Guardsmen, for not even the most wildly misdirected bullet could have reached outside the coombe to an inhabited area, while its steep sides were adequate protection against the intrusion of casual wanderers during the course of an exercise. It was inside this coombe, therefore, safe in the use of live ammunition and sheltered for camping, that the first attempts were made to see how the Battalion would react to the experiment of being set in the field and made to live of its own. Against its virtues as a site for advanced weapon training, however, there must be set the serious disadvantages of the area as a tactical training ground. For exercises involving the movement of troops under cover, for example, its disadvantages were manifold. Troops who chose to move through the trees or the bracken could not possibly be spotted; those who moved out on to the open valley bottom could not achieve concealment. Consequently any attempt to use the site for tactical manoeuvres would have inevitably generated into a form of hide-and-seek, quite apart from the fact that a valley of that description would hardly be used during active warfare as anything but a hiding place of reserves in the rear; it was essentially a place to avoid when in contact with the enemy, because he would not come through it to be ambushed and the defenders could not come out of it without being seen.

Both as a preliminary training ground, however, and as a first camp site, quite apart from its virtues as a rifle and bombing range, Coed Coch was excellent. During the early days of the Ministry Wing and Battalion, a fair number of camps were held there which received steadily improving service from the catering and transport sections. It is interesting, however, by way of contrast to the camps so successfully run in the following year at Pentre Foelas, to look at a specimen camp run during the first days of May, 1943, by "B" Company. They moved up in the evening, two five-ton lorries lent by the Army and the Battalion's Vauxhall truck taking up stores, equipment and greatcoats. There would have been room for a good many of the men as well, but the lorries had been issued for transport of stores, and to the transport of stores they were confined. Consequently, with the exception of 14 cyclists, the Company marched up. Upon arrival they were fed, rested and invited to take part in a night exercise. Unfortunately it does not appear that the period of rest was adequate to offset the preliminary five mile march. After a night exercise, which the C.O. subsequently suggested was not the success it might have been because the men were tired, they retired to sleep in what was, for many of them, their first experience of conditions in the field. The next morning there was physical training before breakfast; a full day's programme and, for some, a march home. Although no doubt the majority of the company who had participated in the week-end enjoyed and profited by it, there were a number of criticisms of the catering, the transport arrangements and the strenuous nature of the programme. It was suggested that food might have been more ample, more transport available and that palliasses might have been provided for the night. It was fairly evident that by this time neither had the level of training of the Battalion reached the height which enabled all comers to enjoy so wholeheartedly the Pentre Foelas camp in the following year, nor had the supply services reached the level of efficiency they were subsequently to achieve. Following camps, however, did successively better; quite a part of the Home Guard became more conversant with the limits of reasonable expectations in a military camp, and cooks, caterers and the transport section gained in experience.

When, therefore, the centre of the Battalion's training moved to Pentre Foelas, the Battalion organisation was ready for operation in the field, and the rank and file were ready to cope with any rigours which this might involve. Moreover, it was time that a new area was found for training purposes. Coed Coch, as suggested above, was far from perfect as regards any tactical exercises, while the country immediately around Colwyn Bay had become so thoroughly known to the more active members of the Battalion that exercises were becoming increasingly unreal. The reasons why Pentre Foelas was a suitable place to stop a west to east invasion, as far as North Wales was concerned, were indicated above. The little village of Pentre Foelas lies at the highest point on the Holyhead road between Bettws-y-Coed and Corwen. To the west lie the Snowdon group of mountains, the Glyder Range and the Llewellyn massif, penetrated only by the Llanberis and Nant Ffrancon passes. These run together at Capel Curig, and they are joined at Bettws-y-Coed by the Blaenau Festiniog road from the south and the Conway valley road from the north. With the exception of the coast road to the north and the Bala road to the south, therefore, all heavy traffic moving east to west must of necessity converge upon the Holyhead road at Bettws-y-Coed. Even such subsidiary roads as that which follows the valley of the Afon Gallt-y-Gwg straight from Llanrwst or that which comes from Festiniog along the upper Conway Valley, converge at Pentre Foelas upon the Holyhead road. Strategically, therefore, this area would, in the event of an invasion from the west, have been of the utmost importance. Not only does the road system converge upon it as described above, but for many miles both to north and south, with the exception of a few miles of cultivation on the lower land through which the Holyhead road runs, it is flanked by marshy moorland over which even tracked vehicles would have to keep strictly to the poor and infrequent roads on pain of being bogged.

Whether in fact there was ever any danger after 1941 of the Germans landing on the west coast of Wales, whether the War Office plans for the use of Home Guard in defence had, in fact, caught up with the situation two years too late, is not so important as the fact that Pentre Foelas was an ideal centre for tactical training. The village itself, standing in the midst of trees and approached from several directions by the valleys of streams and rivers, was nevertheless surrounded by an outer belt of open country and was dominated by a number of minor hills in the immediate vicinity, one of which had indeed been utilised by the Observer Corps as an observation post and one of which was crowned by a clump of trees affording admirable cover. Moreover, all the fields in the cultivated lands under the hills were surrounded by stone walls of a solidity and height not often encountered even in North Wales. Consequently it was ideal ground for infantry manoeuvres. Given sufficient care, troops could infiltrate without observation from the actual place to be approached up to almost any point which could be selected. Stone walls, river valleys, hedges and trees afforded admirable cover. On the other hand, given a really well conceived plan of defence, there were so many natural vantage points that any body of troops must, in moving across that landscape, have inevitably given itself away to some near or remote observer, either at some point where the rolling landscape rose or fell suddenly, or where a high wall had to be crossed, or where progress had to be along the bottom of some steep declivity from the brow of which all movement could have been observed. Neither the perfect defence nor the perfect attack was, in fact, developed during the course of the manoeuvres centred upon Pentre Foelas, which is perhaps just as well as either checkmate and stagnation would have resulted or risks would have been taken which would have driven umpires to distraction, but the most surprising feats both in defence and attack were brought off at one time or another. (This does not include reference to the occasion when a Platoon Commander with long and varied farming experience made skilful use of a herd of young bulls in his plan of defence)

The first step which had to be taken in order to establish the Battalion in its new defence zone was to survey the ground and to select company and platoon headquarters. This task was undertaken by a body consisting of practically the whole of the officers of the Battalion, who spent a week-end in Pentre Foelas very shortly after it had been committed to the charge of the Battalion. The various headquarters were located, contacts with the local vicar, the local publican and those responsible for the village hall and school were opened, which were to be of very great value to the Battalion in its subsequent intimate acquaintance with the village. The week-end was strenuous, a Saturday afternoon's work being succeeded by an evening in the Voelas Arms and a night on the floor of the village hall. As a result of this preliminary survey it was possible, very shortly after, to move the main body of the Battalion up into the area to make its first acquaintance.

The first of the exercises centred upon Pentre Foelas were jointly designed to acquaint the troops with the vicinity and to afford them facilities for training of the kind which their new role necessitated. They tended therefore at first to follow a somewhat stereotyped pattern. One or more bus loads would be despatched in advance, up one of the only three practicable roads leading to Pentre Foelas, with instructions to seize upon a suitable place and ambush the main body of the troops who would be proceeding later. This gave rise to a good many interesting incidents, particularly when the ambush was framed along the Bettws-y-Coed/Pentre Foelas road where overhanging rocks and steep, wooded ravines afforded admirable opportunities for a surprise of this nature, even allowing for the fact that the lorry-borne infantry preceding the second wave were expecting to be attacked. As a matter of fact, the process of getting out of a Crosville bus with full arms and equipment was so protracted that any but the elastic-sided umpires provided for the occasion would have inevitably given out the whole of the ambushed party. Then, normally, upon arrival at Pentre Foelas the different companies would disperse to the defence points allotted to them, and proceed to explore the surrounding country. This was undertaken very thoroughly as the nature of the country, abounding in cover of all kinds, necessitated. Machine gun units found suitable sites, and infantry platoons established suitable battle positions, Signals worked out lines of communication, Intelligence, according to their custom, wandered all over the place, and the whole scene was dominated by Company Commanders attempting to find the units committed to their command. A reference has already been made to the nature of the country which rendered mass reconnaissance of this kind an absolute essential for successful defence. This was carried out very thoroughly indeed. A great deal of hard physical slogging was expended in "beating the bounds." An account follows showing how thoroughly, on one occasion, "B" Company undertook this task.

"After 'B' Company had spent half a dozen trips to Pentre Foelas in manning company and platoon positions, alternately attacking and defending them, until everyone was browned-off, 2 i/c hit

THE BATTALION IN THE FIELD   133

on the idea of exploring the 2,000ft. hills lying three or four miles south of Pentre Foelas and overtopping Garn Prys (1,761ft.), point 1059, and the rest of the ridge immediately dominating the Foelas stream and A5 highway.

"A Sunday in June, 1944, in consequence, found one busload of 'B' Company dumped at Yspytty Ifan and another busload dumped near Geeler Arms, with directions to proceed south to the 2,000ft. ridge, climb it and patrol along the crest, the parties to meet halfway, cross, and utilize each others' outward transport for their homeward journey. The writer accompanied the Yspytty Ifan patrol, and, climbing the road eastwards out of the village, took the trackway leading to the lonely farm at Cerrig-Cellgwm-Isaf (1½ miles) which, although 936 feet above sea level, nestles halfhidden in a fold in the hills, beside a clear bubbling stream, the Nant-Llan-Gwrach. Crossing this, we started the climb proper with halts (for breath) about every 15 minutes. Large tufts of carrageen moss made the climb easy on the feet, but the going was very soggy, and one had to beware of dark pools of bog water. The little stream roughly kept us company—it is here known as Nant-y-Gylchedd, presumably because it rises in Gylchedd just beyond the crest of the massif, through which it tunnels its way out along a course or courses some of which have high peaty banks with occasional white marble slabs showing through their beds—possibly once a glacier.

"To our right rose Foel Goch and an unnamed point (2,059ft.) whilst ahead of us was Carnedd-y-Filiast (2,194ft.). Here we turned north-eastwards along the crest to point 2,112ft., keeping along the northern slopes of Bwlch-y-Pentre for a couple of miles, to drop steeply, through fields of waving bog cotton, down to Pentre Cwm. From the crest of the ridge, Pentre Foelas lay in a hollow to the north, whilst to the south rose the giants Arenig Fach (2,600ft.) and Arenig Fawr (2,800ft.). The crest is pitted with bog holes and crossed by a number of steep-sided old river beds, the climbing into and out of which is not too easy with a rifle. As we snaked round the bluff overlooking Foel Goch we sighted the other patrol led by Capt. Hitchcock (who conceived this toughguy stunt) and soon we had joined up and were swopping yarns about the heavy going ahead. Hitch also brought the glad tidings that the transport could not get through to Pengwern, as arranged, so that we had an additional 3½ miles' walk. The scramble down the steep hillsides was hectic, but no limbs were broken. Soon we saw a tree and were glad. But we had not done with the hills. Over the shoulder of Garn Prys (1,761ft.) we climbed from Pengwern, down through Bryn, and so back to Geeler Arms (approximately 10 miles, the bulk of it tough going) and still no transport! Eventually we got back to Pentre Foelas in time for lunch and a warm welcome from the C.O. at 16.00 hours.

"Anyhow, the Company had been warned that this was a he-man's job, and as usual, all the old stalwarts turned up for a basinful, including R.S.M. Hall. Have 'B' Company ever had a tough job of work at Pentre Foelas without the Regimental being in on it?

"Was it foolhardy to take 50 men over unknown mountain tracks in bad weather?—well, Hitchcock, Training Officer Chart, and the writer vetted the course the previous Thursday night after office hours, reaching the end of our climbing 15 minutes over schedule and two minutes after closing time! Hard luck? Not a bit of it! Our chauffeur, Arnold Thomas, had made a pre-emptive purchase of three pints and provided sandwiches. Some Transport Section! And, as a Sussex man, may I be forgiven if I misquote Hilaire Belloc: —

"The swipes they sell at the Yspytty Inn
"Is the very best beer I know."

Apart from this extensive survey the Guides and Intelligence Sections did a very good job of work in mapping and surveying the area, work in which the assistance of the Auxiliaries was of very great value. Apart from this work at Battalion level, similar surveys were undertaken by each Company and even the humble Platoon Intelligence N.C.O.s were observed to be drawing maps and making sketch plans of the neighbourhood. On the first occasion on which "C" Company visited the locality in strength the Company Intelligence Officer collected his forces, and proceeded in the face of steadily worsening rain to explore the area for which he was responsible. All day they steadily worked their way round the confines of "C" Company's territory, exploring every river valley, estimating the possibilities of every farm yard as a likely place of concealment, climbing every hill, and getting steadily wetter and wetter. Finally, very wet and very hungry, they climbed the last stone wall separating them from the waiting bus, now nearly full, and crossed the last field, where improvised latrines had been erected. Troops were engaged in the task of removing the canvas screens, and as the leader of the Intelligence party, wet and unrecognisable in his gas cape, reached the gate of the field he was greeted by a harassed Sergeant with the words, "How many are there in there still?" Naturally the N.C.O. in question thought that his tired and lagging party were the object of the enquiry, and said, "Ten." "Then," said the Sergeant, "why the Hell aren't you carrying one?" "What the Hell do you think we are," was the answer, "cavalry?"

So the Battalion proceeded to enlarge its acquaintance with its new defence area. At this point, however, it should be noted that the acquaintance thus commenced was not only with the physical characteristics of the neighbourhood. The inhabitants of Pentre Foelas were extraordinarily friendly and hospitable, and for the first time made the Home Guard feel something like a liberating army. Any who had previously had doubts as to the genuineness of the Welsh tradition of hospitality realised that if one seeks the real character of a country one finds it in its villages. Reference has already been made to the contact which was established, by the first officers' group to arrive, with the local hotel keeper and those responsible for the village hall and school. Inside the Foelas Arms a warm welcome from the local shepherds and farmers awaited the troops of the Home Guard, and on Sundays, when the hotel was closed, beer from their meagre war-time stocks was also available in the village hall, forming a very pleasant and tangible manifestation of local good will. The village hall had been placed at the disposal of the first party for sleeping; it was subsequently utilised for stores, as a dining hall and later, in the days when the camp was in progress, as the social centre of the Battalion. The village school opposite was also utilised both as a kitchen and dining room during the first visits of the Unit, and in so far as it operated as a kitchen, once more the presence of the Auxiliaries brought life to the proceedings.

Moreover there was a group of Home Guards of the 2nd Denbigh Battalion living in the village and the surrounding farms. These were incorporated in that part of the training programme of the Ministry Battalion which involved the defence of the Pentre Foelas area, and acquaintance between the local Home Guards and members of the Ministry Unit became close and intimate. Sergeant, later Lieutenant, Roberts in particular, the senior N.C.O., was invaluable as a source of local information, and he and his men co-operated admirably in all the exercises based upon Pentre Foelas. A great asset of course was their intimate knowledge of the countryside, but they had others. The writer has vivid recollections of being allocated a local Lance-Corporal, slight and short of build and agile as a deer, as guide in the course of an exercise in which he was responsible for moving a platoon over some three miles of very difficult country in order to out-flank a position. The guide, his bent head affording adequate cover behind the not excessively high stone wall from behind which the platoon first moved, ran lightly and effortlessly across the rolling landscape, leaving the writer with the unenviable task of keeping his collection of six-foot, fourteen stone toughs in contact. But although contact on this occasion was not easily maintained, contact both with the local Home Guard and with the people of Pentre Foelas, particularly the children who watched every movement of the Battalion with great interest, was close and intimate, and the whole of the life of the Battalion in Pentre Foelas proceeded in an atmosphere of good will, which not even the temporary loss of wooden spoons and dixies from the kitchen of the village school could dispel.

In matters less material we received encouragement from the Vicar, the Rev. T. Morgan-Jones, who arranged a special service for the Unit in Pentre Foelas Church on the National Day of Prayer.

Despite the numerous trips which were made to Pentre Foelas during the first months in which the area was allotted to the Battalion, it is probable that the name is most closely associated in the minds of most members of the Battalion with the standing camp which was held there in the summer of 1944. This constituted almost the most ambitious piece of organisation which the unit undertook, and deserves mention at some length. Work on the organisation of the camp preceded by a very long time the first material signs of its appearance. Indeed, we find Maclean writing about the possibility of holding a camp at Pentre Foelas more than a year before the first tent peg was driven. Further, before that happy event took place a great deal of administrative work was involved, and it is perhaps fitting at this point to refer once more to the very considerable volume of office work which the organisation of a body the size of the Battalion involves. Although the Battalion had by this time an office in Erw Wen Road and a permanent clerical staff in addition to the Adjutant and the Captain A. and Q., there was almost as much administrative work of the kind needing decisions by senior officers as would be the case with a Battalion of the Regular Army; in some ways, because of the necessity of making administrative arrangements through the Territorial Army Association, there was more work. This work was intensified very considerably by the decision to hold a camp, and for a time the files of the Battalion were stiff with correspondence with the T.A.A., with local landowners, and with those local authorities whose co-operation was essential. Moreover, estimates and requisitions had to be duly completed in considerable number; the amount of paper involved was prodigious.

Finally, however, a suitable site was obtained, situated about a quarter of a mile from Pentre Foelas, on Colonel Wynne-Finch's estate, at an altitude of some hundred and fifty feet above the village. It was sheltered by trees from the prevailing wind (although at times one thought that nothing could possibly have sheltered anything from the prevailing rain) and ironically enough, in view of the fact that Pentre Foelas enjoys one of the heaviest average annual rainfalls of any place in the British Isles, its only drawback was that there was no local water supply. A stream some 200 yards distant across the fields provided water for washing but, like much of the water coming off the heavy bogland of the surrounding Denbigh Moors, it was hardly suitable for drinking. Before the troops moved in all necessary arrangements had been completed under the superintendence of the Adjutant and Captain Hewett, aided by the permanent staff of the Battalion and Corporal, later Sergeant, Owen and Private Paterson, Regulars from the Lancashire Fusiliers, who were loaned to help us in running the camp. Bell tents for sleeping purposes and store-tents as dining rooms were erected. Moreover, for the first time in the history of the Ministry Home Guard, a rigid line was drawn between officers and other ranks. One tent was set aside as an Officers' Mess and in the latter stages of the camp even the further "refinement" of a Sergeants' Mess was introduced.

During the period from July to September, in which the camp was open, nearly 2,000 attendances were registered. Nearly all the use which was made of the camp was during the organised week-end

11th Denbighshire on Parade

Auxiliaries inspected by Controller Chitty

visits, comparatively few of the Battalion taking the opportunity to spend their leave in camp. The camp was visited by many distinguished soldiers, including Col. A. M. G. Evans, Commanding Cambrian Sub-District; Col. J. S. Barton, O.B.E., M.C., Home Guard Adviser; Col. J. R. Shennan, O.B.E., M.C., Commanding Conway Valley Sector; Lt.-Col. Mark Wardle, D.S.O., M.C., S.O. 1, Western Command; Lt.-Col. Sir William Jaffray, Bart., S.O. Mid-West District; Major J. G. Perry, M.C., G.S.O. 2, Cambrian Sub-District; and Major C. T. Clegg, Sector Training Officer. In addition visits were made to the camp by several Ministry notabilities, including Sir John Bodinnar, Mr. Alexander Greig, Mr. John Loudon and Major Pemberton. The camp was also visited and an exercise witnessed by a party from the American Forces stationed in the district.

Life in camp is perhaps best epitomised by going through a normal day in the life of the camp. Usually transport, either in the form of buses or army lorries, started from Rydal on a Saturday afternoon, and there was a general sense of going on holiday about the proceedings. Quite a few members of the Battalion chose to augment their official equipment by a suit-case, usually containing sports items, which did not do much to ease the overcrowding problem which the lorries in particular usually presented. The drive up was always pleasant, the Conway Valley being fascinating in all weathers. Sometimes the top road was taken, giving a magnificent view of the Llewellyn massif on the other side of the valley; sometimes the lorries took the valley road via Bettws-y-Coed. On arrival at camp troops were divided into platoons, and in the later camps this was so done that those who had previously attended camps were segregated from the newcomers. Blankets and ground sheets were issued from the store in the Village Hall, and the campers trooped their way in single file up a steep and stony track to their built-up camp.

Many of the Unit had had little or no camping experience, and those who had, had very often gained their experience under civilian conditions. Both the expert camper, who knew how to do everything, and the complete novice who knew how to do nothing, were all right; the one was knowledgeable and the other tended to be docile. As usual, however, those not wholly without experience constituted the principal difficulty. When the camp was only partially occupied, so that two or three men could have a tent to themselves, a certain amount of slovenliness did not matter very much, but when it was full it soon became apparent that sleeping eight men in a bell tent had to be done strictly to rule, with equipment properly stacked and left for the day. Not for the first time the R.S.M. showed how it should be done—the camp was instructed to go and take a look at his kit, neat and orderly in his solo tent, and then go and do likewise. Everyone looked, but it is doubtful if many achieved the same degree of order. (It is not true, however, that the R.S.M.'s boots stood to attention all night at the door of his tent). As soon as kit had been dumped and tents allocated, Standing Orders were read and supper followed, officially at 21.00 hours. The first evening was usually spent partly playing games and partly in the Foelas Arms. In the early days of the camp a great deal of football was played, but the unfortunate ball did not stand up to the impact of army boots for very long, and it was never replaced. Rounders finally became accepted as the standard game of the camp—the principal object was either to hit the ball into someone's tent, or into the deep grass outside the mown strip on which play took place; either of these happy events involved a rest while the ball was being retrieved.

The only casualties which took place during the currency of the camp were indeed those arising out of football and rounders, with the exception of the constant attacks from the air. Mosquitos, horseflies, midges, and almost everything that bites abounded in the camp, and there was a constant procession to the nurses' tent, where sting lotion flowed like water. In passing, mention must be made of the sterling service which the parties of St. John's Ambulance Sisters, under Miss Price and Miss Middleton, gave to the camp. They turned up and sat in their tent all day waiting for casualties; they dressed minor injuries, and probably prayed for something interesting to happen; moreover, they did all this wearing the full nursing regalia which, although calculated to inspire respect in the brutal and licentious soldier, is hardly an ideal costume in which to go camping in mid-summer. As soon as parades were dismissed the Home Guard proceeded to take off nearly everything on the hotter days, and the scene was transformed from a reasonable uniformity on the parade ground to a complete harlequinade as battle-dress blouses came off and displayed shirts of every conceivable colour underneath. Not so the Sisters; they were nurses and they looked like nurses, and they never relaxed.

Games usually continued while there was light to see—so did the shooting which was the other permanent spare time occupation. A set of targets was erected by the stream at the far end of the camping field, and nightly, cows who appeared to resent interference with their attempts to commit suicide were chased away by the indefatigable Bishop. Half a dozen .22 rifles were usually in camp, and, by way of pleasant contrast to the early days, an almost unlimited supply of ammunition. Shooting on an improvised range, however, did not exhaust the use to which these guns were put; every morning one or two optimists, seldom the same two mornings running, elected to go rabbit shooting, or rather rabbit-shooting-at. Hitting a rabbit with a .22 rifle is no mean piece of marksmanship, particularly if the rabbits are as nervous as they tended to be when we were at camp, and there were no presentations from local farmers to the Home Guard for services rendered in destroying rabbits. With the last of the light, however, the shooting too finished, and some resorted to such indoor sports as bridge, poker and pontoon, while others lay on the hay and smoked a final pipe.

Last post was 22.00 hours in the Camp Standing Orders. Owing to the fact that the Battalion, even at the last, never possessed a bugle, nothing was ever done about it. Officially lights out was at 23.00 hours, but this again in fact was honoured more in theory than in observance. However, noise at night was not encouraged; some of the members at least wanted to go to sleep.[1]

Reveille was at 6.45. In point of fact it usually consisted of a yell of "tea up" as the early rising hard working cooks produced the first fruits of their daily labours. Thus fortified the camp trooped some quarter-mile through long dewy grass to wash and shave in cold water by the side of the brook, where washing accommodation (i.e., tin bowls) and, after some field engineering, a small swimming pool had been improvised. Breakfast was, in theory, at 8.15 but physical training intervened from 7.45 to 8.10. The various officers who in turn took charge of this ritual had very different ideas; some liked games, some liked Swedish drill, and Selby liked "O'Grady Says." All of us pretended not to like any of these, but on the whole most of us enjoyed them much more than a great many things which are officially good for one.

After breakfast the day's work commenced, the training programme of the camp concentrating particularly on those items which could be more effectively or realistically carried out at Pentre Foelas in camp than in Colwyn Bay. Since civilian working conditions did not permit of complete sections and platoons being available to come to camp and train together at one time, instruction was largely conducted on the "school" principle. While this contravened the basic principle that as far as possible men who work together should train together, it probably enabled the best possible use to be made of the Battalion experts. Lectures and instruction were largely based on the tactical teaching at G.H.Q. (Home Guard) Courses at Onibury and Bridge of Earn, and in weapon training in the methods in use at the Command Weapon Training School at Altcar.

The morning might be spent in one of two ways; either an exercise employing the whole body of troops at one time would take place, or the camp would be split up into platoons each doing a different training job, or having a different lecture. To illustrate the range of work which was covered it might be as well to give the programme of a specimen day. On Sunday, 13th August, for example, the morning was spent in an exercise—the "Defence of Cefn Garw," in which all troops took part. This occupied the whole of the morning. Meanwhile, however, those Auxiliaries who were in camp were themselves hard at work training. From 9.30 to 11.20 they took part in an observation march under Lieut. C. A. Stock, and from 11.30

(1) LIGHTS OUT
    Hush, hush, whisper who dares,
      The R.S.M. is saying his prayers,
    A pious chap, but regrettably shirty,
    If one ventures a hymn at eleven-thirty !

to 12.30 they were lectured on First Aid by Miss Price. After lunch the troops were free until 14.15 hours; then they split up into platoons and some went over the assault course with the Adjutant, others did bayonet fighting, or were lectured on "Co-operation with Civil Defence" by Sgt. J. O. Hughes, the able Training Officer of the Denbigh Constabulary. Incidentally, tribute must here be paid to the ability with which this Police Officer handled a subject which might have been dull if handled less ably, and in which he had to awaken the interest of a somewhat reluctant audience. This continued until 16.30 hours when the day's work was complete.

Several interesting innovations in the training of the Battalion were also introduced into the camp routine. For example, on one occasion Major Clegg, the Sector Training Officer, on the 17th July, lectured to the entire camp on "The Company and the Platoon in Defence." The lecture was one normally delivered to Officers, and dealt with the subject from the point of view of the Company Commander. This was a distinct innovation, and most of the troops found it of very great interest, particularly as it gave them some insight into the considerations which were likely to be taken into account when directing their movements in the exercise which followed. It was part of the general problem of keeping the Home Guard together and enthusiastic that an element of repetition tended to creep into the Battalion's training, and lessen the interest of the troops. An enormous amount of ingenuity was exercised by the C.O. and the Battalion Training Officers to vary the programme, and this particular innovation was welcome.

Training at Pentre Foelas inevitably recalls the name of our Permanent Staff Instructor, Rowlands. All of us came into contact with him in some capacity or another, but probably only the more senior officers, who saw all sides of his work, could pay adequate tribute to it. Here then, is an appreciation by one of them.

"My first contact with Coy-Sgt.-Major Rowlands was at Pentre Foelas on one of my early visits there. We had scheduled an exercise one Sunday in the early spring of 1943 and he headed up early in the scheme and ably fulfilled the function of umpire by proceeding to 'paint pictures' in the approved style of all good umpires. He at once struck me as a most energetic and enthusiastic fellow, always willing to put out that extra ounce of blood, sweat and tears to accomplish the desired end.

"In Rowlands we gained an insight into the new type of army instructor, painstaking, sympathetic and encouraging. His talents were in great demand with the companies, with the Battalion Training Officer, and at Battalion H.Q. Rowlands never grudged time and was always willing to assist on any useful assignment.

"On one occasion a demonstration was being arranged following a course for Company Commanders at Altcar. Preparation to 'put it across' meant extra parades for the picked squad and for the instructor, not to mention the O.C. Company concerned. Rarely have I seen a squad respond so well to an instructor. There was an air of real enjoyment about the members, and Rowlands, following the main lines suggested by the instigator, instructed, improvised, and sweated with such zest that the squad were genuinely sorry when, the demonstration over, they were dismissed and their enthusiastic little coterie broken up.

"His understanding of the difficulties of men in training was well brought out by his treatment of those who were fortunate enough to come under his care, and his treatment of those who came before him in proficiency badge tests was equally sympathetic. His contribution to the efficiency of the Battalion was much appreciated, and we were only sorry that his services had not covered a longer period of our existence as a unit."

Another innovation which was part of the same week-end's training was a tactical exercise without troops, in which paradoxically all troops took part. The general idea of a "T.E.W.T." is to provide Officers in training with opportunity for appraising a situation and evolving a plan of action without the use of troops. Normally this is carried out in the field. The group is taken to the site to be attacked or defended and given a limited time to reinforce map reading by observation after which, normally within a time limit, each member of the party produces his plan and these are mutually discussed. On this occasion it was decided to march the whole camp to the village of Rhydlydan. Halting outside the village they were given the story. "Enemy airborne troops and paratroops have landed in various places in North Wales during the past 36 hours; the Pentre Foelas Garrison of two Home Guard Battle Companies is actively engaged with about a Company and a half of enemy troops to the west of Pentre Foelas. The O.C. Pentre Foelas Garrison received information about five minutes ago from a reliable local inhabitant that a party of 25 paratroops was engaged with a small reconnaissance patrol from the 2nd Denbigh Home Guard five miles west of Corwen at 08.00 hours. The patrol, after suffering casualties, retired in the direction of Corwen; the enemy, after sustaining light casualties, occupied Rhydlydan and was holding the road junction in the village and also that a quarter of a mile north where a local road crosses the main Holyhead Road. O.C. No. 8 Platoon 'B' Company is ordered to clear the village of Rhydlydan of the enemy and the two roads from the village leading north and east respectively to the Pentre Foelas—Cerrig--y-Druidion Road." The party then split into groups of six or seven, each led by a Senior N.C.O., and proceeded to explore the village in order to work out a plan of attack. It was not an easy village for this purpose; stone walls surrounding and intersecting the fields afforded ample cover for the presumed defenders. There was long grass in the river valley; one house at the road junction formed an ideal machine gun site from which the road through the centre of the village could have been covered, and at the crossroads, a quarter of a mile away, a tall house with a walled garden provided the vantage point from which the attackers could have been easily sniped. The troops swarmed over the village like flies and sounds of debate were loud and continuous. The villagers did not know quite what to make of it, and the rumour went around that we were a party from the Ministry of Food (which was true) searching the village for illegally slaughtered mutton. Finally, the parties re-assembled and the C.O. invited the spokesman of each group to give his account of the plan which had been jointly evolved within it. The result was a surprising display of unanimity; very few of the suggestions put forward were impracticable, and it was apparent that the average Home Guard Sergeant or Corporal as there represented could have been quite safely trusted with a command of any size which the fortunes of war were likely to place in his hands.

Reference has already been made to the general nature of the ground surrounding Pentre Foelas, and to its suitability for infantry training at the tactical level. As an example of the way in which it proved itself to be so in practice, the story of the exercise in defence of Cefn Garw may be briefly outlined. This exercise was directed by the C.O., with the assistance of Major Moore and Captain Hunt. The "British" troops, who were under the command of Major Wheatley with Major Cessford as Umpire, were told that there had been landings of airborne troops in various parts of England intended to weaken our offensive operations on the continent. The Home Guard had been at "Action Stations" since 17,00 hours on the previous day. Two battle platoons and various details of the Home Guard had slept on the previous night at Maes Gwyn. At 09.30 hours their Commander had been informed by a reliable local inhabitant that German paratroops, estimated to number about 40, were at Cefn Garw. He had decided to attack and destroy them. The "Enemy" troops, under the command of Captain Spencer with Major Holt as the Chief Umpire, were told that they had been dropped at the first light of day near Pentre Foelas with orders to get to Cefn Garw and to await the arrival of a party of German sappers, when they were to proceed at dusk to Corwen to destroy the railway junction. At 09.50 hours the Officer commanding the paratroops had been informed by the English speaking N.C.O., who had been on a reconnaissance in civilian clothes, that a party of from 80 to 100 "British" troops were under arms at 09.30 hours in the neighbourhood of Maes Gwyn.

The parties set off to await zero hour at their rendezvous after breakfast, on what was already a very hot morning, which was to become much hotter as the day wore on. (Incidentally, local Home Guards were attached to the "British" forces). Starting from Maes Gwyn one party took to the hills under expert local guidance and made a very strenuous trip across difficult and broken country in record time, emerging unseen on to the high road overlooking Cefn Garw under cover of a wood. They had done a lot of climbing but had managed to work their way round to the far side of the farm and were able to open their attack from the east. The position was not easy either for defence or attack with the limited troops at the disposal of both sides; on the whole the advantage lay with the defence. There was little dead ground in the immediate vicinity and most of the approaches could be dominated by the machine guns with which they were provided. Moreover, attacking troops had to expose themselves almost inevitably before getting within striking range.

The other attacking party meanwhile had worked its way on to the north-western side of the farm, and attacked across the open fields, the attack being admirably co-ordinated with that coming from the east, which was able to find itself a little more assistance from cover, except in the concluding stages of its attack. Finally, after what had been two very strenuous hours indeed for everyone concerned, the troops sat around and heard all the pieces put together and judgment delivered on the degree of success which had attended both attack and defence. There were quite a lot of distinguished visitors present at the concluding stages of the battle, from Western Command, from the Ministry in Colwyn Bay, and from the American Forces. Finally, the troops marched back to camp very hot, tired and thirsty, marched to attention past the C.O. and were dismissed, only to find the distinguished visitors who had preceded them by car finishing off the last of the beer.

Mention of beer recalls to one the social life of the camp. This may have seemed spontaneous but it depended in fact on the very hard work put in by the Welfare Officer, Captain Richardson, who worked that others might play. Most evenings troops foregathered together with Auxiliaries and nurses for some kind of a social occasion in the Village Hall. Dancing was popular, in spite of the fact that there was a shortage of female partners, all of whom were to be congratulated on the temerity with which they risked the impact of army boots, and indeed the skill with which they appeared to avoid them. Normally the Battalion brought its own barrel of beer. Indeed on one occasion a lorry turned up containing the R.S.M., a barrel of beer, and about 15 women. (One spectator who did not take kindly to discipline was heard to remark that it just about balanced things up). The problem of the barrel of beer appeared to overshadow completely the life of the Welfare Officer of the period, who drove alternately on the brake and the accelerator. First it would appear that the barrel would not hang out and appetites were gently curbed; then it seemed that some might be left to go bad, and Battalion funds would suffer; consumption was therefore stimulated. Incidentally, the good nature of the inhabitants of Pentre Foelas was proved by the complete absence of criticism with which they watched the Home Guard drinking beer on Sundays when their own bar was shut, and in their own Village Hall. Pentre Foelas was a kindly place. The atmosphere of the camp in general was an extremely happy one, long days of fairly strenuous exercise in the open-air, rations on army scale, and well cooked at that, sleep under canvas and the exhilarating air of the

Denbigh Moors, combined to provide a real tonic for all who attended.

In those days at Pentre Foelas the Unit undoubtedly reached its highest level of efficiency; all branches of the force collaborated to make for the success of the camp, and the measure of its success is the measure of their effectiveness. Pausing upon this peak, therefore, the achievement which it embodied may tentatively be evaluated. We had commenced in 1940 as an accidentally accumulated body of individuals, some with and some without army experience, all without arms, without officers, without organisation, without experience of common action and without a tradition. Most of us were strangers one to another: before any of these deficiencies could be remedied we were translated to a part of Britain, far from our homes, of which most of us knew nothing. We were all, meanwhile, wrestling with the vital job of ensuring the maintenance and equitable distribution of the national food supply at the most critical phase in the history of the war, when failure upon our part would have meant the betrayal of the fighting forces and the collapse of the war effort in a welter of inflation and malnutrition. From this collection of harassed, worried, and overworked strangers and "aliens" had been evolved a fighting force of a sort, capable of co-ordinated action, acquainted with the use of many modern weapons, and enjoying an intimate knowledge of their adopted countryside. The unity of purpose, which was all we had in common in 1940, had been enriched by comradeship, fortified by training, reinforced by weapons in the use of which we were no longer amateurs. Leaders had emerged in whom we had the most complete trust born of experience: we had toughened our physique and our powers of endurance, and in the process confidence in ourselves and in each other had increased.

What were the weaknesses which offset this acquired strength? In the first place our training had, of necessity, been discontinuous. Particularly in our weapon training had this been a handicap: the fully trained soldier knows his weapons not with his brain but with his hands, and his motions are automatic and unimpeded by reflection or hesitation. This prowess cannot be imparted by instruction or example; it is the fruit of constant and frequent practice, without pauses during which the reflex actions can be lessened in their sureness. But in many of the Battalion, who were old soldiers, this foundation had been so well and truly laid in the past as to be wellnigh indestructible. In any case it was a weakness shared by all Units of the Home Guard.

Secondly, it was difficult for many of the staff of the Ministry to put in absolutely regular attendances at parades because of the exigencies of the service: this in particular affected those senior officers of the Ministry whose duties called them away at frequent intervals. Consequently team work inevitably but unavoidably suffered.

Reference has already and repeatedly been made to the handicap of operating upon a strange terrain. Perhaps, however, this was the least of the Unit's disadvantages; it could be, and was, offset by the organisation of an intelligence section which would probably have stood comparison with that of any other Home Guard Battalion in the country. For work of this kind the Unit was admirably equipped: the standard of education in the ranks was somewhat above the national average, and the many members of the Unit with experience of the precise use of maps as climbers and travellers constituted a valuable asset. The fact that constant map work had to be done on all operations from the beginning saved the Unit from slovenly habits which familiarity with the countryside might have engendered. Operating in an area strange to both sides, we should certainly have held our own against most Home Guard Units, as indeed we did with marked success against regular troops in these circumstances during the exercises centred upon the village of Newmarket.

Finally, what of the cement which held the able structure together, the discipline of the Battalion? Here two factors must be taken into account from the beginning. The discipline of a war-time army, regular or auxiliary, is not that of peace-time. Lawrence of Arabia in one of the most penetrating passages of the "Seven Pillars" analyses the difference, in the course of reflections born of his experience of the guerrilla warriors of the desert. Rigid, "barrack square" discipline is, in his view, a peace-time device, necessitated by the need to maintain the soldier in a way of life which peace renders unnatural. In war, to a degree varying with the nature of the force concerned, it is inevitably and safely relaxed, its place being taken by the sense of common purpose with which an army in the field is inspired. Now the nature of the Home Guard organisation, and the legal framework within which it functioned, from the first precluded the exaction of rigid discipline of the type associated with the Brigade of Guards. All that held the L.D.V. together in the early days was the enthusiasm which led men to select their best to lead them in the defence of their homes. With the coming of compulsory service this voluntary basis was in form abandoned, but in fact remained, since the machinery of sanctions was so ponderous and remote. In the Ministry Battalion the task of maintaining discipline was complicated by the fact that all the Unit was in common employment, and the order of the Ministerial and the Military hierarchy was far from identical. (Indeed the early days saw a Lt.-Colonel doing arms drill under the instructions of an office messenger). Throughout it was the respect which the leaders could inspire, and the spirit of devotion to the common cause, upon which discipline rested. It is here that the second factor comes into the picture. The Battalion was never in action, never under fire even from aerial bombardment: it was operating in one of the safest areas in the kingdom, remote from war's alarms. Lawrence's "common purpose, inspiring the army in the field," was not immediately present in North Wales. Consequently it was only by an effort of the will and the imagination that it could be maintained. It was maintained with a force and vigour that kept seven hundred men in training for four years, willingly accepting a discipline which was essentially voluntary.[1] Those of us who escaped the ordeal of the last war trusted that it would have been strong enough to see us through active service in this had it come our way. Of our older comrades we had no doubt.

---

(1) No prosecution was instituted against any member of the Battalion for non-attendance at parade or for any other offence.

CHAPTER 9.
STANDING DOWN.

"Trail all your pikes, dispirit every drum,
March in a slow procession from afar,
Ye silent, ye dejected men of war!
Be still the hautboys, and the flute be dumb!
Display no more, in vain, the lofty banner;
For see! where on the bier before ye lies,
The pale, the fall'n, th' untimely Sacrifice."

Anne, Countess of Winchelsea.

D-Day might have started anything in the way of a counter-offensive from the Germans; in fact, shortly before the landings, orders had been issued for the partial muster of the Battalion on the public alert being sounded, and for the complete muster to take place in the event of any attempt to make airborne landings in order to hamper the invasion. As we now know the enemy were planning an attack, not by means of airborne troops or ordinary aeroplanes, but by means of the flying bomb and the rocket, and both these attacks, vicious as they were, were not launched in time to imperil the success of the invasion, although they caused a great deal of damage, almost wholly to civilians and dwelling houses.

By the time that the British and American Forces were rolling rapidly eastward through the Falaise Gap, it was evident that many of the duties for which the Home Guard had been training and was held in reserve would not be necessary. Apparently the German air force was not strong enough to launch large scale attacks on the 1940 model, and the Wehrmacht was not strong enough to attempt even the most modest of airborne raids. It seemed, therefore, that the task of the Home Guard was virtually at an end. Moreover, there were massive reasons why the scale of Home Guard activity should be drastically whittled down. Invasion of the Continent meant stepping up rather than relaxing the efforts of the war industries, of transport feeding the invasion ports, and in the field of agriculture, with a view to meeting the food requirements of the areas in Europe which were rapidly being liberated.

It was not perhaps always apparent to Home Guards who earned their bread during the day as civil servants how great a strain Home Guard duties imposed on the ordinary manual workers of the country, particularly those engaged in the heavy industries. After a day on an office chair, even a day of strenuous administrative or statistical work, it was both a change and a relief to be compelled to quit one's office for training in the open air; hours which the sedentary worker would normally have spent throwing cricket balls were spent throwing bombs; young men who might have been running on a football field galloped over an assault course; in either case the effect was salutary and not unpleasant. The circumstances were very different for the miner, who after a hard day at the coal face picked up a rifle heavier than his pick to train over his native slag heaps, or for the steel puddler, who, after an exhausting day manhandling molten steel, had to spend his evening marching across the uninviting landscape of the Black Country. The overworked small farmer too, and farm labourer, after a strenuous day tending his fields, found it neither relief nor relaxation to return to them again after his evening meal, for military training. Consequently, the decision which was made to discontinue compulsory parades, announced in the Battalion Orders dated 6th September, 1944, which marked the end of regular Home Guard activities, probably denoted an increase rather than a relaxation in the National war effort.

Within the Ministry Battalion for a time the future was uncertain; some training activities on a voluntary basis continued; inter-Company and inter-platoon shooting competitions also continued and were well supported; no one, however, was quite certain what was to be the future of the Unit. A meeting had been held in the Drill Hall which Maclean addressed; this coincided, unfortunately, with the announcement of the relaxation of compulsory training. The meeting discussed the future of the Unit, and a number of conflicting views were advanced. One disgruntled private enunciated the view that the time had come for the Home Guards to return to the home, and the women to their typewriters. It was not received with much enthusiasm by the gathering, as it seemed to savour too much of an inverted version of the Nazi view that women's place was in the home, and unkind critics pointed out that supporters of the view were not the most conspicuously home loving members of the Battalion, nor the least likely to lure a young woman from her typewriter. However, the meeting proceeded in an atmosphere of some unreality, as the decision had already been taken. Finally, on Sunday, December 3rd, the "Stand Down" parade took place. Under a leaden sky and to the accompaniment of a steady downpour of rain, the various units assembled at their rendezvous. Small dripping groups of khaki clad figures, exchanging reminiscences, approached the principal Ministry buildings along all the approaches to Colwyn Bay. An indication of their conversation is appended as a footnote.[1]

(1) EXERCISES : 1942/4.

I was shot in the Battle of Blackberry Mountain,
   Stabbed in a skirmish in Hafotty Lane,
Slaughtered in ambushes times beyond countin',
   But always got up to be slaughtered again.

I died in a ditch to please Colonel Llewellin,
   I died on a mountain for Colonel Maclean ;
I survived many battles that other men fell in ;
   I captured a gas-works—and drowned in a drain.

We fought on the beaches (though not on the billow),
   In town and in country, on hill and on plain—
Llanelian, Llandudno, Llanddulas, Llandrillo,
   Pentre Foelas, Bryn Euryn, Coed Coch, Bryn-y-maen.

I remember occasions when Sergeant said, "Blank you!"
   (Occasions on which I prefer not to dwell).
So now we're dismissed, and the King has said "Thank you,"
   I bid my ex-sergeant a Home Guard's Farewell.   A.F.E.

The Auxiliaries March Past—Stand Down Parade 9th December, 1944

Photograph by courtesy of the "Daily Express"

The Last Parade—9th December, 1944

At the same time, in London, preparations were taking place for the National Home Guard Final Parade and March Past. The previous night three "other ranks" representing the Battalion, who had been selected by ballot, Corporals Bishop and Ellis and Private Howard, had proceeded to London with the North Wales contingent, in which were included representatives of the 3rd and 5th Caernarvons, and 1st Denbighshires. At Crewe this contingent was formed into one of the four companies representing the Mid-Western area, and together with others from Lancashire and the North-Western Counties they proceeded to London where they were housed under the command of Lt.-Col. Horton, in Kneller Hall, the Army School of Music. Their hosts were the Queen's Royal West Kents. Next morning the North Wales contingent, under the command of Captain Wright of the Flints., formed up in Hyde Park for the march past, being approximately the centre Company of the parade.

The Home Guard final parade has been described many times. Six abreast and consisting of some 7,000 members of the Home Guard, not specially selected but chosen by ballot, the parade was truly representative of the Force. They marched past the Saluting Base behind the band of the Irish Guards and before their Majesties, the Secretary for War, the Commander-in-Chief of the Home Forces. The route was densely lined with spectators—among whom were many Home Guards in uniform. The parade in spite of its enthusiastic welcome seemed, as one of its members said, to strike a solemn note, rather that of a farewell than an occasion for rejoicing. It is on record that the representatives of the 11th Denbigh. Battalion were at least as smart and and soldierly in their bearing as the representatives of the very many other battalions which took part in the parade.

Meanwhile, in Colwyn Bay the "Stand Down" parade assembled; 53 officers and 307 other ranks represented the battalion, while the platoons of the G.P.O. Unit (22 Cheshire H.G.) mustered 4 officers and 40 other ranks. In a steady drizzle, the Ministry Home Guard marched at attention on what they expected to be their last ceremonial parade. At the Saluting Base, among others, were Col. J. J. Llewellin, Minister of Food; Col. J. R. Shennan, Sector Commander; and Controller A. Chitty, D.D.A.T.S., Western Command. Once past the Saluting Base the 11th Denbighs. and the G.P.O. Unit parted company with the 1st Denbighs., and swung down the road into the grounds of Penrhos College. There, drawn up in a hollow square, Home Guards and Auxiliaries were called to attention by Maclean for the last time, to be addressed by Col. Llewellin and Col. Shennan. It had been agreed the Minister should dismiss us, in order that all, C.O., officers, other ranks and auxiliaries, should be dismissed together. We had started as Home Guards without distinction of rank. In our end was our beginning.

Maclean's Farewell Order of the Day had been previously distributed: —

"Our Final Parade on Sunday would be the appropriate time for me to bid farewell to members of the Battalion and of the Women's Auxiliary Unit but for the fact that we still remain Members of the Home Guard after that. Moreover the Minister and the Sector Commander will be addressing you and further speech from me on what may be a cold day could hardly be welcome. I, therefore, take this medium to send you the message which I would otherwise give orally.

"From an untrained and unarmed mass of enthusiastic volunteers who joined at Great Westminster House four and a half years ago we have steadily progressed in strength and efficiency until to-day we are members of a Battalion of which we have reason to be proud. Progress has not always been easy. There were a variety of weapons to study, difficulties of accommodation to overcome, frequent reorganisations imposed upon us by higher authority to break continuity of training and comradeship, and there have been the insistent calls of official duty only too frequently exacting in its demands upon time and energy. Moreover, many in our ranks might well have sought exemption on the ground of age or disability. Our auxiliaries too received little official encouragement and faced many obstacles when they strove to take a share in our common task. Nevertheless, guidance from the experienced and inspiration from the enthusiastic, *esprit de corps,* and a high sense of duty combined to carry us steadily forward in knowledge and skill and in recent months platoons and sections have given evidence of field craft and technical competence of a high order, and our women's sections have provided a welcome and notable reinforcement in many important spheres.

"Our advance has been particularly noticeable in tactical exercises in which we have been opposed by other units and peculiarly so where the schemes and conditions have been realistic in character.

"This achievement is not without merit and significance. You have been told on the highest authority that the despatch of the Army of Liberation was only made possible by the existence of a large body of trained men and women ready to undertake the major share in the defence of these Islands from raids or invasion. Home Guardsmen and Women Auxiliaries have played no small or insignificant part in advancing the hour of final victory.

"Your zeal, your enthusiasm and your efficiency will be praised by others of greater authority. To me, it is left, however, having served with you from the start, to congratulate you on a job of work well done and to thank you one and all for the unfailing loyalty and support you have given me. I have been proud to command a Unit which has achieved so high a standard. I have been, and shall always be, even more proud to have been one of you."

We stood in our hollow square in the wind and rain and saw

Col. Shennan go through the motions of making a speech. We could not hear what he said, but we knew what he was saying. Then Col. Llewellin presented the Battalion flag to Maclean. We cheered, as self-consciously and unconvincingly as Englishmen always cheer, except at a football match. Maclean said something; we could not hear what it was, but we knew from experience that he was giving the flag away; he always gave things away. We learnt next day that he was giving it to the Imperial War Museum. Then Col. Llewellin made a speech. Again we cheered in the traditional English manner; again we could not hear what he said but we knew what he was saying. The King was saying it. General Franklyn, Commander-in-Chief Home Forces, was saying it. Lieutenant-General Watson, Western Command, was saying it. The Editors of all the Sunday newspapers of that day were saying the same thing, and the B.B.C. was joining in the chorus. "For more than four years you have borne a heavy burden. . . . long hours in.work necessary to the prosecution of the war . . . . patient, ungrudging effort . . . . force able to play an essential part in defence of our threatened soil and liberty . . . . share in the greatest of all our struggles for freedom . . . . for over four years stood prepared to repel any invader of our shores . . . . willingness and untiring enthusiasm . . . . continue to serve your country by providing that steadying influence and retaining that spirit of comradeship, both of which will be so necessary in the difficult years that lie ahead . . . ."

The rain came down harder and harder and the wind rose in intensity. Colonel Llewellin loomed through the driving mist and sleet, becoming more indistinguishable from Carnedd Llewellyn every moment. He concluded his speech. Again we went through the motion of cheering. Colonel Llewellin gave the order, for the last time. "Home Guards and Auxiliaries, dismiss!" Symbolically, the regular rigid lines broke and dissolved into a horde of individuals seeking shelter from the storm. As we turned away it was difficult to get any clear picture of what most of us were feeling. For four years we had given up a very large proportion of the time not claimed by the Ministry to our military training. Now we could do in our spare time all the things we had wanted to do. Instead of lying behind hedges with rifles in the foothills, we could climb the mountains. Instead of reading War Office manuals, we could read real books, and establish again that contact with things of the mind and spirit on which we had turned our backs for so long. Or could we? Was there not a barrier between us and our peace-time activities and interests, which would remain there all the time that our younger brothers-in-arms were laying down their lives on the battlefield? Would not the resumption of the peace-time habit of life constitute the re-erection of that barrier between us and them, which had almost vanished during our years of service? We did not know. The show was over. It was still raining.

M

Battalion Headquarters Officers

The Sergeants' Mess

H.Q. Company Officers

No. 1 Platoon H.Q. Company

No. 2 Platoon (Medium Machine Guns). H.Q. Company

No. 3 Platoon (Signals) H.Q. Company

No. 4 Platoon (Transport) H.Q. Company

No. 6 Platoon H.Q Company

"B" Company Officers

No. 7 Platoon "B" Company

No. 8 Platoon "B" Company

No. 9 Platoon "B" Company

No. 10 Platoon "B" Company

"C" Company Officers

No. 11 Platoon "C" Company

No. 12 Platoon "C" Company

No. 14 Platoon "C" Company

"D" Company Officers

No. 15 Platoon "D" Company

No. 16 Platoon "D" Company

No. 17 Platoon "D" Company

C.O and Auxiliary Unit

ROLL OF HONOUR

This Roll has been compiled from such information as is in the possession of the Unit and cannot claim to be complete

KILLED IN ACTION
or died on active service in His Majesty's Forces or the Merchant Navy

Chopping, S. G.	Holes, P.
Crocker, E. W.	Lyster, A. P.
De Vrye, L. L. F.	Potts, J. W.
Eden, V. G.	Pratt, G. W.
Gracey, H.	Pugh, S. R.
Harman, C. E.	Thompson, B. B.

MISSING BELIEVED KILLED

Carpenter, S.	De Vries, H. A.

HONOURS AND AWARDS

The following Honours and Awards were gained by Members of the Ministry Units

BRITISH EMPIRE MEDAL

Sgt. Edward Waite, "H.Q." Coy., 11 Den. H.G. ... ... June, '44

COMMANDER-IN-CHIEF'S CERTIFICATES

Sgt. H. E. Wilson, "E" Coy., 1 Den. H.G. ... ... June, '42
Pte. D. C. M. Macilquham, "C" Coy., 11 Den. H.G. ... January, '44
Sgt. G. Fowler, "D" Coy., 11 Den. H.G. ... ... March, '45
Cpl. E. W. Alcock, "B" Coy., 11 Den. H.G. ... ... March, '45
Cpl. D. C. Foster, "H.Q." Coy., 11 Den. H.G. ... ... March, '45

CERTIFICATE OF MERITORIOUS SERVICE FROM LONDON A.A. COMMAND

S.Sgt. R. W. McDonald, 107 (County of London) Mixed ZAA Bty.
February, '45

ROLL OF HEADQUARTERS PERSONNEL OF THE MINISTRY OF FOOD WHO SERVED IN THE HOME GUARD

(As far as possible members of the staff are shewn under the Unit in which the bulk of their service was rendered. No persons are shewn in more than one list)

11th (MINISTRY OF FOOD) BATTALION DENBIGHSHIRE HOME GUARD

(The names of those known to have joined the Royal Navy, Regular Army, Royal Air Force, or Mercantile Marine, are marked with an asterisk)

Abbott, J. H.
Abrahams, M.
Abrams, H. V. T.
Acock, E. G. E.
Adams, A. W.
* Adams, E. P.
Adams, G. P.
* Adams, H. W.
Adie, L.
Agius, C.
Albon, W. E.
Alcock, E. W.
Alderman, A.
Aldridge, W. V.
Alexander, C. D.
Alexander, F. A.
Allan, A. R.
Allen, E. P.
Allen, G. J.
Allen, H. A.
Allen, H. C., M.M.
* Allison, D. P.
Almond, A. L.
Almond, C. P. P., M.M.
* Alsop, F. W.
Alston, J. W.
* Alston, M. J.
Amos, G. H. C.
Amos, J. E.
Anderson, E. B.
Appleton, G. A.
Appleton, W. J.
Archer, A. R.
* Arnold, R. D.
Aubrey, R.
Austin, A. A.
Austin, R. W.
Bacon, H.
Bailey, H. E.
Baines, H. E.
Baker, A. B.
Baker, C. J.
Baker, F. C.
Baker, G. W.

Baker, H. P.
* Baker, J. E.
* Baker, J. H. S.
Baker, J. L.
Baker, W. R. C.
Balchin, N. M.
Balfour, F. C. C., C.I.E., C.B.E., M.C.
Ball, G. V.
Balmer, E. W.
Barker, L. S.
Barnard, W. G.
Barnes, E. C.
Barnes, G. G.
Barrell, H. A.
Barron, A.
Barter, P. G. H.
Bartholomew, F. C., M.M.
Bartlett, T. T. B.
Bate, R. C.
Bates, A. C.
Bates, C. J.
Bates, F. W.
Bathurst, F. J. C.
Battson, A. J.
Beckett, T.
Beckett, W. V. A.
Beighton, T. P. D.
* Beken, D. G.
Bell, A. C. G.
Bellenger, A. E.
Bennett, A. R.
Bennetts, E. P.
Bennion, E. B.
* Benson, C. B.
Benthall, F. B.
Bernstein, A. M.
Berth-Jones, H.
Bibby, J. W.
Bickford, A. F.
Biglin, E. H.
Billinghurst, F. W.
Bingham, G. L.
Birch, R. R.

ROLL OF HEADQUARTERS PERSONNEL 155

Bird, H. E.
* Bird, M. D.
Bird, R. H.
Birkbeck, W.
Birtwistle, T.
Bishop, A.
Bishop, G. S.
Blackwood, J. J.
Blagg, A.
Blake, A.
Blogg, F. C.
* Bloomfield, L. A.
Bloomfield, W. L.
Bluhm, J. G.
Bolton, L.
Bolton, R.
Bond, K. H.
Boniface, C. E.
Bonshor, T. W.
Booker, H. S.
Boosey, C. J.
Booth, C. E.
Booth, E. J.
Booth, J. N.
Boty, H.
Boudier, J. K.
Bour, A. P.
Bourne, E. J.
Bowden, H. C.
Bowles, R. S.
Bowyer, A. R.
Boyce, A. G.
Boyce, J. W.
Boycott, W. A.
Boyd, S.
Boyle, M. J.
Boyle, M. J. J.
Boyle-Thomas, R. S. E., M.M.
Brackenboro, F. W. O.
Bradbury, J.
Bradbury, S. L.
Braidwood, A. D.
* Braidwood, D. E.
Branch, W.
* Brech, R. J.
Bremner, R. H.
Brench, C. J.
Brenchley, H. J. A.
Brewer, A. J.
Brickstock, S. J.
Brierley, N.
Brister, C. R.
Bristow, F. J.
Brixey, B. W.
* Brock, N. H.
Brodie, S. E.
Brodrick, W. F. W.
Brown, C. J.
Brown, H. R.

Brown, H. W. F.
Browne, D.
Bryant, A. V.
* Bryant, E. A.
Bryce, J. E.
Brydon, J. B.
Buckley, T. O.
Buckley, W.
Buddin, A. V.
Bull, G. A. E.
Bull, J. L.
Burberry, A. J. R.
Burden, S. H.
Burgess, H.
Burgess, J.
Burke, J. D.
Burn-Callander, F., M.C.
Burnege, R. E.
Burns, D. G.
Burns, J. M.
* Burrows, A. L.
Burstow, H. E.
Burstow, M. J.
Butler, W. S.
Butterfield, W.
Butterworth, A.
Byars, W. A.
Cadman, T. W.
Caesar, A. S.
Cake, G. H. F.
Calder, A.
Callaghan, J. W.
Callin, J. D.
Callinan, E.
Calman, A. B.
Cameron, K. J. N.
Campbell, A. A.
Campbell, A. C.
Camidge, B.
Candy, L. W.
Capstick, E., M.C.
Carnochan, J. G. G.
Carpenter, G.
* Carpenter, S.
Carson, R.
Carter, H. C.
Carter, S.
Casey, G. T.
Casling, H. W.
Catton, L. F.
Cavendish, C. J.
Cessford, H. M.
* Challen, G. C.
Challoner, R. A.
Chandor, A. A.
Chappell, W. P. L.
Charlesworth F.
Chart, F.
Chatfield, R. H.

Chick, P. S.
Chidell, J. W. P.
Chilver, G. E. F.
Chilvers, A. L.
Chimes, D. F.
Chippendale, St. J. A
* Chopping, S. G.
Chubb, J. L.
Clark, H. A.
Clark, W. F. C.
Clarke, L.
Clasper, H.
* Clevely, D. R.
Cleverley, A.
Clutton, W.
Clynch, K. J.
Coates, J. N.
Coke, R. N.
Coleman, B. D.
Collins, H. E.
Collins, J. E.
Collins, S.
Comont, F. O.
Compton, M.
Connoley, C., D.C.M.
Connors, J. P.
Cook, E. J.
Cooke, R.
Cooper, A.
Cooper, H. S.
Coote, J. A.
Coppock, E. F.
Corbett, J. T.
Cornofsky, H.
Cosgrove, T. T.
Costa, M.
Costello, J.
Costin, C. F.
* Costin, J. C.
Couch, L. E.
Coulson, H. O. H.
Court, L. E. S.
Covell, L. G.
Cowie, H. E.
Cowie, W. B.
Cowley, A.
* Cowley, T. R.
Cowling, C.
Cox, A. S. J.
Cox, H. W. G.
Craig-Martin, P. F.
Cramp, F. E.
Cranfield, E. B.
* Crawford, G. A.
Crawford, L. W.
* Cremin, D. J.
* Crocker, E. W.
Crombie, J. I. C.
Cronin, D. B.

Crooks, J.
Croome, J. L.
Cross, H. S.
Cross, L. W. H.
Crotaz, H. J.
Croudace, R. G.
* Crump, W. E.
Curran, W. F.
Currie, C. R.
* Cushion, J. P.
Curtis, W. T.
Dace, A. W.
Dale, C. J.
Dalgleish, G. H.
Dalley, R. C.
Dalton, E.
Dane, T. W.
* Danny, J. R.
Danvers, V. L. D.
Darnell, H.
Davey, J. T.
Davies, B. J.
Davies, C. E.
Davies, D. M.
Davies, E.
Davies, F. E. O.
Davies, I. W.
Davies, H. A.
Davies, J. A.
Davies, T.
Davies, W.
Davies, W. C.
Davis, A. C.
Davis, A. F.
* Davis, D. V.
Davis, G. R.
Davis, H. E.
Davis, S.
Davison, Sir R. C.
Davy, G. H.
Dawson, C.
* Dawson, R. J.
Dawson, S.
Dean, C.
Deane, G. A.
De Carle, H. E.
Dee, W. A.
Deeves, T. W., M.C.
* Defrates, F. F.
* De Freitas, P. B.
De La Perrelle, J. N., D.S.O., M.C.
Desmoulins, W. J.
Devonshire, T. H.
* De Vries, H. A.
* De Vrye, L. F.: F.
Dewey, H. G.
* Dibble, K.
Dickens, E. J. B.
Dickie, R. G.

Dixon, R. L.
Dixon, T. W.
Dobbs, S. P.
* Dobson, J. H.
Dockeray, N. R. C.
Doe, A. G.
Dorward, D.
* Doughton, C. K.
Dowling, G. A.
* Down, S. V. J. E.
Downs, B. E.
Downs, J. T.
Drake, T. O. L., M.C.
Drew, G. R.
Dry, D.
* Du Bois, R. J.
Duckham, A. N., O.B.E.
Duckworth, J. H.
* Dudden, R. H.
Dudley, J. N.
* Duncan, T.
Duncan, W. J.
Dunford, C. F.
Dunlop, J. C.
Dunnett, G. S.
Lunton, R.
Duthie, W. S., O.B.E.
Dwerryhouse, W. J.
Dyer, A. G.
* Easterbrook, B. W.
Easingwood, S. E.
Ebert, A. F.
* Eden, V. G.
Edgington, T. W.
Edwards, D. L.
Edwards, F. S.
Eley, W. H.
Elliott, H. E.
Ellis, C.
Ellis, C. D. B.
Ellis, F. H. W.
Ellis, G.
Ellis, T. H.
Elvidge, A. R.
Emanuel, A.
Embury, L.
Emmerton, H. H.
England, A. W.
Essex-Lopresti, H.
Etnall, G. W.
Evans, A. E. J.
Evans, E.
Evans, F.
Evans, H. H.
Evans, O.
Fairclough, A. D.
Farquharson, A. E. T.
Featonby, W.
* Feaver, E. A.
Felton, B. I.

Ferguson, A. K.
Field, H. A.
Figg, E.
Fillmore, A.
Finch, E. G.
Finch, H. J.
Findlay, R. M.
Finn, D.
Firth, A. L.
* Firth, P. J.
Fisher, S.
* Fishpool, F. H.
Fitzpatrick, E. P.
Fleet, J. A.
Fletcher, B. F. C.
Fletcher, D. H.
Flint, C. S.
Foley, H.
Forbes, R. A.
Ford, E. T.
Forsberg, E. O.
Forster, B. A.
Forward, H. R.
Foster, D. C.
Foulkes, H. E.
Fowler, G.
Fowles, A.
Fox, E. T.
Foy, G. M.
Frampton, B. R.
Frampton, H.
Franklin, F. E.
Franklin, W. G.
Fraser, W. F.
Frears, J. N.
French, G. R.
Fryatt, W. H.
Fuller, H. E. A.
* Fursman, K. W.
Fyvie, H. A.
Gage, H. L.
Gair, W. A.
Gaisford, A. L.
Galbraith, W. G.
Gale, P.
Gamble, F. C.
Gardiner, J. C.
Gardner, J. W.
Gargrave, P. W. J.
Garland, P. J.
Garnett, R. L.
Garnham, R. R.
Garrard, L. A.
Garrett, H. H.
Gasson, W.
Gauntlett, J.
Gavin, M. J.
Gayfer, E.
Gemmell, R. R.
Gibbon, J. T.

* Gibbons, F. C.
Gibson, E. W.
Gideon, C. G. A.
Gilbert, A. E.
Gilbert, F. L.
Gilks, R. A.
Gill, S. H.
Gilliam, P. J.
Ginn, A. P.
Glaser, G. A.
Glover, H. D.
Glushanack, M.
Godbold, E. E.
Goddard, E. G.
Gomersal, G. P.
Goodchild, A.
* Goodliffe, W. L.
Goodman, A.
Gordon, W. H.
* Goss, E. V.
Gould, W. E. T.
* Gowans, J.
Gower, B. A.
Grace, L. B. A.
* Gracey, H.
Graham, John
Graham, John
Graham, J. B.
Grainger, C. F. H.
Graneek, J. J.
Grant, D. A.
Grant, J.
Gray, E. J.
Green, J. W.
Green, S. A.
Greenslade, J. W. D.
* Greenwood, C. W.
Gregory, B. F.
Gregson, H. J.
Gresty, S.
Griffin, R. J.
Griffith, E.
Griffith, R. H.
Griffiths, T. W.
Griggs, N. E.
Grisdale, G.
Grove, R. C.
Guy, G. K.
Gwilliam, J. H.
Hack, C. S.
Hall, A. H.
Hall, J. W.
Hall, P. T.
Hall, S. W.
Hamilton, C.
Hamilton, J.
Hamilton, W. A. B.
* Hammond, C. J.
Hammond, J. W.

Hammond, W. R.
* Hampson, G. C.
* Hancock, B. W.
Hancock, W. M.
Handforth, H. A.
Handley, D.
Hands, A. S.
Handslip, S. A.
* Hansford, G. W.
Hanson, A. R.
Harden, E. C.
Harding, E. H. C.
Harding, G. C.
Hardman, H.
Hardwidge, R. E.
Harker, G. H.
* Harman, C. E.
Harman, H. P. T.
Harmer, E.
Harmer, T.
Harmer, V. F.
Harmston, C.
Harper, C. F.
Harper, W. G.
Harris, A. E.
Harris, A. E. G.
Harris, C. A.
Harris, J. H.
Harrison, A. R. W., O.B.E.
Harrison, C. R.
* Harrison, G. E.
Harrison, John Stewart
Harrison, John Stuart
Harrison, T. W.
Hart, T. A.
Harvey, E. B.
Haslam, J.
Hatch, W. H.
Haydon, E. M.
Hayman, P. A. E.
Head, L. G.
Heath, A. F.
Heath, D. J. D.
* Heather, J. R.
Hechle, H. R.
* Height, E. J. St. J.
Hendry, H. F.
Henlen, G. W.
Herbert, A. H.
Herbert, F. W. C.
Hewitt, J. W.
Hewlett, W. J.
Hewson, L.
Hickey, A. E.
Hicks, G. H.
Higginbotham, R. H.
Higgins, M. E.
Hill, H. G.
Hill, L. V.

ROLL OF HEADQUARTERS PERSONNEL 159

Hill, Sir T. St. Q.
Hill, W. H.
Hiram, A. W. M.
Hillhouse, A. D.
Hilton, W. B.
* Hinton, E. W.
Hinton, R. C.
Hitchcock, R.
Hoare, A. B.
Hockley, W. J.
Hodge, W. K. C.
Hodges, A. S. H.
Hodgson, F. D.
* Hodkinson, W. F.
Holben, F. G.
Holden, H.
Holden, W. S.
* Holes, P.
Holgate, P.
* Holland, P. A.
Holliday, C. A.
Hollins, F.
Holloway, W. H. C.
Holroyd, J. E.
Holt, J. C. W.
Homan, T. E.
Hood, H. G.
* Hood, J. H.
Hooker, A. G.
Hooker, D. M.
Hooper, J.
Hooton, G. W.
Hope-Jones, A.
Hopkinson, W. J. B.
* Horn, E. C.
Horner, J. E.
Horrigan, P. S.
* Hoskins, J. O.
Hosler, R.
Houlding, L. T.
Howard, T.
Howard, W. E. S.
Howe, W. J.
Howell, W. A.
Howells, H. R.
Howes, F. W.
Hudghton, A. R.
Hughes, A. H.
Hughes, C.
* Hughes, G.
Hughes, H.
Hughes, H. W. J.
Hughes, I. E.
Hughes, R. W.
Hughes, W. H.
Hughes, W. O.
Humphrey, F. R.
Humphreys, L. D.
Humphries, H. R.

* Hunt, D. P.
Hunt, E. G.
Hunt, H. J.
Hunt, J. E.
Hunt, R. J.
Hunter, W. E.
Hunter, W. H.
Huntingdon, F.
Huntingford, C. L.
Huntley, C. F.
Hurley, A. R.
Huskisson, G., D.S.O., M.C.
Hutt, J., M.B.E.
Hutton, C. C.
Hutton, M. I., C.M.G.
Hyams, D. A.
Idle, A. E.
* Ingram, R. P.
Inskip, S.
Ivey, W. L.
Izod, A. G. B.
Jackson, N. H.
* Jackson, T. F.
Jaeger, H. G.
James, A. F.
James, E. I.
James, R. H.
James, W. H.
Jefferson, H.
Jenkins, W. J.
Jenner, J. W. C.
Jennings, A. M.
Johns, D. C. E.
Johnson, A. E. C.
Johnson, E. M. C.
Johnson, P. M.
Johnson, R. H.
Johnstone, H. R.
Jolley, F. L.
Jolliffe, J. H.
Jones, E.
Jones, E. L.
Jones, E. P.
Jones, G. W.
Jones, H. H.
Jones, J.
Jones, J. M.
Jones, L. V.
Jones, R. A.
Jones, T. C.
Jones, T. H.
Jones, W. D.
Jones, W. D. S.
Jones, W. S.
Jones-Parry, E.
Jordan, H.
* Jowett, L. G.
Juniper, E. F.
Kane, M.

Kay, G.
Keddie, G.
Keely, E. P.
Keen, L. W.
Kelham, A. E.
Kellaway, O. J.
Kemsley, W. F. F.
Kendall, L. T.
Kendall, W. L.
Kennard, C. C. B.
Kennedy, A. B.
Kenny-Levick, W. G. A.
Kenshole, F.
Ker, R. R.
Kerin, J.
Kerr, J.
Kettle, W. H.
Kift, A. P.
King, A. H.
* King, J. W.
King, S. N.
* Kingsland, W. N.
Kirby, W. C.
Kirkconnell, H.
Kirkham, C. G.
Kirwin, J. J.
Knight, H. V.
Knight, J. F.
Knowles, A.
* Knowles, E. N.
Knowles, F. B.
Knowles, M. B.
Knowles, S. J.
Knox, G. K.
Kochanek, C. T.
Kydd, C. T.
Lamont, A. W.
Langley, G. W.
Large, H. T.
Larking, E. F. B.
Latchford, G. H.
Latham, G. J.
Latham, P. S.
Lawrence, G. N.
Lawrie, G. A. M.
Lawson, A. G.
Lawson, E.
Lawson, W.
Leach, G. C.
Leason, A. W.
Leathers, H. S.
Ledbetter, H.
Lederman, E.
Lee, A.
Lee, E. H.
Lee, H. V.
Lee, J.
Lee, W.
Lehane, T. G.

Le Marquand, C.
Lengyel, A. E.
Leon, R. M.
Le Poer Power, V. B.
Lester, A. M.
* Levett, G. E. F.
Lewis, J. T. S.
Liberman, R.
Lilly, A. C.
Lindsay, J.
Little, G. L.
Liversidge, J. A. C.
Livingstone, A. M., C.I.E., M.C.
Llewellin, Rt. Hon. J. J., C.B.E., M.C., T.D.
Llewellyn-Jones, J. W.
* Lloyd, A.
Lloyd, E. M. H.
Lloyd, J. B.
* Lloyd, J. S.
Lloyd, R. M.
Lloyd, W. W.
Locke, A. L.
Logan, O.
Long, E. J.
Long, R. J.
Looker, R. H.
Loombe, C. A.
Loomes, R. H.
Lovett, E. A.
Lowe, C.
Lowe, H.
Lowe, L. H. H.
Lundie, G. D.
Luscombe, A. V., M.M.
Lyle, C. J. L.
* Lyster, A. P.
Maas, W. A.
McAvoy, W. D.
McCulloch, G.
McDermott, F. J.
* McDermott, P. N.
MacDonald, M. W.
* McDonald, T. G.
* MacFarlane, C. M.
McGillivray, A. W.
* McGowan, J. E.
Macilquham, D. M. C.
Mackay, J.
Mackersy, W. R.
Mackie, D.
McKinlay, K. G.
McLaren, J. L.
MacLean, K.
Maclean, L. F. C., O.B.E., C.St.J.
McPherson, D. M.
Madden, F. M.
Magee, D. N.
Majumdar, B.

ROLL OF HEADQUARTERS PERSONNEL 161

Malloy, C. J.
Mann, C.
Marchant, L. S.
Marcus, A. W. R.
Margach, P.
Margetts, J.
Marris, E. D.
* Marshall, H. A. J.
Marshall, W. H.
* Marshall, W. R.
Martin, W. B.
Marwood, C. T.
Mason, C. W.
Mason, F. A.
Massey, O.
May, R. P.
Mears, L. A.
Meen, R. H. P.
* Meerza, N. T.
Menheneott, F. E.
Menzies, R. M.
Meyer, D. E.
Middleton, C. A.
Middleton, J.
Midwood, J. N.
Mileman, H. S.
Millard, G. R.
Millman, R. J.
* Mills, A. J.
Mills, T. H.
Milne, E. F.
* Mims, J. H.
Minns, H. J.
* Mitchell, E. W.
Mitchell, R. M.
Moleshead, J. R.
Molock, R.
Monger, E. W.
Monro, A.
* Moodie, T. A.
Moolenaar, R. W.
Moore, A. G., M.C.
* Moore, E.
* Moore, G. D.
Moore, R. E.
Moore, S. H.
Mordecai, M. J.
Morgan, C. W.
Morgan, W. F.
Moriarty, J.
Morison, E.
* Morley, F. A. J.
* Morley, G. W.
* Morrin, L. A.
Morris, D. J.
Morris, I.
Mortished, G.
Morton, F.
Moxey, F. C.

Moynihan, B.
Moyse, W. S.
* Mudie, D. J.
Mudie, J.
Mullins, E. J.
Munds, A. B.
Murdoch, W.
Muirie, J. R.
Myerscough, W. F.
Myhill, F. E.
Nash, E. F.
Neal, J.
Neathey, W. J.
Needham, A. O., C.B.E., M.C., D.L., J.P.
Neville, G. J. E.
Newey, F. C.
Newman, H. S.
Newman, L.
Newnes, W. G.
Nice, W. H.
Nicholls, E.
Nicholson, N. C.
Nobbs, F. W.
Nolan, L. J.
Noon, G. S.
Norman, L. H.
Nunn, C. H.
Nutting, V.
O'Brien, B.
O'Brien, R. A. G.
O'Dea, M.
* O'Hare, J. B.
* Osborn, G. F.
Owen, F. B.
Owen, J. H. V.
Pankhurst, E.
Parkinson, J. C.
Parry, E. E.
Parry, G. I.
Parry, R. E.
Parry, R. J.
Parselle, A. R.
Parsons, A. E.
* Parsons, A. V.
Parsons, D. H.
Partridge, T. F.
Pascall, P. J.
Pask, S.
Passmore, A. E.
Paul, A. M.
Paul, J. E.
Paull, H. J. M.
Payton, R. H.
Peacock, J. A.
Pearson, F. T.
Pearson, W. E.
Peck, N. N.
Peers, C. F.

Pender, W. J.
Pendlebury, W.
Penn, E. W.
Percival, L. F.
Periam, H. E. L.
Perkins, G. V.
Perritt, J.
Perry, R. C.
Pettingell, W. E.
Pexton, R. S.
Phillips, D. M.
Phillips, L. W.
Phipps, A. H.
Pickering, L. C.
Pierce, L. B.
Pinner, E. J.
Pitcher, W. G.
* Plant, J.
Platt, A. P.
Polfrey, J. H.
Polhill, R. D. A.
Pomeroy, R. W.
Poole, W. C.
Pooley, P. H.
Pooley, W. M.
Porter, E. R.
* Potts, J. W.
* Pratt, G. W.
Price, A. E.
Price, G. R.
Price, H. W.
Price, W. V. T., M.B.E.
Pritchard, E. M.
Pritchard, G. S.
* Prouse, F. J.
Pugh, K.
* Pugh, S. R.
* Purssell. F. R.
Purves, F.
Quastel, D.
Quastel, G.
Quin, J. P.
Radford, H. C.
Raeburn, J. R.
* Rainger, A. E. V.
Ramsey, D. E.
Randall, I. I.
Randall, L. E.
Rankin, R.
Rastrick, T.
Raven, F. P., M.B.E.
Rayner, H.
Razzell, L. G.
Read, P. A.
Read, P. I.
Read, T. W.
Redman, D.
Rees, D. J.
Rees, J. T.

Rees-Davies, R. F.
Reeves, E. L. F.
* Reffold, R. L.
Reid, J.
Reid, J. O.
Reiss, P. M.
Renvoize, D. R.
Revill, J.
Richards, J. H.
Richardson, A.
Richardson, A.
Richardson, A. G.,
Richardson, R. M.
Riddell, A. P. C.
Riggs, E. H.
Ritchie, J. H.
Rixon, L. C.
Roberts, C. J.
Roberts, E. K.
Roberts, G.
Roberts, G. T.
Roberts, J.
* Roberts, J. G.
Roberts, J. H.
Roberts, N. H.
Roberts, R.
Roberts, R. S.
Roberts, T. H.
* Robinson, P.
Robinson, R.
Rock, J. H.
Rogers, H. G.
Rolfe, K. J. H.
Rolls, W. A.
Rooksby, E. W.
Ropson, E. F. L.
Rose, C. A.
Rose, G. A.
Roseveare, M. P.
Ross, R., I.S.O., M.
Routley, L. F. C.
Rowdon, A. E.
Rowland, H. W.
Rowlands, W.
* Rowley, D. J.
Rowley, N. S.
Rudderham, J. A.
Ruff, F. M.
Rumble, W. E.
* Rundle, D.
Rushforth, W. E.
Russell, W.
Rutland, E. H.
Ryan, C. N.
Sales, A. W.
Sales, C. W.
* Salton, D.
Saul, R. E.
Sayer, G. R.

Sayers, H. J.
Scanes, H. H. P.
Schiele, T. A.
Scholefield, J. B.
Scott, J. K.
Scott, J. W.
Scott, Sir R. R.
Scott, S. B.
Scott, W. S.
Seager, J. E., M.C., D.L., J.P.
Searle, G. H.
Searle, W. F.
Selby, G.
Seldon, W. J.
Sermon, F.
Serpell, D. R., O.B.E.
Settle, R. H.
Shannon, R. A.
* Sharkie, J. A.
Sharp, T. H.
Shaw, H. N.
Shayler, W. A.
Shearman, W. J. G.
Shelley, L. D.
Shephard, H. T.
Shepherd, H. G.
Shepherd, L. E.
Sheppard, F.
Sherman, A.
Shields, F. R.
Shoulder, R. W.
Sidwell, F. W.
Simmonds, C. E.
* Simmonds, D. A.
Simpson, R. H.
Sinclair, W. R.
Skilton, T. F.
Skippins, C. G.
Slack, A.
Slade, G. H. L.
Slowman, R. W.
Smart, G. M.
Smith, A. G. R.
Smith, Albert J.
Smith, Arthur J.
Smith, A. W.
Smith, B. L.
Smith, C. S.
Smith, D. J.
Smith, E. C. F.
* Smith, E. H.
Smith, H.
* Smith, P. H. C.
Smith, R. T.
Smith, W. S.
* Snell, E. R.
Sonn, M.
Soppitt, H.
Sparkes, C. H.

Spencer, H. E.
Spencer, R. R., M.M.
Spinks, A. F.
Stanger, A. F. G.
Stansfield, G.
Stanwix, G. H.
Starnes, K. B.
Steabben, H.
Steadman, P. V.
Stears, E. P.
Stembridge, L.
Stephenson, D.
Steven, D. H.
Stevenson, N. B.
Stewart, C. F.
Stewart, D. G.
Stewart, D. M.
Stewart, T. J.
Stock, C. A. C.
Stocker, J. G.
Stockil, C. J.
* Stoddard, J. P.
Stott, F. L.
Streek, S. F.
* Stretton, G. W. P.
Stubbings, R. H. T.
Suckling, H. N.
* Sugden, M.
Sumering, B. W.
Sutcliffe, A. C.
Sutherland, J. E. W.
Swan, K. T.
* Swarbrick, E.
Sykes, H. W.
Syme, A. H.
Syme, D. A.
Symes, O. E.
Symons, R. W.
Tarrant, S. E., M.C.
Tate, C. T.
Taylor, F. H.
Taylor, H.
Taylor, J. W. H.
Taylor, S. H.
Tees, S.
Telfer, G.
Templeton, R. S.
Tennant, S. W. J.
Theobald, L. C.
Thieme, A. H.
Thomas, A., M.B.E.
Thomas, A. D.
Thomas, D. J.
Thomas, E. J.
Thomas, E. L.
Thomas, G.
Thomas, H. M.
Thomas, J. B.
Thomas, L.

* Thomas, S.
* Thompson, B. B.
Thompson, C. L.
Thompson, J.
Thompson, J. F. G.
Thompson, L. J.
Thompson, S. H.
Thomson, G. B.
* Thorley, D. F.
Threlfall, T. C.
Tidder, L. R.
Timewell, W. H.
Timpson, E. M.
Tinlin, W. R.
Toft, D.
Toft, F.
Tooth, W.
Toseland, C. S., M.B.E.
* Townsend, E. A.
Townsend, H. J.
* Townsend, R.
Townshend, G. J. W. A.
Trevor, J. P. H.
* Truman, H. W. H.
Tunstall, P. E.
* Turnbull, F. M.
Turner, A. A.
Turner, A. J.
Turner, H. S. E.
* Turner, J. E. B.
Turner, T.
Turpin, D. H.
Twigg, G.
Tyack, P. H.
Tyrrell, H. R.
Valentine, L.
Van Zwanenberg, L. F.
Veale, C. W.
Venn, A. W.
Verden, G.
Vernon, J. W.
Vieweg, A. R. C.
Wadham-Smith, W. T.
Waite, E., B.E.M.
Walker, G.
Walker, H. F. H.
Walker, J. E.
* Walker, R.
Walker, S. C.
Wall, G. R. P., M.C.
Wallace, W.
Walls, J.
Walmsley, W. J.
Ward, A. G.
Ward, C. P.
Ward, E. F.
Ward-Smith, C. O.
Warden, C. E.
Warland, A. C. G.

Warn, R. P.
Warren A. S.
Warren, E. W.
Warter, P. A.
* Warwick, R. W.
Waterland, H.
* Waterton, E. T.
Watson, D.
Watson, H. W.
Watson, T. C. B.
Watterson, J. W.
Weatherley, C.
Weatherley, F. R.
Weatherly, G. H.
Weaver, S. E.
Webb, A. W.
Webster, F. E.
Webster, H.
Weight, J. A.
Weir, A. H.
Welfare, C.
Wells, C.
Wells, E. I., M.C.
Welsh, M. R.
Whalley, P. G. R.
Wheatley, A. F.
Wheeldon, P. J., O.B.E.
Whitaker, E. G.
White, F. C.
White, M. J. D.
* Whittaker, G. H.
Wicks, J. E. M.
Wiffen, H. C.
Wiglesworth, G.
Wildman, W. E.
Wilkin, H. J.
Wilkin, W. H.
Williams, A. E.
Williams, A. L.
* Williams, D. L.
Williams, E. A.
Williams, F. R.
Williams, G. H.
Williams, K. E. J.
Williams, P.
Williams, P. M.
Williams, R.
* Williams, R. J.
Williams, R. O.
Williams, S. T.
Williams, T. G.
Williams, W.
Williams, W. A. S.
* Williams, W. O.
Wills, C. B.
Wilson, F. S.
Wilson, H. E.
Wilson, L. S.
* Wilson, R. G.

ROLL OF HEADQUARTERS PERSONNEL

Winch, A. D.
Winn, L. C.
Winter, F. L.
Witherspoon, J.
* Witton, G.
Wood, C. E.
Wood, C. S. V.
Wood, E. T. A.
Wood, N. W. F.
Wood, R. O.
Wood, V. F., M.B.E.
Woodbridge, V. A.
Woodham, G. A. H.
Woodhouse, A. J.

* Woodruff, T. D.
* Woods, S. W.
Woollacott, B. H.
Woolland, C. E.
Woollcott, P.
* Worden, N. S.
Wright, A. M.
Wright, W. F.
Wright, W. F. M.
Wrigley, A.
* Wynne, A.
Young, C. T.
Young, R. D.

The following although not members of the Ministry Staff served with the 11th (Ministry of Food) Battalion Denbigh H.G.

* Appleton, A. T. (son of Appleton, G. A.)
* Broom, L. E. (Bacon Imp. Nat. Def. Assen. Ltd.)
  Coleman, F. (Admiralty)
* Grainger, R. E. Bacon Imp. Nat. Def. Assen. Ltd.)
  Greenaway, W. J. (Hollerith Co.)
  Howard, A. O. (Union Cold Storage Ltd.)
  Jennings, S. S. Weddle & Co.
* Mudie, D. J. (son of Mudie, J.)
  Stockil, C. J. (Treasury)
  Thorn, J. M. (Smithfield & Argentine Meat Co.)
  Williams, J. (Tpt. driver)
  Williams, W. O. (Tpt. driver)
  Wythe, E. W. Bacon Imp. Nat. Def. Assen. Ltd.)

ROLL OF WOMEN AUXILIARIES
WHO SERVED WITH THE 11th (MINISTRY OF FOOD) BATTALION DENBIGHSHIRE HOME GUARD

Adams, V. S.
Alexander, P. I.
Andrews, C. M.
Anstee, K. M.
Baker, E.
Bales, N.
Beale, A. E.
Benbow, M. C.
Bishop, D. L.
Bridgman, L.
Brunning, M. W.
Canney, R. M. L.
Casey, G. M.
Clutton, M.
Cook, A.
Corbet-Owen, E.
Cornell, O. E.
Cross, G.
Davies, C.
Davies, D. A.
Davies, H.
Dear, J. R.
Devonshire, L. A.
Doran, M. E.
Eden, D. F.
Edwards, M. N.
Ellis, D. M.
Fallows, H. B.
Finney, G. G.
Fraser, C. E.
French, A. E.
French, G. M.
Gale, O. B.
Garnett, G. F.

Gerrans, J.
Glinnan, H. M.
Goodinson, D. G.
Harcombe, M. D.
Higgins, P. E.
Hollingworth, K.
Hopkins, L.
Hughes, D.
Hughes, D. I.
Jaques, B. E. M.
Jarvie, C.
Jenner, M. K.
Jones, D. M.
Jones, K.
Jones, P. G.
Keeling, A. A. F.
Large, L. M.
Lawrence, M. B.
Leech, O. H.
Lilburn, D. K.
Lilburn, U. G.
Lindsey, H. V.
Livermore, M.
Livingston, J. M.
Lock, I.
Lockwood, S.
Lord, A.
Maclean, I.
McPherson, M.
Malyon, M. A. E.
Marovitch, D.
Middleton, J. E.
Mitchell, B. C.
Moon, J.

Nousiain, B.
Ogilvy, O.
Orrell, J. T.
Owen, M. M.
Page, J. D.
Pearce, M. J.
Phillips, J. M.
Price, L. E.
Rayner, G. M.
Roberts, A.
Roberts, B. V.
Roberts, M. E.
Rolls, J. M.
Ross, G. E.
Shamash, E.
Shergold, E.
Skilton, M. I.
Skilton, O. J.
Somerville, G.
Stapleton, I. K.
Stock, M. E.
Tammadge, D. F.
Taylor, B. J.
Thomas, D.
Thomson, G. E.
Tinker, E. G.
Walker, A. M.
Watmough, J. E. M.
Whitmore, L.
Williams, F. M.
Williams, M. E.
Wood, E.
Worley, J.
Wright, C.

OTHER NORTH WALES UNITS

Campbell, J. G.	1st Denbighshire
Chapman, A.	1st Denbighshire
Clegg, H.	1st Denbighshire
Dally, L. E.	22nd Cheshire
Davies, D. E.	1st Caernarvonshire
Davies, J. T.	1st Denbighshire
Davies, R. T.	1st Denbighshire
Davies, W. J.	1st Denbighshire
Dean, K. J. J.	1st Denbighshire
Desmond, H.	3rd Flintshire
Ellard, P.	1st Caernarvonshire
Evans, A. R.	1st Denbighshire
Evans, H.	1st Denbighshire
Fisher, N. R.	1st Caernarvonshire
Fraser, W. R.	1st Denbighshire
Goss, H. H.	1st Denbighshire
Henry, N.	3rd Flintshire

OTHER NORTH WALES UNITS 167

Hollis, L.	1st Denbighshire
Hunt, A. G.	5th Caernarvonshire
Irving, C. A. Le M.	1st Caernarvonshire
Jackson, D. G.	5th Caernarvonshire
Jones, A. G.	1st Denbighshire
Jones, M.	1st Denbighshire
Jones, R. J.	1st Denbighshire
Jones, T.	1st Denbighshire
Jones, W. P.	1st Denbighshire
Locke, R. H.	3rd Flintshire
Macadam, N. E.	3rd Flintshire
McKee, A. H.	3rd Flintshire
Marriott, B.	1st Caernarvonshire
Nutting, F.	1st Denbighshire
Pickup, G.	1st Caernarvonshire
Prytherch, M.	1st Caernarvonshire
Roberts, A. L.	1st Denbighshire
Roberts, W.	1st Denbighshire
Robinson, W. C.	1st Flintshire.
Wardle, S. G.	1st Denbighshire
Watson, A. J.	1st Denbighshire
Watson, A. E.	1st Denbighshire
Watson, B. A.	1st Denbighshire
Willey, P.	1st Denbighshire
Williams, J. H.	22nd Cheshire
Wrigley, F.	1st Denbighshire

2nd CITY OF LONDON (CIVIL SERVICE) BATTALION
(AND THE ORIGINAL L.D.V. UNIT AT GREAT WESTMINSTER HOUSE : MAY/JUNE, 1940)

Barnett, S.A.
Brett, G. A.
Corden, B. W., M.C.
Crawhall, T. C.
Drummond, Sir J. C.
Ellard, P.
Hains, J. H.
Harman, H. R.
Harrison, A. R. W.
Hill, J. H.
Jones, A. G.
Kenna, G. W.
Mackay, H. D.
Marshall, H.
Mensing, C. W.
Metcalf, M. R.
Moore, E.
Seymour, J. W.
Sheldon, W. J.
Sykes, S. T. L.
Taylor, F.
*Truscott, G. A.
Vincent, H. G., C.B., C.V.O.
Waterer, V. A.
Westerby, R. J.
White, E.
Williams, J.
Woon, J. A.

101 (COUNTY OF LONDON) HOME GUARD, MIXED 3" A.A. BATTERY

Conoley, D. J.
Dagnall, T.
Fisher, J.
Harrington, C. G.
Hill, W.
Lamerton, C.
Macdonald, R. W.
Matheson, N. S.
Mills, G. T.
Oake, G. R.
Pace, J.
*Peters, C. P.
Petrie, J. B.
Rainer, J. S. W.
Redgrove, J. G.
Roots, H. E.
Stanhope-Palmer, R. E. S.
Taylor, A. G.
Turner, H. G.

9th SURREY (OXTED) BATTALION HOME GUARD

Lacey, W. C.
Klaiber, J.
Drynan, D.
Brown, A. W.
Harris, W. S.

Bell, J.
Brown, S. A.
Lemarie, L. J.
Holmes, J. M.
Marshall, A. R.

OTHER HOME GUARD UNITS IN THE METROPOLITAN DISTRICT

Atkinson, G. C.	"E" Coy. East Surrey Regiment
Bell, D.	"H" Coy. 8th Battalion, Wilts.
Billardis, G.	Essex 202
Druce, W. B.	"B" Troop, 458 Battery H.A.A.
Evans, J. C.	"B" Platoon 11th Coy. 20th Battalion, Middx.
Fitzgerald, H.	193rd (101st) C.O.L. H.G. M. "Z" A.A. Battery
Fitzgerald, L. W. A.	221 (101) Surrey H.G. "Z" A.A. Battery R.A.
Holcombe, R. S.	29th Middx. Battalion "D" Coy.
Hughes, H. T. W. S.	No. 2 C.O.L. Battalion
Jacques, N. C.	58th Surrey
Johnson, G. F.	8th Surrey (Reigate) Battalion H.G.
Johnson, N. E.	"B" Coy 56th Surrey.
Leach, R. G.	E.C. Surrey VII. Battalion
Mesner, C. H.	29th Battalion, Middx.
Nicholls, L. L.	20th Battalion, Kent
Plumbridge, J. L.	"D" Coy. 60th Surrey
Pyke, Dr. M.	Hammersmith Coy. 6th Battalion London H.G.
Rennie, P. J.	"C" Platoon (2003) Bucks. H.G., Motor Transport
Roberts, J. E.	No. 9 Platoon "D" Coy. 13th Battalion Middx. Regt.
Ryder, E. M.	11th Battalion, Herts.
Scott, L. T.	63rd Surrey Battalion "A" Coy.
Seers, J. C.	Mounted Patrol "E" Coy. 59th (Addington) Bn. Surrey
Thomson, M. M.	"A" Platoon, No. 15 Coy. 20th Middx. Regt.
Valentine, D.H.	"D" Coy. 5th Battalion, Cambridgeshire
Warner, J. H.	53rd Surrey Battalion—Intelligence Section
Woodhouse, A. J.	101st C.O.L., A.A. "Z" Battery
Woomack, S. H.	"T" Garrison, 11 Coy. 24th Middx. Regt., Totteridge.
Wright, J. M.,C.B.E., J.P.	1st C.O.L. (Westminster) Battalion, Coy. No. 2

OXFORDSHIRE UNITS

Arnold, G. G. F.
Beckett, H.
Bowles, S. G.
Cook, J. M.
Dean, J. E.
Dunlop, J. P. C.
Gough, G. A.
Greenhalgh, C. H.

Holliday, A. E.
Lee, A. R.
Mullis, H. J.
Myres. J. N. L.
Robinson, A. G.
Robinson, R. K.
Sable, A. E.
Sutcliffe, J. S.

www.ingramcontent.com/pod-product-compliance
Lightning Source LLC
Chambersburg PA
CBHW070534090426
42735CB00013B/2975